In Memory Of

W. Russell Johnston

Lamar University Library

Dr. R. B. Thomas

Donor

Longhorns North of the Arkansas

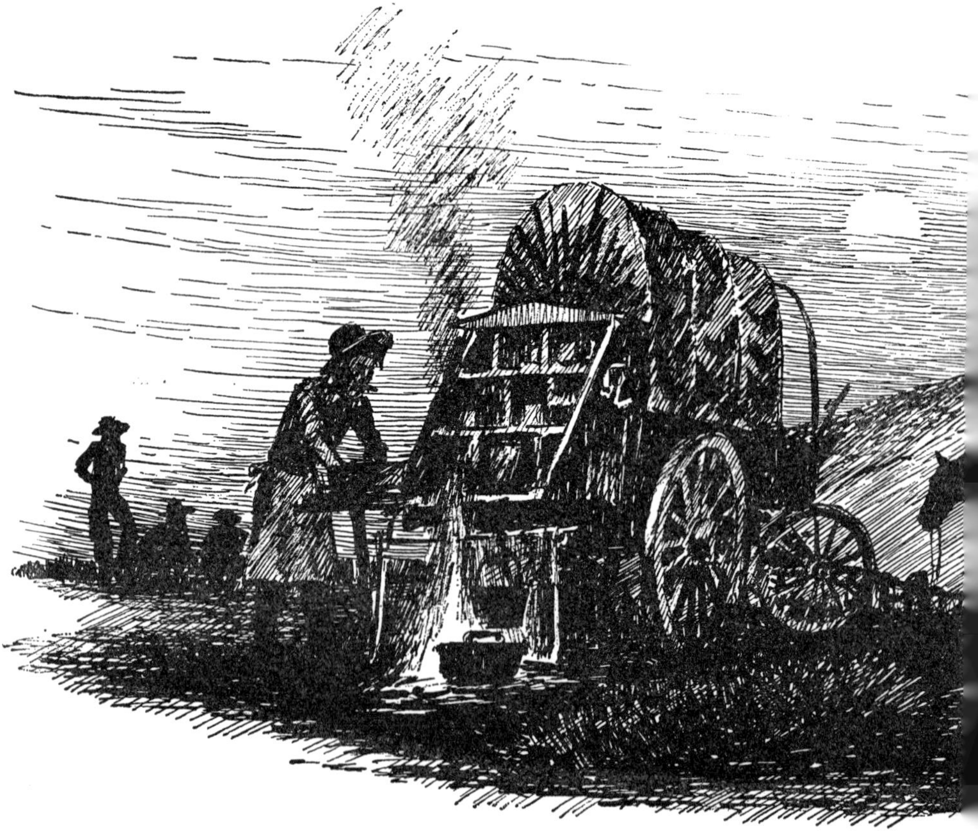

Longhorns North OF THE Arkansas

RALPH F. JONES

The Naylor Company
Book Publishers of the Southwest
San Antonio, Texas

Copyright ©, 1969 by THE NAYLOR COMPANY
This book or parts thereof may not be reproduced without written permission of the publisher except for customary privileges extended to the press and other reviewing agencies.
Library of Congress Catalog Card No. 70-86885
ALL RIGHTS RESERVED
Printed in the United States of America
SBN 8111-0305-6

List of Illustrations

Picture section between pages 40 and 41

Page 1 Swan Land and Cattle Company Headquarters at Chugwater, 1884, with Cheyenne-Deadwood stage barn and office in foreground
Chugwater Station, First Division, Cheyenne-Black Hills Stage & Express Line, fifty miles north of Cheyenne; George Lathrop, driver, 1884

Page 2 Dinner during roundup
Last Black Hills coach leaving Cheyenne, February 19, 1887

Page 3 Branding calves at 66 Ranch
The Longhorn and the Hereford

Page 4 Cheyenne Club, 1883
Ralph F. Jones, 1948

Introduction

The purpose of this book is to set forth in true perspective a factual and authentic account of the West as it was, and of the developments, changes and activities which occurred in the northern high plains country of the West (including the states of Montana, Wyoming, northeastern Colorado, western Nebraska and the western part of North and South Dakota), in the period from the time of the end of the Civil War to around the turn of the century. This also involves describing some of the people, places and events that went into the making of this very colorful period in the history of the West.

The upper Arkansas River was a natural division point between the area to the south where the early Spanish culture and settlements had been established for over two hundred years (with these settlements extending into the valleys of the Sangre de Cristo ["Blood of Christ"] mountains on the headwaters of the Arkansas), and the vast, rolling grasslands of the northern high plains country; which extended for a thousand miles northward to the Canadian border, and from the Missouri River on the east to the Rocky Mountains on the west.

This land "North of the Arkansas," at the beginning of the period covered by this writing, was a land that was inhabited principally by the many tribes of Plains Indians, including the Arapaho, Sioux, Cheyenne, Crow, Kiowa, and Pawnee. These Indians depended almost exclusively upon the great herds of the millions of buffalo for almost everything that they used to sustain life, from the meat and tallow for food, to the heavy hides which were cured and tanned and made into clothing, robes and bedding, for protection from the bitter cold northern winters. In addition, these hides were also used for coverings for their teepees, as well as for many other items.

During this period of time the buffalo were being rapidly killed off by the buffalo hunters for their hides. At the same time the Indian wars, which were caused to a great degree by the slaughter of the buffalo, were also occurring in the northern high plains country. After the beginning of the slaughter of the great herds of buffalo, great quantities of grass became available for cattle on the open range.

The story of the coming of the great open-range cattle companies, with many of these outfits being multimillion dollar British syndicates, is also told in this book, with detailed explanations of the methods of operation which were used by the cattlemen and cowboys in handling the roundup wagons, trail drives and other activities necessary for a large cattle outfit running many thousands of head of cattle on the open range.

Many of the hardships and challenges which were experienced and endured by these first pioneer settlers and cattlemen, in the northern high plains country of the West, are also told by the writer. He presents a thorough analysis of the causes and effects of the major conflicts and controversies (many of them violent) which actually occurred, in this very turbulent and lawless period of the cattle country.

Recognition is also given to many of the individuals (on both sides of the law) who attracted public attention, with special emphasis upon some of the many strong and fearless leaders who were prominent in the events of that very colorful period, which became a very definite part of the Great American Heritage.

1 In any factual and authentic account of *the West as it was*, in the northern high plains country during the period from 1868 to 1908, it would be necessary to give proper recognition to the impact of the Texas-Montana Cattle Trail, upon this great and important area lying north of the Arkansas River and including the states of Wyoming, Montana, eastern Colorado, western Nebraska, and western North and South Dakota.

The first trail herd, of record, to move over this trail, all the way from the Panhandle of Texas to the Yellowstone country in Montana, was in the summer of 1876.

This herd, headed for Paint Rock, Montana, traveled a total distance of over fifteen hundred miles, across country that, up until that time, had been occupied almost exclusively by buffalo and Indians.

Prior to 1876, several herds had moved over what was known as the Ogallala Trail running from Dodge City northward to the Pine Ridge Indian Reservation near the Black Hills of South Dakota. However, no herds had legally gone north beyond that point before 1876 due to a treaty that had existed with the Sioux and Cheyenne Indians. However, within the following twenty-five years, hundreds of thousands of Texas Longhorn steers moved over this famous old Texas-Montana Cattle Trail. In the summer of 1891 alone, thirty-five large herds of Texas dogies crossed the North Platte River at the regular crossing of the trail, which was located about four miles above where the city of Torrington, Wyoming, now stands. All of these herds were headed for the good grass country in northern Wyoming and Montana.

There were also several other old cattle trails which originated in the Panhandle Country of Texas, such as the Chisholm Trail and the Tascosa Trail. The ultimate destination of herds moving over these trails was generally Dodge City, or points eastward from Dodge, where the Santa Fe Railroad was under construction. However, none of the other old cattle trails were as long or as hazardous as the Texas-Montana Cattle Trail. Herds moving up this trail had to contend with large, turbulent rivers, oftentimes at flood stage; blizzards in the early spring; shortages of water due to droughts; hostile Indians; and many other emergencies of the long trail, such as stampedes and gunfights, while standing off gangs of outlaws who were bent on stealing all or part of the herd.

The Texas-Montana Cattle Trail passed through the

watersheds of six major rivers: the Canadian, Arkansas, South Platte, North Platte, Powder and the Yellowstone. These large rivers, of course, created a hazard for herds moving up the trail, particularly during periods of high runoff. However, cattle have to have water, and it would have been impossible to move large herds over this trail without the rivers and their tributaries.

The average trail herd moving out of the Panhandle of Texas would be made up of around three thousand head of two-year-old Longhorn steers, handled by a trail crew of about twelve good trail drivers.

When the big herds were swung out on the trail and pointed northwards, there would be two top hands riding point, with two swing men and two flank men keeping the herd pinched in and strung out on the trail. About four more cowboys (generally "green" men) would bring up the drag, eating the dust which would be kicked up by the big herd moving up the trail. Off to one side, or probably in front of the herd, would be the horse wrangler with the cavvy, or remuda, of about a hundred head of good cow ponies, including a few additional horses or mules, broken to harness, to be used for pulling the chuck wagon.

The chuck wagon, with its arched wagon bows, covered with a canvas wagon sheet, with a mess box in the rear, and with water barrels strapped to its sides, would be loaded with enough grub and supplies to last to the next supply point. Loaded in the wagon, on top of the supplies, would also be the bedrolls which were the personal property of the trail drivers. Seated on a spring seat in the front of the chuck wagon would be the crusty old trail cook, handling the lines on a *four-up* or rough-broken harness horses, with the cook's helper, generally called the pot wrestler, seated on the spring seat beside him. Asleep in the back of the wagon would be the *night hawk*, or night horse wrangler.

Soon after the herd was pointed northward out of the Panhandle of Texas, the trail boss, who was always a salty, experienced, and hard-bitten man of courage who knew the trail and how to handle both cattle and men under any unusual and difficult circumstances, would shove his herd across the Canadian River at Adobe Walls, about thirty miles north of Dalhart, Texas. A couple of days later the slow-moving herd would move out of the state of Texas and into the neutral strip. The Strip was a rectangular area of land, about thirty-five miles in width by two hundred miles in length, bounded by Texas on the south, the state of Kansas on the north, New Mexico on the west and the Cherokee Strip on the east.

The neutral strip resulted from disputes which had arisen between Texas and the adjoining states of the Union, over boundary lines, following the Mexican War of 1848. These disputes caused a buffer zone, or no man's land, to be created between the states involved. This buffer zone was known as the neutral strip for many years. Not being subject to law of any kind, it soon became a natural hideout for rustlers, outlaws and fugitives from all over the nation. The Strip eventually became a part of the state of Oklahoma, and it is now referred to as the Panhandle of Oklahoma.

On the second day after crossing the Canadian, the herd would move in for water on the Beaver River, a tributary of the North Canadian; this crossing of the river was only a few miles from where the city of Guyman, Oklahoma, is now located.

The Texas-Montana Cattle Trail was often referred to in this area as the Western Trail, due to herds being pointed westward from this point to avoid crossing the state of Kansas, where cattle quarantines were oftentimes in effect against Texas cattle. This was due to the fear by the local cattlemen of tick fever which was sometimes carried by Texas cattle.

When the herd moved out from the Beaver River crossing, it would be pointed in a northwesterly direction towards the headwaters of the Cimarron River. A couple of days later it would cross over into the extreme southeastern corner of Colorado at a point just west of the old landmark known as Point of Rocks.

The Cimarron was the last stream on the Canadian River watershed to be crossed by the herd. The next dependable water would be on Two Butte Creek, tributary of the Arkansas River, about fifty miles distant from the crossing of the Cimarron. Between these two streams was a semibarren, short-grass country which, during dry seasons, was completely without water.

The trail boss would have a scout out looking for water in this barren country a couple of days in advance of the herd reaching the Cimarron. If there had been recent rains, water holes would be found and there would be no problem in crossing this country. However, if the scout had not found water, then it would be necessary to make the long fifty-mile drive without water and also to make dry camps between the two streams for the next couple of nights. In the event that a dry crossing was to be made, the herd would be held on the Cimarron until about noon and then drifted slowly out onto the trail where it would be kept moving until late in the evening. Then the herd would be thrown off from the trail and bedded down for the night.

The trail cook and his helper would have filled the water barrels, which were strapped to the side of the chuck wagon, from a spring near the river and would also have gathered some wood from the nearby hills where there was a thin stand of scrub pine and cedar timber. Then he would have pulled his chuck wagon out on the trail ahead of the herd, bound for some point on up the trail designated by the trail boss for an overnight dry camp.

When the trail drivers came into camp, the cook would set out a bucket of the precious water where the men could wash off some of the trail dust before eating the good, well-cooked meal of beans, beef, and potatoes washed down with plenty of good, strong coffee. The horse cavvy would be brought in by the horse wrangler and the cowboys would catch out their night horses, tying them to anything around camp that was solid enough to hold them, including trees, brush, or the wheels of the chuck wagon. Sometimes picket lines were also used. The trail boss would set up a schedule for night herd duty for the cowboys where each of them would be assigned his hours on duty. This schedule would include at least two men riding night herd at all times. As the men rode slowly around the herd, in opposite directions, they would naturally pass each other about every half hour, visit for a few minutes, then continue to ride quietly around the cattle throwing back any animals that were on their feet and straying away from the herd. At the same time, these cowboys would generally be singing softly or humming, as they rode. This was referred to around cow camps as singin' 'em to sleep.

Early the next morning, before daybreak, the herd would again be strung out on the trail, pointed northward, and driven steadily all day. The trail drivers would ride in to the chuck wagon in small groups around the noon hour for a cold handout. Shortly afterwards, they would ride on back to keep the herd moving, and to eat more trail dust. By the afternoon of this second day without water, coupled with the hard driving to which it had been subjected, the herd would be getting dry and thirsty. Before the day was over they would become quite trail weary and increasingly hard to handle. Another dry camp would be made on the trail that night. The herd would again be bedded down. The night guard holding the thirsty cattle would be doubled. The steers, by this time, would be restless and jumpy and the slightest unusual disturbance could set them off and result in a stampede.

Again, long before the break of dawn, the trail boss would shake out his riders and get the herd of thirsty cattle on up the trail, towards Two Butte Creek in an effort to get them on water before the hot part of the day. As they approached the small stream of Two Butte, and before they were close enough to the stream for the cattle to smell water, the herd would be broken up into small bunches. These bunches would then be led down slowly and allowed to go to the small stream only a few at a time, in order not to stir up and muddy the water for the cattle still to follow.

The following day the herd would be drifted slowly across to the Arkansas River. Here, in the valley of the Arkansas, the northbound trail herd would cross the old Santa Fe Trail running east and west from Independence, Missouri, to Santa Fe, New Mexico. Moving over the old, well-known trail would be many kinds of vehicular traffic including freight outfits, stagecoaches, and army transport wagons, oftentimes with military escort, as well as vehicles in use by many other people on the move to various destinations in this new and developing country.

The herd would swim across the Arkansas at Trail City, near the site of the present town of Holly, Colorado. The wild cow town of Trail City was considered by many of the old-timers to have been the toughest cow town on the Arkansas, with the possible exception of Dodge City. Also, this crossing of the Arkansas was known to the old trail drivers as one of the most dangerous river crossings on the Texas-Montana Cattle Trail, especially when the snow was melting in the mountains about two hundred miles to the west.

The northbound herds were generally held here on the Arkansas, on the good grass along the river, for two or three days. This would give the trail drivers an opportunity to ride into town and celebrate, and blow in any money they might have at the saloons, honky tonks, gambling houses, and other attractions of Trail City. The trail cook would drive into town and restock his chuck wagon and mess box with enough grub and other supplies to take care of the needs of the outfit during the long hard drive ahead, before another supply point would be reached on the trail.

After the perils of the river and particularly of Trail City, the trail boss would consider himself lucky if he moved out on the trail with a full crew. When the big herd was out of the valley, pointed northward and strung out on the trail for over a mile, the trail boss would probably ride his horse up on top of one of the rolling hills and, looking northward, give some thought to the problems which he might expect on the trail ahead. With his herd moving into that vast northern high plains country, referred to by the old trail drivers as the *Country North of the Arkansas*, he would know that in this big country, which extended northward a thousand miles from the valley of the Arkansas, emergencies could occur. He would also know that it was over three hundred miles from the valley of the Arkansas to the North Platte River. Between these two great river basins was a big, well-grassed, open country of rolling hills with plenty of water. For centuries, this country had been the good hunting ground of the Arapahoe, Pawnee, Kiowa, and Ogallala Sioux, and they could give plenty of trouble.

The first live water to be reached after leaving the

Arkansas would be Big Sandy Creek, one of the northern tributaries of the Arkansas. A few days later the herd would be in on the south fork of the Republican River and would then be moved on out into the big divide country lying between the headwaters of the Republican and the headwaters of the South Platte Rivers. Several days later, after the drive was over the divide, the big herd would be thrown in on Sand Creek, one of the principle tributaries of the South Platte. They then drifted slowly on down that small stream to where it empties into the main stem of the Platte, a few miles downstream from Fort Morgan, Colorado.

The South Platte River, at this point, flows down a wide valley with good grass growing in natural meadows. The wise old trail boss would know that cloudbursts frequently occur upstream, bringing the big rivers to flood stage and blocking the crossings. Consequently, the herd would usually be shoved across the big rivers before nightfall and before the trail hands were allowed to ride into the town and blow off steam.

The experienced trail boss would probably decide that Fort Morgan, where the cattle were on good grass and where there were corrals and a blacksmith shop, would be a good place to bring in the horse cavvy and reset the shoes on all of the cow ponies, as well as to make any necessary repairs to the chuck wagon, saddles, harness, or other equipment.

The next overnight camp after leaving the South Platte, with the herd traveling toward the north fork of the Platte River, about a hundred and fifty miles distant, would be on the north fork of Pawnee Creek. The following morning, the drive would cross over into the southeastern corner of the Territory of Wyoming, with the point men heading the herd towards Pine Bluffs, a wooded area covered with scrub pine near the present town of the same name. That night, the trail cook would set up his pot racks and Dutch ovens on Pole Creek, a few miles beyond the bluffs. The next day, the trail boss would make a hard drive across the high divide country that lies between Pole Creek and Horse Creek. When he was over this divide he would drop the herd in on Bushnell Creek, a small stream that empties into Horse Creek from the south.

At this point on the trail the herd would be getting onto the home range of the writer. I was born on the old Y Cross Ranch alongside of the Texas-Montana Cattle Trail in 1895, at a time when my father, Frank E. Jones, was ranch foreman for H. B. "Hi" Kelly, owner of the Y Cross. I can still remember seeing as a small boy several trail herds in sight at one time, where they could be spotted by the great dust clouds that were being kicked up by the hooves of the thousands of head of cattle in each herd moving up the trail.

The next day, after reaching Horse Creek, the herd would pass just to the east of the little cow town of LaGrange where the cook would pull into town and restock his chuck wagon at the Robb Mercantile Company, owned by S. J. Robb. The saloon in the little cow town would do a rushing business for a few hours until the herd had moved on up the trail toward what was known to the old trail drivers as Horse Creek Gap.

At this point on the trail Horse Creek flows between two low mountains of white sandstone with Bear Mountain on the west and Sixty-Six Mountain on the east. This Gap is one of the few breaks in the south rimrock of a very fine grass country known as Goshen Hole which extends northward for over thirty miles from the Gap to the North Platte River valley.

Just to the west of the trail where it passes through the

Gap was the Y Cross Ranch with its good log house and very fine natural meadows. To the northeast of the Y Cross Ranch buildings was a large area covered with good grass where several large springs of clear, cold water, furnishing adequate water for a large trail herd, came boiling up out of the ground, creating a small stream which ran westward for a short distance to Horse Creek. Here, at Hawk Springs, was naturally a favorite overnight camping spot for trail bosses moving herds up the trail. However, around the turn of the century, these fine springs were completely buried under the large Hawk Springs Reservoir, built for irrigation purposes.

When the herd was again on the move up the trail, with the trail boss slowing down the drive to permit the cattle, horses, and men to get some needed rest, the first overnight camp would be set up at Big Willows, a good camping area on Horse Creek. For the next few days the herd would be drifted slowly northward across the well-watered and heavily grassed Goshen Hole country to where Horse Creek makes a big bend to the east. At this big bend the trail cook would set up the last overnight camp on Horse Creek. The following morning the trail boss would point the herd over the divide toward the well-known crossing of the North Platte River.

Shortly before reaching the river crossing about twelve miles downstream from Fort Laramie, the northbound herd would cross the old Oregon Trail running east and west on the south side of the river with the long trains of emigrant Conestoga wagons moving slowly westward toward Fort Laramie. From there the emigrants would cross over the mountain ranges on their way to the West Coast in search of a home and a new way of life in that fabulous, new and rapidly developing country.

By the time that the herd, traveling at an average

speed of about fifteen miles a day, reached the North Platte, it would have been on the trail for about six weeks. If it had left the Panhandle in early May, which was the usual time for moving herds out on the long trail north, it would now be mid-June, with the snow melting rapidly in the mountains and the river at flood stage. At the North Platte crossing, which was known as the toughest and most dangerous river on the trail to cross, several cowboys going north with trail herds had lost their lives. With this river just ahead, the trail drivers would know that trouble could occur at the crossing.

When the trail boss was ready to make the crossing the horse cavvy would be shoved into the river, along with a small bunch of cattle broken off from the main herd. When these cattle were in and swimming, the main herd would be thrown in slowly behind them and the entire herd of Longhorns would then have to swim the main channel of the river, a quarter of a mile in width, with a strong current running. The experienced trail boss would know, of course, that sometimes in midstream some of the swimming cattle might take a sudden notion to turn back. When this occurred a milling herd in the main channel of an angry river would be the result.

All cattlemen knew that there was nothing more dangerous in the life of a cowboy than trying to straighten out a milling herd in midstream. The cattle could become weak and exhausted from swimming against the strong current to the point where they could be sucked under by the turbulent river and swept downstream, taking any unfortunate cowboy who happened to be on the downstream side of the herd with them. When this occurred, unless that cowboy happened to be an exceptionally good swimmer, he would have made his last trail drive.

If a ferry was not operating near the river crossing at

that time so that the chuck wagon could be ferried across the channel, the cook and his helper would have to pull out with the wagon immediately after breakfast and drive the twelve miles upstream to where they could cross the river on the steel military bridge at Fort Laramie. Then, after restocking the chuck wagon at the sutler's store at this historic old army outpost, they would have driven back downstream on the north side of the river in time to set up camp and to have a hot meal, along with dry clothes, ready for the trail drivers when they came up out of the river.

The next stream, after leaving the North Platte, where the herd would be bedded down for the night, would be on the clear little Rawhide Creek near the well-known landmark of Rawhide Buttes where small round hills were visible for great distances in any direction. Located at this point on Rawhide Creek was the Rawhide Stage Station of the Cheyenne and Deadwood Stagecoach and Express Line. The large, colorful, six-horse Concord Stagecoach regularly pulled in and out from this stage station, heavily loaded with wild-eyed and eager gold seekers who had been bitten by the gold bug, rushing madly to the newly discovered gold strikes on French Creek in the Black Hills of South Dakota.

The next supply point where an overnight camp would be made, with the herd bedded down on the headwaters of the Niobrara River, would be at the small mining camp and cow town of Silver Cliff near the site of the present little city of Lusk, Wyoming. Then there, as it moved on north, the herd would water on Lance Creek, and during the next few days would cross several other small streams on the headwaters of the south fork of the Cheyenne River before reaching a point on the north fork of the same river where the Chicago, Burlington and Quincy Railroad later built stockyards and a railway station. This place, called

Moorcroft, became a major shipping point for mature cattle to livestock markets in cities to the east along the Missouri River valley.

At this point on the long trail northward, the herd would be getting into the well-grassed and well-watered valleys which lie between the lofty and majestic Big Horn Mountain Range with its snow-capped peaks on the west and the beautiful pine-clad Black Hills of South Dakota on the east. These mountain ranges formed a gateway to that vast cattleman's paradise of rivers and grass, five hundred miles across in any direction, lying in the watersheds of five great river basins, composed of the Little Missouri, the Yellowstone, the Powder, and the Big Horn rivers, and the main stem of the upper Missouri in northern Montana, and all of their tributaries. This great country, lying mostly in the Territory of Montana, had long been the homeland and good hunting grounds of the Cheyenne, Sioux, Crow, Shoshone, and several other tribes of plains Indians; and they were not giving it up to the invasion of the white man without a fight. The Battle of the Little Big Horn, where Lt. Col. George A. Custer and his entire command lost their lives, had been fought in 1876 in this country north of the Big Horns and, although the Indians won that battle, in the end they lost the war.

Just to the north of the Cheyenne River, the Texas-Montana Cattle Trail forked in three directions. The fork bearing eastward passed that famous landmark later dedicated as a national monument, known as Devil's Tower, which could be seen for almost fifty miles in any direction. Its stone walls rose almost perpendicularly for over six hundred feet above the surrounding plains. Herds moving to the northeast up this fork of the cattle trail were usually turned loose on the Belle Fourche River or some of the other tributaries of the Little Missouri in the good cattle country north of the Black Hills.

Trail herds bound for the Judith Basin, Sun River Valley or other ranges in the west-central part of Montana would cross Crazy Woman Creek and go up the fork of the trail bearing northwest to the headwaters of the Tongue River, before moving on and swimming the swift and turbulent waters of the mighty Yellowstone at Terry's Crossing. Many of the herds that were moved into that part of the high plains country would be turned loose on the Musselshell or the other tributaries of the Missouri in northwest Montana.

The herds pointed northward up the main or middle trail would cross the main stem of the Powder River about twenty miles above the little cow town of Powderville. The Powder River, although not deep, was a very dangerous river, with flash floods and quicksand, famed up and down the trail from the Yellowstone to the Panhandle as being a mile wide and an inch deep.

When the cowboys were in the little cow towns and it was their night to howl, the wild cowboy yell of "Powder River" could always be heard up and down the streets, as well as in the saloons and honky tonks. "Powder River" was the battle cry of Teddy Roosevelt's Rough Riders when they went up San Juan Hill during the Spanish-American War. Also, during World War One, that yell of "Powder River" could be heard in France wherever troops from the cow country were quartered. The French girls naturally concluded that Powder River must be at least as large as the Mississippi.

After crossing the Powder River, the herds bound for ranges to the north would be pointed toward a crossing of the Yellowstone, located a short distance downstream from Fort Keogh near the big cow town of Miles City, Montana;

named in honor of General Nelson A. Miles who, following the death of Colonel Custer, became the commander of all of the troops in the military outposts of the upper Missouri River Basin, including Fort Keogh on the Yellowstone. After crossing the Yellowstone on this trail the cattle would be turned loose on some of the many streams to the north in central Montana, including the Big Dry and its tributaries.

As the herds were being trailed northward over a period of from two to four months, depending upon when they moved out from the Panhandle and where they were turned loose on the range, the cattle would naturally become trail-broken and were inclined to stick together in a herd. Consequently, when they were turned loose on the range, the chuck wagon would generally camp in the area for a couple of weeks while the cowboys would break up the herd into small bunches and scatter them over the range in localities where the shelter, water, and grass were the best, with particular attention being given to shelter. Winters in this northern high plains country were generally rough and losses in cattle were particularly heavy. These winter losses sometimes ran in excess of twenty-five percent of the herd, especially with southern dogies on this northern range for their first winter.

These cattle would usually be kept on the same range until they were three or four years old, with the Texas Longhorns becoming quite large and rangy and oftentimes developing horn spreads of six to eight feet. Seldom seeing a man, they would become as wild as deer and would be extremely hard to handle when they were picked up in the fall roundup, until they again became trail broken, as they were trailed eastward to a railroad shipping point where they would be shipped out to an eastern livestock market.

By the time that the herd was settled it would usually be late August, and the trail drivers faced a long ride back to Texas. However, it was customary during that period of time for almost all of the big outfits with cattle running on the open range in the northern high plains country to operate from line camps, consisting of a log cabin and a corral built near where the herds were to be turned loose. Consequently, the trail drivers going north with trail herds would generally make their headquarters at these line camps until their outfit was ready to hit the long trail back to Texas.

A couple of the cow punchers who had come north with the herd would usually be left in the line camp for the winter where there would not be much that they could do except to scare off rustlers, cut ice for the cattle, see which way they went when they were hit by one of those terrific northern blizzards, and then, to go out when the snow went off in the spring, and try to shake the live ones out of the badlands. The chuck wagon would also sometimes be left at the line camp, to be used by the cowboys who were wintering there, for hauling wood and other supplies needed at the camp, and also to be available as a chuck wagon for the spring roundup.

When this occurred, the trail boss would soon be busy putting a pack outfit together for the return trip. The horse cavvy would be brought into the pole corral with the horses that were to be taken back to Texas as pack animals, as well as the cow ponies that were to be used for changes by the trail drivers on the return trip, being caught out and reshod with light plates. Some of the horses that were to be used as winter horses at the line camp during the coming months would be rough shod with long calks for traveling over frozen snow and ice. All of these horses that were to be used for either purpose would then be held in a small horse pasture, near the line camp, until they were needed, while the balance of the cavvy would be turned out on the range with the cattle, where they could be picked up in the spring for use with the roundup wagons.

Light camping equipment, including cooking utensils and a good supply of grub, would be loaded, by the use of pack saddles, on a couple of the gentle horses that had been used, coming up the trail, for pulling the chuck wagon, while at the same time each of the trail drivers who was returning to Texas would be busy packing his bed on a pack horse assigned to him by the trail boss, to be used for that purpose on the return trip.

There were two things that a cowboy always owned: his saddle and his bed. With his bed he always had a large tarpaulin, called a tarp, which was used to protect his blankets from the weather regardless of whether he was sleeping in the bed, had it rolled, or had it packed on a horse. Packed in the bed he would always have a flour sack, referred to as his "war bag," containing his clean socks, his razor, and all of his other personal belongings. Whenever the bed was being packed on a horse, it would be so folded that the tarp was always on the outside and that no part of the blankets was ever exposed to the weather. Then it would be thrown over the back of the pack horse and secured in place with a diamond hitch.

When the pack outfit was ready to move out on the trail, the trail boss would pay off the cowboys who were remaining in the line camp for the winter, step up on his big horse, and lead out his trail drivers, with all the pack horses and other cow ponies that were being taken along for changes of mounts being driven ahead of them, as they began the long ride back down the trail to Texas.

When they were a few miles out on the trail, the horses would seem to get the general idea that they were headed back to the tall grass country in the Panhandle of Texas. Then, as their pace quickened, their ears would begin to point forward, with their heads lifted high and sniffing the morning air; a reaction on the part of the horses that was referred to by the cowboys as headin' for home with their heads up and their tails a risin'. From here on the cow ponies would not require much crowding by the trail drivers.

At this time of year there would always be twenty or thirty outfits strung out on the trail between the Yellowstone and the Panhandle, all of them making their way back to Texas. Some of these trail outfits would have chuck wagons while others would be traveling light with pack outfits. However, any cowboy was always welcome to eat at any of the camps of the cow outfits along the trail. Consequently, if some cowboy tarried too long with a hangover in some of the wild cow towns along the trail and became separated from his own outfit, he could always eat at the other camps until he caught up with his own bunch of trail drivers.

The southern cowboys always attracted a lot of attention in the northern cow towns when they rode into town with their double-rigged, two-cinch saddles with colorful Navajo saddle blankets and long, tapered, fourteen-inch leather tapaderos (called taps) covering the front of their stirrups and hanging almost to the ground. They would wear heavy, drop-shanked spurs with three-inch rowels, and large silver conchos, in addition to bat-winged chaps. Their bridles would have spade bits and instead of the usual hemp rope an occasional braided rawhide saddle rope.

The people who lived in the little cow towns along the trail always figured that there were two ways that they could tell for sure when winter was coming. One by the honking of the Canadian geese heading south, and the other by the thin-blooded Texas trail hands trying to get out of the north country ahead of the winter blizzards.

One thing was certain, the trail hands would all get back to Texas by the time that the trail boss came in at the headquarters ranch to pay them off for their summer's work, after which they would start looking around for another trail herd that would be going up north in the spring.

2 Among the first of the great pioneer cattlemen to come into the northern high plains country of the West was H. B. "Hi" Kelly, who was born in Sheridan County, Missouri, on October 14, 1834. Hi first crossed the plains and passed through Fort Laramie in 1849. At that time, this tall, likable, fifteen-year-old boy, with smiling brown eyes, who was destined to live one of the most adventurous and colorful lives in the history of the West, was traveling with a wagon train bound for the West Coast at the beginning of the California gold rush.

Three years later, Hi again passed through Fort Laramie, this time with an east-bound wagon train going through to St. Louis, Missouri. He had spent these three very exciting years in the gold fields of California, without fortune having come his way. However, this impressionable youngster had been very much impressed and fascinated by his experiences in crossing the vast, rolling plains, with the great herds of buffalo and the wild, colorful, untamed and oftentimes hostile Indians. This was a land where the wagons would roll along for hundreds of miles without any sign of habitation. Danger was always present; in this big land anything could happen at any time. It had been an exciting way of life and an experience that he would not soon forget.

After returning to Missouri, Hi worked for a short period of time on a farm near his birthplace. However, the love of adventure and the challenge of life on the plains was in his blood to the point where he soon found his life on the farm to be very unexciting and monotonous. Consequently, in the spring of 1853, still only nineteen years of age, this restless young man took a job as a bull whacker with a large wagon train moving merchandise over the Santa Fe Trail from Independence, Missouri, to Santa Fe, New Mexico.

Among the many stories which Hi Kelly told the writer about his early experiences on the plains and wagon trails of the West was one of an incident which occurred while he was with one of these wagon trains on the old Santa Fe Trail.

As Kelly told the story, this event occurred when the heavily loaded wagon train was moving up the valley of the Arkansas and had stopped about noon near the mouth of the Little Arkansas; the wagons drawn up in a circle, while the men were cooking their noon meal over an open fire and the oxen were being permitted to graze within the circle of wagons. While these activities were still under way, a large party of about two hundred painted Comanche

Indians who had not been previously observed, suddenly made their appearance on a hill overlooking the camp. They sat on their horses quietly for a few minutes and then, at a signal from their chief, with their horses running at full speed and with wild Comanche yells, swept down and surrounded the wagon train. A small party of the Indians, headed by the chief, then rode into the camp under a white flag, where the chief demanded an immediate powwow with the boss of the wagon train.

In the conversations which followed in sign language, the chief proceeded to make threatening demands for food for his entire party. While these arguments were still under way, one of the Indians walked over to where a bull whacker was busy frying bacon over the open fire and deliberately kicked the frying pan out of his hand, burning him with the hot grease. The bull whacker jumped to his feet and hit the Indian a hard blow with his fist, knocking him to the ground under the feet of a pony that was tied to a wagon wheel. The frightened pony kicked the Indian in the head, killing him instantly.

After this unfortunate incident had occurred, the chief, with a great show of anger, demanded that the white man who had struck the blow be turned over to the Indians. The boss of the wagon train angrily refused to comply with this demand. The chief took his small party of Indians and sullenly withdrew, taking the dead Indian with them, and rejoined the main party still waiting in a circle around the camp of the white men.

The Indians continued throughout the afternoon to ride circle around the camp. Meanwhile, the bull whacker who had hit the Indian was hidden under a canvas cover in the back of one of the wagons. The boss of the wagon train gave orders that the oxen be chained to the wheels of the wagons in such a manner that if a fight with the Indians did develop and the oxen should be killed by the arrows and rifle fire of the Comanches, the bodies of the dead animals would be lying in such a position that they would serve as cover for the men who would be making their last stand within the circle of wagons.

Kelly said that, with the coming of night, the Indians withdrew a short distance, held a powwow which continued far into the night, and kept their fires burning in a circle around the wagons all night long. With the coming of daylight the next morning, the chief, with his small party of Indians, again rode into the camp under the white flag. After several hours of bickering and bargaining, the boss of the wagon train finally gave them a rather large quantity of merchandise consisting of food, calico, and trinkets. The wagon train once more moved out on the long, hazardous trail to Santa Fe.

After continuing his work with this freighting outfit on the Santa Fe Trail for almost two years, Hi took a job in the summer of 1855 as a pony express rider carrying the mail between Independence, Missouri, and Santa Fe. He often told the story in his later years about being taken prisoner in the valley of the Arkansas at dusk one evening by a large band of about a hundred painted and hostile Cheyenne Indians. When it became dark, he was bound and placed in a circle of fire with two other white men who were also prisoners. A council meeting of the Indians, who claimed that eleven of their people had recently been killed by the white man, soon got under way, and the Indian braves demanded revenge.

With his experience on the Santa Fe Trail, Hi had become a very calm and fearless young man accustomed to dealing with Indians, and had learned to use the Indian sign language very effectively. He knew that under circumstances of this kind, to show any sign of fear or weakness was almost certain to be fatal. As the council meeting proceeded he told the Indians that he was a personal messenger of the great white father who had sent him with messages to his people, which were written on the white pieces of paper which he carried in the mail pouches; and that, if the Indians were to kill him, the great white father would send many thousands of his soldiers to kill all of them and their women and children.

Early the next morning, the three prisoners were released upon the condition that the other two white men, who were buffalo hunters who had been killing buffalo for the hides and leaving the meat for the wolves, immediately leave the land of the Cheyennes and never return and that Kelly was to see that this occurred or he himself would pay the penalty.

In the summer of 1858, after two years as a pony express rider, Hi decided to make a change and, along with his brother-in-law, Tom Maxwell, took a wagon train of twenty-four wagons owned by Ford and Smith, tandem drawn by thirty-six mule teams, from Atchinson, Kansas, to Salt Lake City, Utah.

It was late summer when the wagon train left Atchinson. Winter caught them at Fort Laramie, where they were forced to stay. No hay was available, so they wintered the mules on grass in the Goshen Hole country near the fort.

During that long winter at Fort Laramie, Hi Kelly came to a very definite conclusion which was to have a certain effect on his life. He decided that it was possible to winter livestock in large numbers in that part of the country without feed other than the rich grass which grew in abundance on the plains and in the mountain valleys.

With the coming of spring, the wagon train moved westward over the mountain ranges to Salt Lake City. Here, they unloaded part of the merchandise which they were hauling, then continued southward about fifty miles to Camp Floyd, near the site of the present city of Provo, Utah, where they unloaded the balance of the merchandise. They then returned with their mules to Salt Lake City where these animals were sold to the United States government for use by the army in that area. The contract completed, they returned with their teamsters, using light equipment, to Independence, Missouri, that same summer.

Two years later, in the spring of 1860, Hi again left Independence with a wagon train owned by Hi Harrison and Sid Barnes, loaded with merchandise bound for Denver, Colorado. When they pulled into this flourishing little town in the foothills of the Rockies, the gold fever was running high. Several major strikes had been made in the mountains to the west, and everyone in town who could get away was rushing madly to these new diggings.

Hi had never entirely recovered from being bitten by the California gold bug. After spending a few days around Denver, he decided to again try his luck at gold mining. The result was that he spent that summer and fall prospecting in the mountains around Leadville, without making a strike of any consequence.

Winter came to the high country and mining activities were closed down for the season. Hi returned to Denver where he took a job with the Ben Halliday Stagecoach and Express Company as a pony express messenger between Julesburg, in the extreme northeast corner of Colorado, and South Pass in central Wyoming.

Not long after he started, his pleasing personality attracted the attention of the management and he was named superintendent of the Julesburg-to-South Pass Division of the company. This covered a distance of about three hundred miles, and had a stage station about every twenty miles, to accommodate stagecoaches and freight wagons, where at least one man was always on duty to assist with fresh horses for the stagecoaches and fresh mules and oxen for the freight outfits. Several teams of horses, mules, and oxen were always kept available.

This was during that period of time in the early sixties, before any railroad had been built into the territories of Colorado, Wyoming, Montana or Utah. All passengers and freight traffic coming into this vast area of the West, including the heavy mining equipment for the rapidly developing mining activities in the mountainous areas of Colorado, were being moved over the rugged wagon trails by horse-drawn stagecoaches and mule- or oxen-drawn freight wagons.

The mining activity around Denver continued to gain momentum. The Ben Halliday Company moved its headquarters from North Platte, Nebraska, to Denver in 1862, and also changed the route of its stagecoach and freighting operations so that the traffic moving over the new line would pass through this booming little mining town as it continued westward through Fort Bridger in central Wyoming, to Salt Lake City, Utah. The total mileage for this new line was approximately seven hundred miles.

There were three basic requirements in establishing a long distance freight and stagecoach operation in the West at that time: grass, wood, and water. All of these necessary items were available in abundance along the two hundred miles from Julesburg to Denver, which closely followed the South Platte River.

In the fine, wide valley of the South Platte, with its winding, slow-moving stream, the beaver, over a long period of years, had built hundreds of dams which caused the water, during periods of high runoff, to back up and overflow the rich bottom land along the stream. In the process, it created fine natural meadows, where the grass grew thick and heavy and stayed green almost all summer. This was, of course, an ideal location for the new stage line, but westward from Denver to Salt Lake City, the route was over country which was far more rugged and difficult. Hi Kelly, who had become recognized as one of the best operators of stagecoach and freight lines in the West, was made superintendent of this new division. He soon began organizing the operation with his usual efficiency and devotion to duty, and found the challenge and responsibility of this new job very much to his liking. While the stage stations were being built every twenty miles, he maintained his office at Virginia Dale, about thirty miles northwest of Fort Collins, where the new stage line crossed over the mountain range lying between the headwaters of the South Platte and the headwaters of the Laramie River.

There was a good stand of pine and fir on the mountain range in this area, and while the building of the stations was under way, Kelly had crews working in this timber, cutting long logs and poles. These logs and poles were loaded on the running gear of freight wagons, which were coupled together by long coupling poles, or reaches, so that the distance between the front and rear axles was about twice the usual length. This was done to balance the long logs and poles when they were loaded on the wagons. Each of these heavily loaded wagons was drawn by several teams of mules or oxen. The large logs would be used to build the main building for the accommodation of passengers, while the smaller poles would be used for the building of barns and corrals for the shelter and control of the livestock.

For many years, while working for the various freighting and stagecoach outfits, Kelly had been saving his money and dreaming of having a freight outfit of his own. Thus it was that, in the summer of 1863, he showed up on the streets of Fort Laramie with a small freight outfit of his own, consisting of a few freight wagons and several yoke of oxen. Hi, now twenty-nine years old was a tall, bronzed, soft-spoken, and distinguished-looking young plainsman who had seen the rough and seamy side of life in mining camps from Colorado to California. He had slept on practically every major wagon trail west of the Missouri River, and had encountered about all of the dangers the West had to offer, from gunfights with outlaws and Indian raiding parties to floating large wagon trains across flood-swollen rivers on improvised ferries. He had now returned to Fort Laramie in the hopes of getting a few freighting contracts from the army in that area.

His first major contract was supplying the army with one hundred tons of hay, at twenty-nine dollars a ton. His hay crews cut most of this hay with scythes and cradles along the small streams near the fort, then baled it with a homemade hay press. However, some of the hay was cut on Fox Creek and hauled the thirty miles to Fort Laramie with bull teams.

When this contract was completed, Hi took his profits and bought more bull teams and freight wagons, and furnished hay and wood to other army outposts in that part of the terriory. He learned that there was a strong demand for fresh beef at the army outposts. He had never forgotten the idea which had occurred to him, several years before when he had wintered the mules on grass in the Goshen Hole, about the possibility of raising livestock on the open range in that part of the country. Therefore, he began to buy cattle wherever he could find them, and to make plans for handling livestock at Fort Laramie in large numbers.

Fort Laramie at that time was a major supply point on the Oregon and California emigrant trail. Many of the people on the trail found that by the time they reached Fort Laramie they had more horses and cattle than they could take over the mountains. Hi bought or traded hay for this surplus livestock, which he then turned out on the good grass near the fort. Before many weeks, they would gain sufficient weight to become good beef animals. This enterprising young man was soon in a position to furnish a limited amount of beef to the army and to furnish other types of livestock to anyone needing them.

As he continued to expand his operations, Hi soon had a very profitable livestock trading business going and was well on his way to becoming one of Wyoming's first big cattlemen. He did, however, have two major problems which gave him considerable trouble. One of them was heavy losses of both horses and cattle to Indian raiding parties; the other was the tendency of his cattle to mix with the great herds of buffalo and follow them out of the country. He found the answers to both of these problems in a rather unexpected way in the spring of 1864. He was camped on Chugwater Creek, about twenty miles southwest of Fort Laramie, when a small party of peaceful Sioux Indians set up their teepees in a meadow a short distance from his camp. Hi had learned to speak both the Sioux and Cheyenne languages very fluently during his fifteen years on the plains; so, after he had cooked and eaten his evening meal, he strolled over for a visit with the Indian chief. During the course of the evening, he noticed a very beautiful Indian girl, whom he later learned was a granddaughter of the great Indian chief Red Cloud.

Hi had hay crews working in the meadows near the camp of the Indians, and during the next few weeks he found occasion to spend a considerable amount of his time in that area. A romance quickly developed between the tall, handsome plainsman and the beautiful little Indian princess. Before the summer was over, Hi had asked her to marry him. She was willing, but she told him that before she could marry a white man it would be necessary to get the approval of the chief. When Hi went to the chief and asked for his permission to marry the princess, the chief called a council meeting. After the pipes had been smoked, the chief indicated a willingness for the princess to marry the white man, but he wanted horses. Kelly was willing to talk about horses, but said he wanted the raids on his camps and the stealing of his horses and cattle stopped. After the powwow had lasted almost all night an agreement was finally reached, based upon the proposition that the buffalo belonged to the Indians, but the horses and cattle on the range belonged to Kelly. Kelly agreed to give the Indian chief twenty-three ponies in exchange for permission to marry the Indian princess. The chief promised that not only would the raids on Kelly's livestock by his tribe be stopped, but that they would also help him to run off any raiding parties from other tribes in the future. Kelly and the Indians also mutually agreed that when any large herds of buffalo came on Kelly's range he would get word to their tribe, and they would then come in with hunting parties and run the buffalo off from his range.

Hi and his Indian princess were married at Fort Laramie in the summer of 1864, and they became one of the happiest and most respected couples, by both Indian and white people alike, in that part of the Territory of Wyoming.

Hi continued to expand his operations very rapidly. He established a headquarters ranch on Chugwater Creek, near the site of the present town of Chugwater, and only a short distance from where he first met the Indian maiden who was destined to become his wife. This headquarters ranch continued to be the home of his family and the base of his operations for many years.

There is the story of how Chugwater Creek got its name. It seems that when their oldest boy was about two years of age, the Kellys were camped near a waterfall on the small stream when the little boy, playing nearby, started saying, "Chug, chug, chug." So they named the boy "Chug," and the stream "Chugwater."

Both of the parties to the agreements made at the council meeting on Chugwater Creek kept their commitments down through the years, with one exception. As Hi Kelly told the story to the writer many years later, his wife had one relative who, since he was a member of the family, seemed to feel that he was entitled to special privileges. When he would get tired of eating buffalo meat he would come in on Kelly's range and kill a beef, take all of the good meat he wanted and leave the rest for the wolves and coyotes. Hi finally warned the Indian not to do it again but a few weeks later he found where another beef had been butchered, with indications that the same Indian had done the butchering. Kelly took his rifle and started out on the Indian's trail. Later he said that he was on the trail for about a week, but after he returned he never had any more trouble with that Indian.

Although Kelly's personal problems with the Indians were satisfactorily resolved, the Indian problem in general continued to be quite serious. About twelve years prior, a treaty council meeting of all the high plains Indians had been called by the army to meet at Fort Laramie on September 1, 1851, with high United States government officials.

Almost ten thousand Indians gathered in the Fort Laramie area. Represented in this large gathering were the Sioux, Crow, Cheyenne, Arapaho, Gros Ventres, Arikara,

Mandam and Shoshone, as well as many other smaller tribes of plains Indians. It so happened that at the time there was a shortage of grass in the Fort Laramie area for so large a gathering, and the meeting was moved down the North Platte River about thirty miles to the mouth of Horse Creek, where there were many fine springs and an abundance of grass in the large natural meadows.

After all of the preliminaries and pipe smoking had been taken care of, the meeting got under way with D. D. Mitchell, commissioner of the Bureau of Indian Affairs, from Washington, D.C. representing the United States government. After about two weeks of almost continuous powwows a treaty, which was to prove very ineffective, was finally signed, on September 17, 1851. Within five years this treaty had been broken by almost all of the Indian tribes who had participated in the council meetings and by most of the white people in that part of the country, especially white trappers, buffalo hunters and gold miners and by the troops of the United States Army.

Pressures built up; there were demands that the Indians be brought under control. Another treaty council was convened at Fort Laramie, on April 6, 1868, with twenty-three men and nine women from Washington, D.C., representing the United States government. Present at this meeting were several high-ranking army officers, including General Phil Sheridan of Civil War fame, General W. S. Haney, and Generals Angus, Terry, and Gibbon. As a result of this treaty council meeting, another and very important treaty was signed with the Indians, which was known as "The Treaty with the Sioux, Brule, Ogallala, Minicoujou, Yonktori, Huckpapa, Cuthead, Two Kettle, Sansarcs, Santee, and Arapaho of 1868." One of the principal provisions of this treaty was that it stipulated that each of the Indian tribes would have a reservation; and it defined in very general terms the boundaries of these reservations. Hi Kelly assisted at this meeting in various ways. Under army contract, he moved white settlers from Fort McKinney to Fort Smith and Fort Reno, as a provision of the treaty.

For the next twenty years Hi Kelly served as a neutral mediator. He was able to establish contact with any tribe of Indians, and act as interpreter. His counsel was treated with due accord by both parties.

During this time, the army maintained general headquarters at Omaha, Nebraska, and from this point regulated army operations in the northern high plains country. Fort Laramie was the army outpost from which a major portion of the field operations in connection with the control of the Indians was being conducted. In order to establish a direct contact by wire between these important military establishments, the army, in the summer of 1869, let a contract to Ed Creighton of Omaha for the completion of the telegraph line from North Platte, Nebraska, to Fort Laramie, with this contract providing that the army would furnish the poles and wire.

At about the same time the army also let a contract to Hi Kelly for furnishing the telegraph poles, cut to certain specifications, to be delivered to Ed Creighton in the North Platte River valley. Some of these poles were planned to be cut on the slopes of Bear Mountain near the south rim of the Goshen Hole, and hauled the thirty miles to the mouth of Horse Creek.

The Indians resisted in every way possible while the building of the telegraph line was under way. Besides cutting wire and burning poles, they killed and scalped two of Kelly's pole haulers who were camped on Horse Creek at the big willows about ten miles north of Bear Mountain, burned the wagons loaded with poles, and ran off the oxen. It was late fall when this occurred, with the temperatures running far below freezing; when other pole haulers came along the next day they found the burned wagons with the frozen bodies of the scalped men, which they took on down to the Kelly pole camp in the valley of the Platte for burial.

In the late sixties and early seventies, other changes were occurring in that part of the country. Close upon the heels of the gold seekers of 1849 came the emigrant wagon trains making their way toward the West Coast. As these long, slow-moving wagon trains moved up the valley of the Platte over what later became known as the Oregon Trail and on through Fort Laramie, they were in effect passing through the "Cumberland Gap of the West." It was here at Fort Laramie that the people in the long, white, canvas-covered Conestoga wagons would make their last stop before starting over the rough and dangerous mountain trails on their way to the land of their dreams in California, Oregon, or Washington.

When these wagons were out a few miles beyond Green River, after crossing over the Continental Divide, they would come to a fork in the historic Oregon Trail. One of the forks bore to the northwest down the upper Snake River; the emigrants taking this fork in the trail headed into the beautiful valley of the Willamette or some of the other highly productive valleys in Oregon or Washington. Those taking the other fork in the trail, to the southwest, headed into that fabulous country of rich gold strikes, old Spanish missions and haciendas, and vast unclaimed deserts in the booming, new state of California. Through Fort Laramie came most of the pioneer settlers who crossed the plains before the turn of the century, and who were the forefathers of most of the first generation of native-born residents of the West Coast states.

With this increasing movement of people westward up the valley of the Platte, there was naturally a rapidly developing demand for merchandise of almost all kinds. Hi Kelly, who never hesitated when an opportunity presented itself, made a quick trip in the summer of 1869 to Nebraska City, near Omaha, where he bought a large train of oxen-drawn wagons that he loaded with the merchandise most in demand at the time. He then unloaded this merchandise at a warehouse which he had built about four hundred miles to the west at the mouth of Horse Creek in the Platte River valley. Kelly established a retail store at this point, and used the warehouse as a distribution center for merchandise that he sold wholesale and moved with his own freight wagons to other retail outlets on up the trail. At the same time he had other wagons constantly on the trail, bringing in merchandise in large quantities from Missouri River points, four hundred miles distant, and unloading it at the Platte valley warehouse. A few years later, he moved his retail store and wholesale merchandising operations on to the west about fifty miles, to a point on Chugwater Creek, later known as Bordeaux, only a few miles from the headquarters ranch of his cattle operations.

It was here at Bordeaux, on Chugwater Creek, that three heavily traveled wagon trails forked in different directions. The trail northward, down Chugwater Creek, was the route of the Cheyenne to the Deadwood Stagecoach line, which ran from Cheyenne northward through Fort Laramie to the Black Hills of South Dakota. Forking off and bearing to the northwest was the Bozeman Trail, which ran past Fort Fetterman and skirted the western edge of the Sioux and Cheyenne country before reaching Bozeman, Montana; from there it continued westward to the rich gold fields around Virginia City. The other trail, which was established at a later date, ran to the southwest from Bordeaux, up the Sybille Creek, crossed the Squaw Mountains, then ran westward across the Laramie plains, passing Fort Bridger, before reaching Salt Lake City.

By the time the Longhorn steers began coming up the Texas-Montana Cattle Trail in large numbers, this enterprising pioneer cattleman, with his merchandising, freighting, and cattle operations, was already well on his way to becoming a very wealthy man. However, when the trail opened up, he began buying Longhorns by the thousands and expanding his cattle operations still further, with additional ranches and line camps in the Laramie River basin, on the Laramie plains, and in the Goshen Hole country. Within a few years he was running around twenty thousand head of cattle in the Territory of Wyoming.

It was also about this time that the Kellys built a very fine two-story home at their headquarters ranch on Chugwater Creek, where they raised a large family of five boys and three girls. Hi Kelly spent money lavishly on his family, giving them every opportunity, through the employment of private tutors at the ranch on a year around basis, to get the best possible education. Some attended college in St. Louis, Missouri. Mrs. Kelly took advantage of the educational opportunities by studying along with the children, and she became a very well-educated, charming, and cultured woman, who was always perfectly at ease regardless of her surroundings. In later years it was said that Mrs. Kelly was born with some white blood in her veins, due to her mother having been married, at the time of Mrs. Kelly's birth, to John Reshaw, a white trapper who lived with the Indians.

In the summer of 1884, other cattlemen were coming into that part of the territory and Hi Kelly decided that this country, which he had become accustomed to having almost to himself, was becoming too crowded. Also, satisfied that he had all of the money he would ever need, he sold his entire cattle operation to a Scottish syndicate, the Swan Land and Cattle Company, which had offices in Edinburg, Scotland. Alex Swan was president and general manager.

After making this sale at a price of $410,000, which was a lot of money in 1884, H. B. Kelly made a trip to Scotland to close the deal. When he returned from Europe he built a beautiful new home on Carey Avenue in Cheyenne, with the intention of retiring from all types of business activity. However, having lived an exceptionally active and venturesome life, he soon found this retirement program to be quite monotonous, and before long he was back in the cattle business with three large ranches: the "D," on upper Horse Creek; the "LC," about fifteen miles downstream; and the "Y Cross," also on Horse Creek, about five miles northwest of the little cow town of La Grange.

It was here at the Y Cross, where I was born, that I first knew Hi Kelly, who was like a grandfather to me. When I was a small boy, he gave me the first saddle I ever owned, a beautiful, full-stamped, silver-mounted, boy's saddle, with a large, flat horn and low cantle of the type then used in South Texas and the Republic of Mexico. This saddle Kelly had first given to his oldest son Chug when he was a small boy and who had outgrown it several years before. Needless to say, this saddle was one of my most prized possessions for many years.

Mrs. Kelly continued to live in the big house in Cheyenne, even after her husband went back into the cattle business. Hi spent a considerable amount of his time at home, and they moved in the best social circles. Mrs. Kelly seemed to be quite happy. My father and mother visited the Kellys on many occasions when I was a small boy, and I still remember the teepee which Mrs. Kelly always had set up in the backyard in the summertime, where it served two purposes: a sentimental connection with the past; and a guest house for her Indian relatives, where they would feel at home when they visited her.

Many changes were occurring in the northern high plains country in the nineties, with many restrictions and regulations being put into effect by various governmental agencies which affected the operations of the cattlemen to the point that they felt that they, like the Indians, were being restricted to reservations.

Hi Kelly tried very hard to adjust to these changing conditions, but he soon found that the challenge and freedom of action, which he had long known in the cattle business, were rapidly disappearing. In the spring of 1898, then in his late sixties, he again sold all of his ranching operations, including the Y Cross, and for the second time retired to his home in Cheyenne. He had a deep feeling of disappointment at the changes which were occurring, but was reconciled to the fact that these changes were inevitable.

An action which was taken at federal level about this time that had a very definite impact upon the way of life of some of the cattlemen was a law which permitted any squaw man to divorce his Indian wife, with or without cause, if he made a sworn statement that he had married her in order to live at peace with the Indians.

Many of the squaw men took advantage of this law and abandoned their Indian wives. However, there were five prominent cattlemen in the Territory of Wyoming who did not, and Hi Kelly was one of them. When asked whether he intended to dviorce his wife, he said, "Why should I? She is all that I have left of the way of life that I always have loved."

Once more, in 1903, this dynamic and restless man was in action. This time, he went back to his first love, gold mining, with heavy investments in mining ventures in Oregon. However, he wasn't as successful in mining as in the cattle business, and after some disappointing experiences he returned to Denver about the time of the outbreak of World War One. He became interested in some tungsten mines at the little mining town of Nederlands, about fifty miles northwest of Denver, but again his mining ventures did not prove to be successful, and so he ended his mining career.

I last visited with this remarkable man of the plains a few weeks before I left for the service in 1917; he was then in his late eighties, standing tall and straight as an arrow, still with a restless and fearless gleam in his smiling eyes, as though he were ready and eager for whatever the future might hold. He passed away quietly at Fort Collins in 1924, after having lived ninety eventful years.

Swan Land & Cattle Company Headquarters at Chugwater, 1884, with Cheyenne-Deadwood stage barn and office in foreground
(Courtesy of R. L. Staats of The Swan Company, Chugwater, Wyoming)

(Courtesy of R. L. Staats of The Swan Company, Chugwater, Wyoming)
Chugwater Station, First Division, Cheyenne-Black Hills Stage & Express Line, fifty miles north of Cheyenne; George Lathrop, driver, 1884

Dinner during roundup
(Courtesy of Wyoming State Archives and Historical Department)

(Courtesy of R. L. Staats of The Swan Company, Chugwater, Wyoming)
Last Black Hills coach leaving Cheyenne, February 19, 1887

Branding calves at 66 Ranch

The Longhorn and the Hereford

Cheyenne Club, 1883
(Courtesy of Wyoming State Archives and Historical Department)

Ralph F. Jones, 1948

3 The first large (open range) cattle operation to move into the North Platte valley of western Nebraska was the Bay State Livestock Company, owned by John and Mark Coad of Omaha, and branding the "Block Half Circle." The Coads also owned a large farm near Fremont, Nebraska, about fifty miles west of Omaha, where many of the feeder cattle from their open range operation were fattened out on corn.

The first of the Bay State cattle were turned loose on the Platte west of Grand Island in the early sixties. As the central part of the state began to be settled by farmers, the Coads continued to move westward up the river. At the same time, they expanded very rapidly by bringing in several herds of Texas Longhorn steers and turning them loose on the north fork of the Platte and by establishing additional ranches, including one on Pumpkin Creek, in what is now Banner County, Nebraska, and also a very well-improved headquarters ranch in the North Platte valley, south of the site of the present town of Mitchell.

Another large open-range cattle operation which came in on the South Platte in the early seventies was the Ogallala Land and Cattle Company, branding the "Keystone." They were a large British-owned syndicate and established their headquarters at the mouth of White Tail Creek, about fifty miles west of the present city of North Platte, Nebraska, where the small town of Keystone is now located.

The entire area along the South Platte in western Nebraska and northeastern Colorado was known as the Ogallala Country. The name "Ogallala" was derived from the Ogallala-Sioux tribe of Indians, who had long considered the country lying north of the Arkansas over to and including the valley of the South Platte as their own private hunting grounds. It is probably only natural that the Scottish owners of this big open-range cattle operation would name it the Ogallala Land and Cattle Company. Bill Paxton, a very competent cattleman with offices in Omaha, was general manager of the Ogallala for many years.

Both the Ogallala and the Bay State brought their trail

herds of Longhorn steers into the country over a cattle trail leading northwest out of Dodge City (on the Arkansas) to their ranges on both forks of the Platte. This trail was known as the Western, or Ogallala, Trail. There was also a continuation of this cattle trail, leading northward from the Ogallala, that passed Sidney, Nebraska, and crossed the North Platte River on a toll bridge near the site of the present town of Bridgeport. It was known as the Sidney Trail. The official name for the toll bridge crossing the river at that point was the Camp Clark Bridge. However, since it was on the cattle trail between Sidney (the county seat of what was then Cheyenne County) and the Pine Ridge Indian Agency, on the Sioux Indian reservation in South Dakota, it became known as the Sidney Bridge.

Over the Sidney Trail moved thousands of cattle bound for the Pine Ridge Agency, to be sold to the United States Army for use as army rations and for feeding the Indians after they had been confined to the reservations when all of the buffalo had been killed. The principal point of delivery for Indian cattle for the entire Sioux nation was for many years the Pine Ridge Indian Agency. Many southern dogies bound for the Sand Hill country of western Nebraska and for the good cattle country in the West moved over this trail.

At the time that the Bay State and the Ogallala cattle outfits moved in on the Platte in western Nebraska, it was practically virgin cattle country, with a very heavy growth of good grass and plenty of water in the creeks and rivers which drained the gently rolling hillsides. About the only competition for grass were the remaining herds of buffalo, which were rapidly being slaughtered by the buffalo hunters. This situation was due to change very rapidly.

The migration of people westward, which had been going on ever since the landing of the Pilgrims at Plymouth Rock, was temporarily slowed down by the War Between the States. At the end of this conflict many restless men started looking westward again. Out there were hundreds of thousands of acres of land open to homesteaders. Some of it looked very inviting, particularly in western Nebraska and Kansas.

Many of these were servicemen, recently released from the Union and Confederate armies. Many were newlyweds. They came from everywhere; most were from the states along the Mississippi and Missouri rivers and had farming backgrounds. Most were good, God-fearing, hardworking people; there were, of course, some weaklings and drifters. Many headed for that triangular strip of land lying between the North and South Platte rivers in western Nebraska, bounded on the west by Wyoming. This area had long been the home range of the Ogallala and Bay State cattle companies, and they were not going to give it up easily.

These people came over the Ogallala Crossing on the South Platte, or the toll bridge at Clark's Crossing on the North Platte. Their Peter Schutler wagons, equipped with extra sideboards, would be pulled by one or more yoke of oxen, or by teams of horses or mules. The wagon bows, which held up the canvas wagon cover, would be set in the keepers on the side of the wagon box. The really well-to-do had spring seats, mounted on top of the wagon box. The water barrel was anchored to the left-hand side of the wagon. On the right-hand side was a walking sod-breaking plow, with either a rod or solid moldboard, and a two-by-six slab of oak to make an evener for the plow, as well as extra singletrees for the same purpose. Hung on the endgate of the wagon would be a crate of chickens, with the milk cow following on a lead rope. In the tool box, sort of like a woman's handbag, on the front would be a pail of axle grease, a curry comb and brush, a wagon wheel wrench, picket ropes and hobbles, extra singletree clips, plowshares, and a slab of leather for repairing harness and many other things.

The wagon box would contain all of the family's worldly possessions, including a few pieces of furniture, a sheet-iron wood-burning cook stove, seed grain, cooking pots and pans, and a large kettle for rendering lard and making soap. Inside the wagon would be the family bed, and if there were more than could sleep inside, they slept on the ground outside or under the wagon if it looked like rain. Additional livestock would be trailing along behind, probably driven by a teen-age boy. The one thing that the family would be almost sure to have very little of was money. They would probably have just enough for filing fees.

The migration which had started as a trickle in the seventies built up momentum until people were coming into the Platte River valley of western Nebraska by the hundreds. They filed on any land on which they could get a plow in the ground, right up to the Territory of Wyoming. The opinion of the people from the eastern states was, with some justification, that the Territory of Wyoming was a wild country, inhabited principally by Indians, cowboys, and outlaws, all grouped in the same category, where the property rights of homesteaders were not respected and there was no law except cattleman's law. The Wyoming cattlemen did nothing to dispel this opinion.

Under the law, a homesteader was permitted to file on only 160 acres of land. He was then required to live on the land for five years before making final proof and getting a deed. Someone said that "Uncle Sam wasn't giving them a hundred and sixty acres of land; he was just betting them the land against the thirteen dollar filing fee that they couldn't live on it for five years." Some soon decided that they had made a poor bet.

The first problem after filing was getting a supply of water. They hauled it in barrels loaded in the back of the wagon box from the nearest creek, spring, or other living water, which was usually several miles away. Whisky and vinegar barrels were much in demand. When the barrels were filled with water, they were covered with a piece of burlap or carpet held in place by an extra barrel hoop. By the time the wagon had been driven back to the homestead over the rough prairie, most of the water would have splashed out of the barrels.

The homesteader and his family would continue to live in the wagon until a soddy or half-dugout could be built. The material for laying up the walls of the soddy came from the nearest spot where there was a good stand of black-root buffalo grass. The sod would be turned over with the breaking plow, cut in blocks about sixteen inches square, and layed in the wall, using clay for mortar. When the walls were up, the roof would go on, with a ridge pole in the center and two smaller poles on each side. Poles or boards would then be laid, sloping up to the ridge pole and forming a deck; tar paper would be laid on top of this deck and covered over with about six inches of dirt, with a coping around the edges to hold the soil in place. The dirt floor would be soaked down with water, puddled and tamped, then allowed to dry for several days. When completed, the soddy, although not very pretentious, made a very warm and comfortable place in which to live.

The half-dugouts were built in much the same manner as the soddies except that they were dug about four feet into the ground; with the balance of the wall laid up with sod above ground level, to allow for the installation of windows. The dugout was as serviceable as the soddy, except for the problem caused by snow. When blizzards came, the dugouts would oftentimes become almost completely buried under the snow drifts. A shovel was always kept in the dugout in the wintertime, so that the people could dig their way out when the storm was over.

The big problem for the homesteaders was money; they needed a well and barbed wire. There was only one way to get money, and that was to go get a job, and work was scarce. The big ranches did hire a few people at twenty-five to thirty dollars a month including board. There was some work in the towns along the Union Pacific Railroad, but there just were not enough jobs to go around.

The sodbusters raised chickens and pigs. The women sold all of the butter and eggs that they could spare and only bought groceries that were absolutely necessary. They had to buy flour, salt, coffee, baking powder, a little sugar, and calico. Flour cost two dollars and a quarter for a hundred pounds; blue denim overalls were a dollar a pair. They raised small gardens and hunted rabbits and other small game for meat. When there was no rain, they hauled water in barrels to keep the gardens alive. The homesteaders called this dry farming. The horse- and ox-drawn breaking plows went only about three inches deep. The grain drills and corn planters planted the seed practically on top of the ground, and the first hot wind that came along burned up the crops.

After the crops were planted the men went out and tried to get jobs. The women stayed in the soddies, burned cow or buffalo chips for fuel, and hauled water. They tried to chase the range cattle from the crops, without too much success. Once those Texas Longhorn steers got a taste of that green corn they would be back. The cattlemen were not very helpful; in fact, in many instances they were accused of cutting the homesteaders' fences and of burning their crops. If the hot winds didn't get crops, the range cattle often did.

The Indians said, "sodbuster crazy: he plant buffalo grass wrong side up." When the sod rotted, the topsoil blew away. The cattlemen had always said that it was impossible for a man to make a living on a quarter section of land in this country. Many of the homesteaders decided that the cattlemen were right, loaded their few possessions in their wagons, and headed back to the wives' folks. They didn't have much when they came; they had even less when they left. My mother had an uncle by the name of Ben Stone, who homesteaded in western Nebraska. When he left he traded his homestead for a large silver watch with a hunting case. When he died he didn't leave much in the way of real estate, but that watch was in the family for a long time. They called it "Big Ben."

Many of the people leaving had not only lost faith in the country but in themselves as well. They said that homesteading was all right if you had some other way of making a living; and that instead of the homestead supporting them, they had been supporting the homestead. Soon there were more people leaving than there were people coming into the country. At least four out of five of the original settlers left before they had proven up their homestead, or immediately after they had made final proof. Some sold their relinquishments to people coming into the country, taking whatever they could get for their equity. Both parties went to the land office; one signed relinquishment of all his rights to the land and the other then filed a new homestead and started to fulfill his residence requirement.

The stubborn ones stayed on; not necessarily because they were smarter, or had more vision, but because they were just plain bullheaded and couldn't tell when they were whipped. They dug in and worked a little harder.

They would finally get a well down, which took money since they had to drill from fifty to three hundred feet for water. Drilling costs increased with the depth of the well. The usual cost for a two hundred foot well would be around thirty cents a foot, including casing, or sixty dollars for the well, plus another twenty-five dollars for pipe, cylinder, and hand pump. Once the well was down, they would start raising more pigs and chickens, and probably get another milk cow or two. They had to pump the water by hand for the livestock and garden. It meant a lot of pumping, but it was better than hauling the water five miles in barrels.

There was some rough and hilly country in western Nebraska with a rather limited growth of pine and cedar timber. This timber was within twenty miles of most homesteads. The industrious ones started getting fence posts and wood from the hills and buying enough barbed wire to fence in at least the land that they were actually farming. They also started getting out logs, hewing them, and building good log houses and barns. The old soddy was turned into a smoke house for curing meat.

The real symbol of social status in the community was a windmill. It did in some cases create a problem, however: with the farm fenced, no range cattle to chase, and no water to pump for the livestock, the women were about out of anything to do and in some instances they became quite independent. Some of them even refused to gather and burn cow chips in the cook stove; they insisted on wood. Some had new Singer sewing machines and they were beginning to crowd the men to build schoolhouses and churches. It began to look as though the women were going to win the battle for improved living conditions.

As the influx of homesteaders continued to increase,

the Ogallala and Bay State cattle outfits were being forced to move out and hunt new range. The country had become cut up with plowed fields and barbed wire fences. The sodbusters were chasing and dogging the range cattle to the point where a continuation of the open-range type of operation in that part of the country was becoming almost impossible.

The final blow to the big cattle companies fell in 1887 when the state of Nebraska passed a herd law. Previously, it had been the responsibility of the farmer to protect himself by fencing out the range cattle. Under the new law, the burden fell on the owner of the livestock. If cattle or other livestock were found on someone else's property, they were trespassing and the owner of the land had the right to impound or corral them, notify the owner, and feed the cattle until they were redeemed and the feed bill paid. Under these circumstances, the farmer could determine what his feed was worth, which was usually plenty. If the cattle were not picked up and the feed bill paid within a reasonable length of time (generally about ten days) they would be sold by the county at public auction and the money used to pay the feed bill. This law was, of course, the finish for the Ogallala and the Bay State in Nebraska. They moved everything to Wyoming as rapidly as possible except for what few cattle they could continue to run on the land which they owned or controlled under lease.

The Bay State moved across the state line into the Goshen Hole country. They established the old Crockett ranch just over the Wyoming line, about fifteen miles south of the North Platte River; two ranches on Horse Creek, one north of LaGrange near Hawk Springs, and another at the mouth of Bushnell Creek, about ten miles south of LaGrange; and another very fine ranch about twenty miles east of Cheyenne. A gentleman by the name of Snodgrass, who originally came from Virginia, was manager of the Bay State outfit for several years; and Chris Streaks, who came north with a trail herd from Texas, had stayed on as one of the wagon bosses. At one time, the Bay State was reported to be running around forty thousand head of cattle.

Bill Paxton, manager of the Ogallala, scouted out the Powder River country in the eighties and established a Wyoming headquarters ranch on the middle fork of the Powder River near where the small town of Kaycee is now located. Soon after the passing of the Herd Law in Nebraska, trail herds bearing the "Keystone" brand of the Ogallala were moving northward from Nebraska to Converse and Johnson counties in the Territory of Wyoming to be turned loose on the Powder River.

Herds of cattle gathered in Nebraska by the Ogallala and, bound for the new range on Powder River, would leave the Sidney Trail soon after crossing the North Platte River at Clark's toll bridge, then head westward on the north side of the river, stop overnight on Sheep Creek, and then make a hard drive the next day to the Rawhide, making connections there (near Rawhide Butte) with the Texas-Montana Cattle Trail. Paxton had four wagons, with Bill Hanger, Bud Chambers, Gene Hall, and John Hewitt as trail bosses, moving out herds with around three thousand head to the herd. In the spring of 1887, after the passing of the Herd Law in Nebraska, they turned the first four herds loose on the headwaters of the Powder River, then doubled back and picked up another four herds and pointed them up the trail. They moved over twenty-eight thousand head of steers to the Powder River in that one year alone.

In addition to the herds of Longhorn steers that were

coming up the trail from Texas, a few herds were beginning to come into the territories of Wyoming and Montana (in the eighties) from Oregon. These cattle were a different type of animal than the Texas Longhorns. The southern cattle were long-legged and rangy in build, and capable of traveling greater distances without water. The Oregon cattle, originating principally from Shorthorn and Durham stock, were shorter-legged and more stocky in build.

Attracted by the possibilities of the Oregon cattle making better beef animals than the Longhorns, John A. McShane, one of the Bay State managers, contracted, in 1883, for three thousand head of two- and three-year-old Oregon steers, with delivery to be taken at Baker City, Oregon. The Bay State cowboys who were to pick up the herd, sacked their saddles and caught a Union Pacific passenger train to Kelton, Utah. From there they rode a stagecoach to Baker City. The trail boss, J. H. Ford, had gone up a few days before; when the cowboys came in, Ford had bought and stocked a mess wagon, hired a cook, and was in the process of buying a string of rough-broken saddle horses for the return drive. The cattle were soon gathered and tallied out, then branded with an "FF Bar" on the left side. It was about the middle of July when the herd moved out for the Goshen Hole country a thousand miles away. The herd was drifted up the Snake River for several days, more or less following the route of the old Oregon Trail. It forded the Green River a few miles north of Big Piney, Wyoming, crossed the Continental Divide at South Pass, drifted down the Sweetwater, across the Laramie plains, then down the Laramie River to the Sybill, and from there into the western end of the Goshen Hole. There the herd was worked, and about a thousand head of the smallest steers were cut out and shoved off to the southeast about twenty miles and turned loose on the Bay State range on Horse Creek.

After a few days' rest, the remainder of the herd was put on the trail and headed for the Pine Ridge Indian Agency in South Dakota. They swam the steers across the North Platte at the crossing of the Texas-Montana Cattle Trail below Fort Laramie and then drifted them northward on this trail to the Rawhide. There they turned off from the Texas-Montana Cattle Trail and pointed the herd northeast to the headwaters of the Niobrara River, and from there to the Pine Ridge Indian Agency on the White River. Upon their arrival, over two thousand head of Oregon steers were tallied out to the buyers for the Indian Agency. It was now November and they had been on the trail for over four months and had moved the herd over twelve hundred miles.

In 1886, the Bay State Livestock Company acquired the U. P. Noble ranch, in the Big Horn Basin of northern Wyoming, and began moving herds in from Oregon to stock that range.

In the middle eighties, the Coads began selling their Bay State interests in western Nebraska and eastern Wyoming. The Pumpkin Creek ranch in Banner Country was sold to Ben Cross. They sold their headquarters ranch south of Mitchell and the Crockett ranch just over the Wyoming line to Johnnie Boyle, who branded the "OP." When Boyle was asked what the "OP" stood for, he said, "other peoples." Carl Spencer, a very able cattleman, was his wagon boss. The Coads sold their ranches on Horse Creek near LaGrange to the Union Cattle Company, owned by Sturgis and Goddel, who branded the "Bridle Bit."

As the Coads continued to liquidate the Bay State and their other holdings, John Coad (with a large family of five boys) retained the farm at Fremont, as well as other interests in Omaha, including the Packer's Bank in south Omaha. Mark Coad, a bachelor, kept a fine block of land between Horse Creek and Bear Creek, with his headquarters ranch about ten miles southwest of LaGrange. He switched from cattle to sheep and continued to run around ten thousand head of woolies on this ranch for the next twenty-five years.

As the Ogallala and the Bay State were forced to move out of western Nebraska by the filing of homesteads and the effects of the Herd Law, other changes were also occurring. Some of the sons and daughters of the original homesteaders were coming of age and were filing on the adjoining abandoned homesteads. In the process, the homesteaders were getting elbowroom. Soon, they were building up small herds of what the cattlemen referred to as granger cattle, by keeping the heifers from their milk cows, and buying more cattle when they could. They then naturally became principally interested (from a farming standpoint) in raising feed crops for their livestock. Their next move was to improve the quality of their cattle by crossbreeding with a good quality of Shorthorn or other types of beef cattle. Soon, they were in the cattle business.

This was still cattle country but things had changed: where there had been two large outfits in that country, there were now hundreds of small ones. Through one process or another, most of the remaining homesteaders had acquired from one to ten sections of land, and were now running small outfits of their own. With the introduction of power farming equipment, including listers and deep furrow drills, a large part of western Nebraska soon became rich wheat country. When oil was later discovered in the Julesburg basin of northeastern Colorado and western Nebraska, many of the "stubborn ones," or their sons and daughters, became wealthy from oil royalties.

4   The seventies and eighties were a turbulent period in the development of the West. Gold in large quantities had been found in many places throughout the mountainous areas of the country, and names like Deadwood, Cripple Creek, Tombstone, and Virginia City became known everywhere. The Colorado Rockies became a beehive of mining activity; people came boiling in from everywhere in search of fortunes and adventure.

With the buffalo rapidly being eliminated, and with increasing numbers of trail herds coming to the northern high plains country, the cattle business north of the Arkansas was becoming big business. Reports were circulating in Europe of fabulous profits to be made in the open-range cattle business in the plains states of America. The British government sent a parliamentary commission to the

United States in 1880 to investigate the range cattle industry. This commission, headed by Albert Pell and Clare Read, sent back glowing reports stating that profits of a minimum of 33% could be anticipated on cattle-ranching ventures. After this report was released in England and Scotland, money in almost any quantity became available for investment in new cattle ventures, or for the purpose of expanding existing companies.

As early as 1870, the Scottish American Investment Company had been founded, financing, among other outfits, the Wyoming Cattle Ranch Company, and Western Ranches, Inc. Another Scottish syndicate was formed in 1880, known as the Scottish American Mortgage Company, which financed the Prairie Cattle Company, one of the largest British-owned cattle operations.

In addition to the British-owned and financed companies, there were perhaps an equal number of large, open-range cattle operations financed by companies in some of the eastern cities of the United States. They too were attracted by the overstated profit possibilities of the high risk, open-range cattle business in the high plains country. The investors in these enterprises were usually far more interested in increasing the size of the operation than in taking out the accumulated "book" profits. New companies were formed and many individuals who could get financial backing got into the business. This abundance of invested "risk" capital seeking to make exorbitant profits created a boom in the cattle business. This tremendous expansion program hit the cattle industry hard, and a highly explosive situation developed.

The Union Pacific Railroad arrived in Cheyenne in 1866, and the Northern Pacific arrived in Miles City, on the banks of the Yellowstone, in the fall of 1881. These two railheads, seven hundred miles apart, became two of the wildest cow towns in the West. Miles City became known as the Dodge City of Montana. This was a rollicking, free-swinging country, where the sky was the limit. Funerals for gunfighters were not uncommon; and where there were wild men there would always be wild women, with dance halls, gambling houses, saloons and honky-tonks. A person never asked a man where he came from more than once. This was a big, raw country with plenty of room to expand. A man could just cut his hound loose and go as far as he liked; the next time he stuck his pick in the ground he might hit the mother lode. Or he could try his luck and make a killing in cattle.

Everyone found a place in this big, new country, except horse thieves and boys with yellow streaks. Horse thieves were hanged, and the boys with the yellow streaks generally caught the next stagecoach back home if they were still able. Cowboys sometimes became miners; miners, starving out in the diggin's, oftentimes went to work for the cow outfits.

Many of the big outfits established accounting offices and other business headquarters in Cheyenne or Miles City. Freight wagons, some pulled in tandem by several teams of horses or oxen and others by teams of mules on a jerk line, were always in town at the large supply houses loading grub and other supplies for the cow camps and roundup wagons. Other wagons were coming in heavily loaded with buffalo hides for shipment to eastern markets. Stagecoaches pulled out, bound for many different destinations, loaded with restless people on the move. Roundup wagons set up camp close to town, while the beef herds of three- or four-year-old Longhorn steers, bound for eastern cattle markets, were loaded at the stockyards located on the outskirts of town. Cowboys, buffalo hunters, trappers, and miners came to town to raise hell and let off steam. There were few laws in these cow towns other than that one didn't shoot an unarmed man or shoot a man in the back.

While the trail herds were moving into the high plains country and the homesteaders were beginning to settle in western Nebraska, the railroad companies continued to lay steel westward, and the hide hunters slaughtered the buffalo by the thousands. A very critical problem was being created for the many tribes of Plains Indians, whose forefathers had made their homes in this country for thousands of years.

The way of life of the Indians who lived in this vast and colorful land north of the Arkansas had been almost completely dependent upon the great herds of buffalo for everything that they needed and used. The meat from the buffalo provided the greater part of their food supply; the hides were tanned to make leather, and then made into the blankets and robes for protection against the bitter cold winters, and provided the material for their clothing and bedding, as well as the covering for the frame work of the teepee. Some other uses of the leather were as water containers and covers for boats. Dry buffalo hides were very buoyant. Many crossings of turbulent and swollen rivers were made by both Indians and white mountain men, using nothing more than a dry buffalo hide lashed to a couple of small poles.

White buffalo-hunters, with Sharps rifles and long skinning knives, were exterminating the buffalo by the hundreds of thousands. The hunters generally took only the hides and tongues of the buffalo, leaving the fine meat and carcasses to rot or to be eaten by the wolves and coyotes. The Indians were faced with the threat of their buffalo being destroyed and of the white man coming in with trail herds and taking over the grass, in addition to having their land taken by settlers.

To the white man this was virgin and unoccupied territory, but in the opinion of the Indian, this was *his* land. As the momentum of the white man's migration continued to build, a conflict of major proportions was developing, which, over a period of twenty-five years, would result in many hundreds of people being killed and would take a hundred years of peace to reconcile and adjust.

The white man was very methodical and deliberate in slaughtering the buffalo. The hunters hid in blinds downwind from the herd. The sixteen-pound, fifty-caliber Sharps rifles with thirty-two inch barrels were placed on rests mounted on tripods with a turntable. The loads the hunters used were one hundred twenty grains of powder, with a bullet an inch and a quarter in length. By picking off the buffalo grazing on the edges of the main herd, as many as twenty-five or thirty buffalo could be killed from one stand by an experienced hunter without disturbing the rest of the herd.

The average hunting party was made up of six men: one killer, three skinners, one cook, and the wagon man, who picked up the hides from the skinners and hauled them to camp, where he stretched them out on the ground to dry (with the hairy side underneath), pegging them to the ground with small wooden pegs to hold the stretch. There were also larger hunting parties, some with as many as sixteen men. These usually consisted of two killers, nine skinners, one hide-pegger, one cook, one reloader, and two wagon men: one for gathering the hides from the skinners, and the other for freighting the hides to the nearest shipping point on the railroad.

The number of buffalo slaughtered for hides ran into the millions. In the period from 1870 to 1886, over five million dried buffalo hides were reported to have been shipped over the Santa Fe Railroad from one shipping point alone, Dodge City. The heavy buffalo bull hides were very much in demand during that period of time for making heavy leather belts which were being used for driving the heavy industrial machinery and other equipment in use in the eastern United States and in Europe, as well as for other related activities. There was also a strong demand from all over the world for overcoats and lap robes and other articles made from the lighter weight buffalo hides.

The increased killing of the buffalo and the greed of the white man for gold resulted in the invasion of the Indian country lying north of the Platte, which had been closed to the white man by the treaty of 1868. The tension between the Indian and the white man continued to increase.

Many gold prospectors, hearing wild rumors of fabulous gold deposits in the Indian country, took the big gamble and crossed the Platte. Some came back and some did not. A few made their way as far as the Black Hills of South Dakota and told of finding rich placer showings on some of the streams they panned in that beautiful, mountainous area. Soon the pressure was on for the United States government to open this Indian country to gold-mining. It was a touchy and delicate matter; any such action on the part of the government would be construed by the Indians as being in violation of the Indian Treaty of 1868.

The first open and flagrant violation of this treaty by the white man occurred in 1869, when an organization which had been formed in Cheyenne known as the Big Horn and Black Hills Mining Association, was permitted by the United States government to make an exploratory expedition into the area north of the Platte. When the expedition crossed the North Platte it was composed of 127 armed men, some of whom were miners. After a period of several weeks the expedition returned to Cheyenne without having found gold in any quantity. However, a precedent had been established, and the treaty had been officially broken.

Shortly afterwards the Sioux and Cheyenne went on the warpath. They were later joined by the Arapaho, the Pawnee, the Kiowa and other, smaller tribes, until the entire northern high plains country from the Arkansas River to the Canadian border was in a turmoil, with massacres (including the killing of women and children) occurring without provocation on both sides of the conflict.

In the late seventies, Indian raids on wagon trains and settlements were at a high pitch. Flaming headlines in newspapers over the country demanded that the savage and hostile Indians be killed off or brought under control. There were strong political pressures from mining and cattle interests. A major policy was adopted by the war department which encouraged the killing of the buffalo by the hunters as a means of bringing the Indians to their knees. It was a variation of the scorched-earth policy that had been employed during the recent War Between the States, especially in Sherman's march to the sea. This policy had been effective in bringing that war to a close, and it was now felt that the same policy would place the Indians in a position in which they could not continue to resist. It was known that without the buffalo the Indians would soon be forced to either starve or submit to the white man's will; then they could be restricted to small reservations (as virtual prisoners) and made dependent upon government rations for sustenance.

In the campaign of the army, to bring the Indians under control, three principal army outposts were used in the northern high plains area as bases of operation. They were the Pine Ridge Agency on the edge of the Black Hills of South Dakota, Fort Keogh on the Yellowstone near Miles

City, Montana; and Fort Laramie on the North Platte at the mouth of the Laramie River in Wyoming. There were, of course, many smaller army outposts such as Fort Fetterman and Fort McKinney in Wyoming, and Fort Benton and Fort Peck in Montana. The principal function of these small outposts was to protect the wagon trains and white settlements from Indian raids. Many well-known and outstanding generals commanded these outposts, such as the hard-riding General Nelson A. Miles, General George Crook, and, of course, the impetuous Colonel George Custer who met his Waterloo on the Little Big Horn, where he and his entire command were wiped out by the Sioux and Cheyenne Indians fighting under the able leadership of two great Indian chiefs, Sitting Bull and Crazy Horse.

As the army applied the pressure, the many tribes of Indians, particularly the Sioux and the Cheyenne, fought back with everything that they had. What they lacked in fighting equipment and in formal military training they (to some degree) made up for in cunning and in sheer courage. They ambushed numerous army patrols in the field and on many occasions they besieged some of the smaller, isolated army outposts where getting reinforcements was difficult. When these outposts were captured, they were generally burned to the ground and, sometimes, the Indians also killed any women and children who happened to be at the post. The army often retaliated with raids against Indian villages and in turn killed Indian women and children. Probably the most savage and brutal of these attacks occurred when troops under the command of Colonel John Chivington made a surprise attack upon an Indian village. They slaughtered over one hundred fifty old men, women, and children of Black Kettle's band of Cheyenne Indians while they were camped on Sand Creek, east of Colorado

Springs, waiting for government rations which had been promised but never came.

There was also the infamous Battle of Wounded Knee, which occurred in the Black Hills of South Dakota in 1890; when the Seventh Cavalry made an attack upon an Indian village and killed all of the men, women, and children in Big Foot's band of Sioux at Wounded Knee Creek, except for a few who escaped and hid in the wild and rugged bad lands country along the White River.

Several major engagements were fought between large gatherings of well-mounted Indian warriors and troops of the United States Cavalry. There was the Fetterman Battle, fought near Fort Phil Kearney in northern Wyoming; the Wagon Box Fight, in the same area; and the Dull Knives Fight near Fort Reno on the Powder River, also in the Territory of Wyoming. In the southern part of the Territory of Montana, there were the Battle of the Rosebud and the Lame Deer Fight, both fought on Rosebud Creek, a tributary of the Yellowstone; the Wolf Mountain Fight on the Tongue River at the mouth of Hanging Woman Creek, about a hundred miles south of Miles City; and, of course, Custer's Last Stand on the Little Big Horn River, also in the southern part of the Territory of Montana; as well as many other large and small engagements over the entire northern high plains country. In some of these battles, the Indians were defeated, and in some they won.

The final blow to the cause of the Indians fell when (in 1874) Colonel George A. Custer, in direct violation of the Indian Treaty of 1868, was sent by the War Department, with one thousand men into the Black Hills of South Dakota on what was reported to be a "military reconnaissance of that area." This expedition was accompanied by newspaper correspondents and a large group of experienced miners, making the real purpose of the expedition quite obvious.

The miners found substantial quantities of gold on French Creek (in the Black Hills) and the gold rush was on. For a period of time, the United States Army tried to bar trespassers from the reservation, but the lure of gold was too strong; gold miners by the thousands invaded the land of the Sioux. Red Cloud and other Indian chiefs made trips to Washington, D.C., protesting the breaking of the treaty by the white man. Regardless, in the end the political and economic pressures applied by the white man at the federal level prevailed, and in November of 1875, President Grant and his cabinet decided that the Indians must forever relinquish the Powder River country in Wyoming and the Black Hills in South Dakota. The justification for the seizure of these Indian lands was based upon certain claims of depredations, alleged to have been committed by the Indians over a period of time, in violation of the Fort Laramie Indian Treaty of 1868. This was certainly not a proud day in American history. The Indians learned by this and other official actions to be cautious when dealing with the white man's government. It is regrettable, but that same caution still exists today.

I have, during my lifetime, had the opportunity of attending and participating in several council meetings and conferences with different tribes of Indians, and I have always been impressed with their dedication to their purpose and their ability (with the use of few words) to negotiate and bargain in a council meeting to attain that purpose. They have learned that by delaying in accepting a proposal made by the white man, they can usually get even more concessions. They know that the white man is always in a hurry; they are not, so they can afford to wait.

Indians like to use verbal illustrations when discussing

any subject in a council meeting. Some of these illustrations are very pertinent and reflect the accumulated wisdom of their Indian forefathers, which is a part of the Indian tradition and heritage that has been handed down to them, through Indian folklore and mythology (over thousands of years), by people dealing in the simple things of life and living close to nature. I have heard many very beautiful verbal illustrations used in these meetings. I recall one well-educated Indian who said, "It is a very beautiful cover that you have over the work that you have been doing and the proposals that you are making, but we want to see what is under the cover." At another meeting I once heard an Indian say, "It is a very beautiful picture that you are painting, but we want to know about the kind of paint you are using and what all of the lines in the picture mean before we agree to your proposal."

When the treaties were signed with the peaceful Pueblo Indians living in the Rio Grande Valley of New Mexico, President Lincoln sent a cane to each of the tribes as a token of good faith on the part of the United States government, and he admonished the Indians never to break the cane. Many of the tribes still have these canes hanging in the council meeting rooms of their pueblos, and they point with pride to the fact that the cane has never been broken.

The United States government was very slow and dilatory in meeting its treaty commitments with the Indians, particularly in furnishing adequate educational facilities. However, this situation is being corrected and the American Indian is rapidly being absorbed and assimilated into the white man's way of life. It is being learned that an Indian, given a proper education, can compete with the white man in any walk of life.

The Indian is still intensely loyal to his homeland.

The Navajos claim with considerable pride that more of their young men went to the service during World War II, in proportion to total population, than white men, and that they gave an excellent account of themselves.

5

Many of the great cattle companies that operated on the northern plains before the turn of the century originated in the Southwest, particularly in the Panhandle of Texas and the Strip of Oklahoma. Most of them kept their breeding herds in the warm southern climate; moved their steers north when they were two years old to finish them out on the rich, high-protein grass which grew in abundance in the north, and to make them more rugged. Some of these steers would be shipped out at threes and others would be double-wintered and shipped out at fours. Some would be fat enough at the time that they were shipped to go directly to the packing plants, instead of being moved to feeding pens and finished out on corn.

The Hash Knife outfit, which moved thirty-two thousand head of two-year-old steers (in ten trail herds) to Montana in 1880 and turned them loose on Box Elder Creek, one of the upper tributaries of the Little Missouri, was founded in the late seventies by three cattlemen from Weatherford, Texas. Their herds were running on the Pecos River in New Mexico and Texas. Besides the "Hash Knife" brand, this company, with Colonel Simpson as general manager and part owner, also ran the famous "Mill Iron" brand on some of the cattle they turned loose in Montana.

The arrival of the Hash Knife herds on the little Missouri in 1880 occurred only four years after the Indian country north of the Platte had been opened to the white man. This was beautiful, virgin cattle country and the Hash Knife was the first large southern outfit to move in on the headwaters of this fine stream. However, a short time later the OX outfit, owned by Towers and Gudgell, who were operating a big outfit on the Beaver River in the Strip of Oklahoma, moved in about fifty miles to the north. They were just over the line in South Dakota, on the main stream of the Little Missouri. Another company that moved in shortly afterward was the old 777 outfit owned by Berry and Boise, which originated in the Cherokee Strip of Oklahoma; they established their headquarters on the Little Missouri in the same general area.

At about the same time that the Hash Knife outfit moved in on the Little Missouri in Montana, they also moved another thirty thousand head of cows and yearling heifers to northern Arizona, where the Aztex Land and Cattle Company had purchased over a million acres of land in alternate sections from the Santa Fe Railroad.

This purchase of alternate sections gave them control over an additional million acres of land, represented by the other alternate sections of public land automatically included within the outside boundary of the purchase. This fine tract of land was eighty miles long, running west from Holbrook, Arizona; and was forty miles in width, practically all on the south side of the Santa Fe Railroad tracks. The Hash Knife outfit was reported to be running around eighty thousand head of cattle and to be the second largest cattle outfit in the United States (second only to the giant XIT) and to have been operating ten roundup wagons in the states of Texas, Arizona and Montana.

Burt "Cap" Mossman, who became one of the most widely known cattlemen in the country, was, for a period of time, general manager of the Arizona division of the Hash Knife outfit. Young Mossman first came to New Mexico in 1883 as a sixteen-year-old cowboy for the old Bar A Bar cattle outfit, which had headquarters near the little cow town of San Marchael, New Mexico. When Burt Mossman was only twenty-one years of age, he was running the Bar A Bar. When the outfit was liquidated a few years later he drifted into Arizona and took a job with the Thatcher Banking Interests of Pueblo, Colorado, headed by Mahlon Thatcher.

In addition to other interests in Arizona, the Thatchers owned twelve thousand head of over-aged Texas Longhorn steers, running wild in what was known as the Bloody Basin country on the lower Verde River. This was a rocky, cactus-and-brush country, cut up with arroyos and gullys, and covered with a fairly heavy growth of mesquite brush and Sahuaro and Ocotillo cactus; and there was a rim rock running almost all of the way around the basin so that it was practically inaccessible. This was a tough country to work under any conditions; particularly so since these old steers had been in the basin since they were yearlings and were now as wild as deer. A large percentage of them were renegade steers that had been breaking back into the rough country from roundup outfits for several years. Some of them were seven or eight years old, extremely cunning, and hard to handle. If cornered, these old outlaw steers would come out fighting and would gore a horse or a man with their long, sharply pointed horns, if given a chance.

The Thatchers wanted all of these Longhorn steers gathered and shipped out to market. It was impossible to gather this type of cattle, in this kind of country, by using the usual roundup methods. After checking out the country, Burt Mossman sent in a fence crew to build five- and six-wire fences, with a post every rod and two stays between, across the mouths of several box canyons where there was living water, to be used as holding pastures. Mossman, who spoke Spanish fluently, then made a trip south of the border into old Mexico and came back with a half dozen of the wildest and most daring Yaqui Indian *vaqueros* (cowboys) that he could find. He then went into the Basin with a pack outfit and started gathering steers.

Young Mossman split his vaqueros into pairs and, when the big steers tried to break back to the rough country, the vaqueros, who were experts with a rope, would rope, bust and hog-tie them. They let them lie for an hour or two until they had several hog-tied, then they would pull their *piggin'* strings (tie-down ropes) and let the steers up. If they tried to break back again, they would get more of the same medicine until they got the general idea and went along quietly to the holding pastures.

This was hard, grueling and dangerous work. Running a horse at top speed, roping and busting a big steer in this rocky, broken, cactus-and-brush country took a lot of skill and nerve on the part of both the horse and the rider. The horse could at any time be jerked over when the steer hit the end of the rope, and a fall in this rocky country could be extremely dangerous.

When the young boss and his vaqueros got around a thousand head of big steers in the holding pastures, which took at least a month, they would then move them out as a trail herd towards the nearest cow town on the Santa Fe Railroad, usually Prescott, where the steers would be loaded for shipment to eastern markets.

It took the young roundup boss over two years to work himself out of a job with the Thatchers. By that time, he had gained a wide reputation as being a man who knew how to handle cattle and how to handle men. Even before the Thatcher job was completed, he was approached by Colonel Simpson and offered the job of manager of the Arizona division of the Hash Knife outfit.

When Burt Mossman showed up at Holbrook to take over his new job he was thirty years of age, a good looking man with steady steel-grey eyes, of medium build and a very compact body. He moved quickly in everything he did. He never tried to avoid danger, and had proven during his lifetime that he was perfectly capable of taking care of himself with either his fists or a gun, and he was always ready to prove it again should it be necessary.

In addition to serious personnel and operating problems, the Hash Knife had been having considerable trouble with cattle thieves. When Mossman took over, there were eighty-two men on the payroll, many of them friends and relatives of the previous management. Within a month, he had fired forty-eight men, reducing the crew to thirty-four, which he considered an adequate number to handle the operation. He then turned his attention to the rustler problem.

The Hash Knife holdings adjoined the Navajo Indian reservation on the north for eighty miles. There had been some trouble with Indians butchering Hash Knife beef; however, this problem was brought under control by a program of working closely with the Indian Agency and the Federal Bureau of Indian Affairs. The big problem was in the rough country on the southern border of the Hash Knife range where the terrain was similar to that of the lower Verde River watershed, where Burt Mossman spent the last two years combing the big steers out of the rough country for the Thatchers. Pockets in this type of country made good hideouts for rustlers and other outlaws. Many of them were men who had been run out of the tough mining camps scattered over the Territory of Arizona. These outlaws were not only butchering Hash Knife beef and selling the meat to butcher shops in the mining camps and other towns in the area, but they were also altering brands on some of the Hash Knife cattle and running them across the border into old Mexico and selling them.

When Frank Wattron, the recently elected sheriff of Navajo County, learned that the new Hash Knife manager had serious intentions of cleaning up the rustlers, he issued a deputy sheriff's badge to him and assigned a special deputy to work under his direction. Within the first year, Mossman and the sheriff's office obtained the conviction of twelve rustlers who were sentenced to serve terms of various lengths in the old territorial prison at Yuma.

These arrests were not accomplished without a certain amount of gunplay, and word soon got around among the rustlers that Mossman was a man to look out for in any kind of fight. Many of the outlaws soon left the Territory of Arizona and things quieted down on the Hash Knife range.

Shortly before the turn of the century, the owners of the Hash Knife decided to close out their cattle operations in northern Arizona. Burt Mossman started gathering and shipping out cattle at the rate of two trainloads each week. Before the shipping was completed, Mossman was approached by Arizona Territorial Governor Murphy with a request that he organize and head a territorial department of Arizona Rangers, which would operate upon the same basic concept as the Texas Rangers. Its purpose would be to clean up the outlaw and rustler problem in the entire Territory of Arizona.

Burt Mossman had other plans; but under pressure from other cattlemen he finally agreed to accept the appointment, subject to certain conditions. He took a firm position that if he accepted the appointment, he would serve as captain of the company for one year only, and that he would then have the privilege of naming his successor. He also stipulated that he be allowed to pick his own men, that the names of these men be kept secret, and that the company be composed of a minimum of fourteen men who would operate over the entire Territory of Arizona and be placed strictly at the discretion of the captain.

Captain Burt Mossman did a remarkably good job of cleaning up the outlaw problem in the Territory of Arizona not only with the outlaws and rustlers in the cattle country, but with other types of outlaw gangs that were scattered over the balance of the territory as well. Cap Mossman became a man well known and highly respected by law-abiding citizens over the territory and feared by outlaws during the year that he served as captain of the Arizona Rangers. The name "Cap" stuck with Burt Mossman for the rest of his life.

A few months after tendering his resignation as Captain of the Arizona Rangers, Cap Mossman took what he thought was a temporary job as manager for the Scottish-owned Hansford Land and Cattle Company, branding the "Turkey Track" and operating a large cattle outfit in the Caprock Country, east of the Pecos River near the town of Artesia, in the Territory of New Mexico. The Turkey Track cattle also ranged eastward into what was known as the *Llano Estacado* (staked plains) in West Texas, where the Turkey Track range joined that of the great Matador outfit.

The Matador, with its approximately three quarters of a million acres of excellent, deeded grassland on the headwaters of the Pease River in West Texas, and with its fine headquarters ranch located in Motley County, was purchased from the original owners in 1882 by a Scottish syndicate, which incorporated under the name of the Matador Land and Cattle Company, Ltd., with a capital investment of two million dollars. The new owners expanded very rapidly and, by 1892, showed a count of over seventy thousand head of cattle.

In the summer of 1904, a very serious drought situation developed on the ranges of the Turkey Track and the Matador. It soon became apparent that both of their outfits were going to have to either ship out most of their cattle or find more grass. Mr. James Coburn, a former Kansas City banker who represented the Scotch owners of the Turkey Track in the United States, learned that the Bureau of Indian Affairs in Washington, D.C., was interested in leasing a million acres of grazing land on the Sioux Indian reservation in South Dakota, which would be adequate to take care of the pressing needs of both outfits.

Contact was made by Cap Mossman with Murdo Mc-

Kenzie, who was the manager of the Matador and who served in that capacity for a total of thirty-five years. McKenzie was considered to be another one of the really great cattlemen of the open-range period in the West. The two men agreed to meet in South Dakota and go over the range together.

The area being offered for lease on the Sioux Indian reservation was in high plains country lying east of the Black Hills, bounded on the north by the White River, on the east by the Missouri River, and on the south by Nebraska. After the two men had completed their inspection of the range and found it to be quite satisfactory, they entered into a lease with the Federal Bureau of Indian Affairs, with the Matador taking the northern half of the lease and the Turkey Track taking the southern half. Each of the leases covered approximately a half million acres. Mossman and McKenzie agreed to build a line fence running east and west for a distance of forty miles, between their leases, and to share equally in the cost of building and maintaining the fence.

The Matador had been looking northward for several years, with plans for further expansion of their very profitable Texas operation; they were already operating in the Belle Fourche country, lying north of the Black Hills. With the signing of the lease on the Sioux reservation, they immediately began moving sixteen thousand head of two-year-old steers into that area with Dode McKenzie, the son of Murdo McKenzie, as manager. In December of 1909, he was killed in a gunfight in LeBeau, South Dakota. Bud Stevens, a former Matador cowboy, was arrested and tried for the killing, but was acquitted by the jury in March of 1910.

Continuing its expansion program northward, the Matador leased another fifty thousand acres of fine grazing land on the Saskatchewan River in Canada in 1901. In June of that year, Murdo McKenzie moved approximately two thousand head of steers carrying the Matador brand across the border into Canada, to stock that range.

At a later date, the Matador entered into another lease with the United States Bureau of Indian Affairs for the grazing rights on the Belknap Indian Reservation on the Milk River in northern Montana. The Belknap was the reservation of the Gros Ventres and Assiniboine Indians. This lease contained approximately a half million acres lying south of the town of Harlem, Montana. It was excellent cattle country, with plenty of water, grass and shelter. The first summer Murdo McKenzie stocked this range with fifteen thousand head of cattle. The Matador, under the able leadership of Murdo McKenzie, even with droughts, depressions, and other problems, was, on the average, a very profitable operation.

At the same time that the Matador was moving northward, Cap Mossman was doing likewise with the Turkey Track. The lease on the Sioux reservation was bordered on the north by the new line fence, on the east by the Missouri River, and on the south by Nebraska. Cap built an additional twenty-four miles of fence along the west side of his lease to close it off from the Pine Ridge Indian Reservation. He spent the greater part of his time in South Dakota, building up the Turkey Track herds on the Sioux lease. In the winter of 1905, when he was thirty-eight years of age, he was married, for the first time in his adventurous life, to the lovely Grace Coburn of Kansas City. The bride was the daughter of James Coburn, the Kansas City banker and representative of the owners of the Turkey Track. The Mossmans established a home in Evarts, South Dakota, across the Missouri River from the Sioux lease, and Cap used it for the base of his operations.

A short time after he was married, he acquired complete personal control of the Sioux lease and resigned his position as manager of the Turkey Track.

I shall never forget one story that Cap told to me many years ago about crossing the Missouri River between his lease on the Sioux reservation and his home in Evarts, South Dakota, with his entire family, in the spring of the year, when the ice was breaking up on the river and the crossing was extremely dangerous. He said that he sent two men who could swim on ahead, pulling the light family buggy by a rope. Then he followed, carrying his fifteen-month-old daughter in his arms, while the rest of his family came behind carrying a long rope, which they were ready to throw to anyone who should happen to break through the ice. Cap said that the little girl got a big kick out of the trip, and flirted with him all of the way across the river.

He continued to expand his operations during 1906 and 1907, until he eventually had about one million two hundred thousand acres of good grassland under lease. This gave him capacity for fifty thousand head of cattle. In 1907, in cooperation with Mahlon Thatcher of Pueblo, Colorado (the banker who had owned the steers on the lower Verde in Arizona), Cap founded the Diamond A Cattle Company with headquarters in South Dakota. He proceeded to move in cattle until the leases were stocked to capacity. Later, he bought the Turkey Track holdings on the Pecos in New Mexico from the Scotch owners, and stocked them with Longhorn steers trailed in from Old Mexico. However, his principal interest continued to be in South Dakota. Cap eventually lost part of his lease on the Sioux reservation in South Dakota. He then moved fifteen thousand head of his two-year-old steers to Montana and turned them loose on the Yellowstone, about sixty miles below the mouth of the Powder River.

Cap Mossman, always a fighter, stayed with the cattle business through droughts, blizzards, and depressions, until he finally retired in 1944 at the age of seventy-seven. I am sure that when Cap's time came to ride over that last divide he was leaning forward in his saddle in anticipation of another great adventure.

6 The valley of the Yellowstone, in the central part of the Territory of Montana, was considered to be the heart of the cattle country in that area. Across the headwaters of the Yellowstone and Missouri rivers, in the mountainous country of western Montana, was that fabulous gold-mining country around Virginia City. People from all over the world were boiling into this rich mining area when Conrad Kohrs, a Danish emigrant, came to Grasshopper Gulch in the summer of 1862.

Young Kohrs was then a tall, grey-eyed, broad-shouldered and powerfully built man, nineteen years of age, standing six feet three, and reflecting complete confidence in his ability to meet any challenge. His first job at Grasshopper Gulch was working as a helper in the butcher shop at the camp. Con saved his money, and within a few months he owned the butcher shop. He moved it to Virginia City, where new strikes had been made at Last Chance Gulch, Silver Creek, Alder Gulch, Ophir Gulch, and in several other spots. Gold fever was running high. The miners in the camps wanted beef and they had the gold dust to pay for it. The butcher boy from Virginia City started opening up shops in other mining camps and buying butcher cattle wherever he could find them over a large area of country. Cattle were scarce in the Territory of Montana in the early sixties, so this energetic young man soon started bringing in small trail herds of butcher cattle over the mountain passes from Oregon.

In 1863, Con Kohrs formed a partnership with Ben Peel; they began operating under the name of "Con and Peel." By 1864, they were bringing in an increasing number of large trail herds from Oregon and selling butcher cattle to other shops over the entire territory, at the same time continuing to operate several butcher shops of their own, selling beef both wholesale and retail in large quantities. The country lying between the Yellowstone and the big Missouri in central Montana was known as the Big Open. Con Kohrs, as well as many other Montana cattlemen, started his large-scale, open-range cattle operations in this fine strip of good cattle country.

In the period between his arrival in Virginia City in

1862 and the opening of the country north of the Platte in 1876 which permitted the trail herds to start moving over the Texas-Montana Cattle Trail, Con Kohrs made a sizable fortune. In the Yellowstone country, he established a headquarters ranch for his outfit and put together an organization of cowboys, ranch foremen, and wagon bosses capable of handling a large, open-range operation. With the opening of the trail, he immediately began contracting for trail herds of Longhorn steers, from Texas, and turning them loose on some of the streams in the big open country of central Montana.

Kohrs also formed partnerships with several other cattlemen, including a cattle venture with Granville Stuart in the Judith Basin. He became the largest independent cattleman in the Judith Basin of central Montana. He was elected as the first president of the Montana Stockgrowers' Association, when it was formed in Miles City in April, 1884, with four hundred members. The cattle business at that time was growing very rapidly throughout the West. The records indicate that in 1870 there were only 51,000 head of cattle in the entire Territory of Montana; by 1880 this number had increased to 274,000 head and by 1886 there were 663,000 head of cattle. The rapid increase was due, to a great degree, to the opening of the Texas-Montana Cattle Trail in 1876.

Another big pioneer cattleman was John T. Murphy. He first came to Virginia City in 1864 as a merchant with a wagon train. Virginia City had over ten thousand people, and money was flowing quite freely. Murphy established a large wholesale and retail grocery and freight line under the name of Murphy Neil and Company. He was quite successful and soon branched out into other towns and mining camps in western Montana. He established a large mercantile business in Helena. He also helped organize the Helena National Bank, and later became president of the Montana National Bank.

Enjoying his financial success, Murphy established his 79 outfit, under the name of the Montana Cattle Company. The "79" brand, which became quite famous in the West, was adopted by Murphy as indicating the year in which he started in the cattle business. When the fine headquarters were completed, he moved in herds of Longhorn steers from Texas and herds from Oregon. The Oregon cattle were trailed up the Snake River to the Continental Divide and then moved over the Targhee, Raynolds, and Medicine Lodge passes to the headwaters of the Madison and Ruby rivers. If the herds were to be moved further eastward to the Big Open, they would be moved down the same trail through Bannock and Virginia City; then pick up the Bozeman Trail and be drifted on out into the Yellowstone country.

In 1881, the 79 outfit moved its headquarters to Big Coulee Creek, south of Rygate in central Montana. It had other ranches on the White Beaver and on the Yellowstone, between Reedpoint and Columbus; also the Painted Robe ranch on a stream of the same name, the River Ranch west of Broadview, and the Cross S on the Musselshell. In 1883, the 79 outfit established another ranch on the head of the Big Dry, known as Dugout Ranch.

In addition to their cattle activities, the 79 outfit also had one of the largest horse operations in the West, running thousands of head of good saddle-bred horses on some of their good ranches in central Montana. The original breeding stock for the 79's horses had been trailed in from Oregon; while the foundation breeding of the Oregon saddle-bred horse had been done in California, where fine horses had been the pride of the Spanish rancheros for generations. These horses came from mustang stock that had been crossed and graded up with Claybank and other types; some of the stallions had been imported from Spain by the Spanish rancheros. The California horses had then been brought up the coast to Oregon by boat many years before and turned loose on the range in eastern Oregon.

The Oregon horse was broad chested, with clean limbs and good feet, standing well over fifteen hands in height and weighing from 1,050 to 1,200 pounds. Being short-coupled, sure-footed, and active, these horses had the strength and stamina to fight their way through the deep snow in the north country. There was a good market in the high plains country for all good, clean, well-broken saddle horses with other cattle ranches and with the United States Cavalry. The need for straight colors was always observed in breeding; any horses that were too heavy or found unsuitable for saddle horses were broken to harness and sold in matched teams for pulling stagecoaches, freight wagons, and chuck wagons. The 79 outfit made one sale of three thousand head of horses to an Omaha horsebuyer one year.

The 79's horses were recognized by the cattlemen as being tough and salty. When the big three- and four-year-old broncs, never having felt a rope except once at branding time, were brought into the breaking pens, they were snaky, mean, and hard to handle. It took a real good *bronc peeler* (horse breaker) to handle those big 79 broncs; and it took a special type of cowboy to make a good bronc peeler. He had to be a good rider, cool-headed, and had to like the challenge and ever-present danger of his work, as well as understand the individual horse's temperament and reactions.

There was always plenty of action around the breaking pens at the 79 outfit, and good bronc peelers were hired on a year-around basis. After the broncs were roughed out by the peelers, they were turned over to the cowboys working with the roundup wagons to be used as circle horses;

after they were finished out and well-broken, some would become good cutting ponies and rope horses.

Cowboys working with the 79 wagons had a rough string to ride. The cowboys said that it sure took a good bronc stomper to punch cows for the 79, that the horses were snaky and the country was big, that the wagon bosses were tough and it took a good cowboy to stay with the outfit, but that they did give a man enough to eat.

A young Frenchman, Pierre Wiboux, the son of a large textile manufacturer in Rouboix, France, was a highly educated, serious-minded young man who, with the benefit of a college education, a natural business ability, and financial resources accumulated by his family, was in a position to take advantage of any opportunity that might present itself.

His interest in the cattle business in the high plains country of the United States developed while he was traveling in England. He was studying the operation of the English textile mills with the expectation of continuing in the family business. He heard stories which were going around the wealthy English families about the fabulous fortunes to be made in the open-range cattle business in the United States. His curiosity was aroused and he decided to investigate. With a new wife, a lovely English girl, Mary Ellen Cooper, he arrived in Miles City in 1883. He went over the range country very thoroughly, and liked what he saw. He was particularly impressed with the country along the Little Missouri River in eastern Montana, and after spending some time studying the situation in that area, he returned to Chicago where he spent another several months around the stockyards and livestock markets, asking questions of the people around the Livestock Commission firms or of anyone from whom he could get information about the different breeds of cattle and their relative market values. He spent a considerable amount of time around hotel lobbies, visiting with the many cattlemen and cowboys who came into Chicago with cattle trains, asking them their opinions on the open-range cattle business and its possibilities. He even bought and sold a few carloads of cattle to get a feel of the market and some experience in cattle dealing. When his decision was made, Wiboux left for Montana with the ten thousand dollars he had brought from France, his entire personal capital. He had made up his mind that he would bet that amount on the hunch that he could make a success of the cattle business in this new and interesting country.

The young Frenchman built his first log cabin on Beaver Creek with one large room and a dirt roof, then brought his beautiful bride of a few months out to their new home.

In later years, the Wibouxs liked to tell the story of their first Christmas dinner in this log cabin. Their table was beautifully set with the fine china and silver they had brought over with them from Europe, and the turkey dinner was on the table when, suddenly, a great quantity of water that had been accumulating on the dirt roof, caused by the melting snow, broke through and came down in sheets all over the beautiful table. Although it was a disaster at the time, the memory of that first Christmas dinner was one of the highlights, in future years, for the Wibouxs' stories of the pioneer life that they lived together on the plains of eastern Montana.

Two years after their arrival in the country, the young couple built a large, three-story, frame house on Beaver Creek, and painted it white. In later years, it was the scene of many beautiful social affairs and became known as the White House of eastern Montana.

Pierre Wiboux had shown considerable foresight and judgement in his choice of the Beaver as a location for the headquarters of his W Bar Ranch. It was about twelve miles upstream from Mingusville, near the site of the present town of Wiboux. This part of eastern Montana was a gently rolling country, with a heavy growth of good grass and excellent shelter. Growing in the draws and coulees along the streams were wild fruit thickets, willows, and other brush, providing good shelter for cattle during those severe blizzards which frequently hit the northern plains in the spring of the year. The Northern Pacific Railroad had spanned the Little Missouri River only a few years before, and was reaching westward from North Dakota.

He proceeded slowly in stocking his range, and when the hard winter of '86-'87 occurred, he was not overstocked. His losses were heavy but not disastrous, as were the losses of some of his neighboring cattlemen.

In the summer of 1887, following the hard winter, Wiboux decided that it was time for him to expand. He made a trip to France and secured several hundred thousand dollars. Upon his return, he started buying remnants of herds whose owners had been hard hit by the storms of the previous winter, and were either being forced to sell by the bankers, or had become disillusioned and discouraged by the heavy losses and had decided to get out of the business. Wiboux felt that the demand for feeders and cattle from the northern ranges would continue, and that the recent depletion of the herds would be to his benefit. The strong cattle had lived through the extremely hard winter, and he was sure they would have the stamina to go through other hard winters in the future.

One of the first outfits that he bought was the remnant of the once great Hash Knife outfit which, in addition to their Arizona operations, had at one time been running around sixty thousand head on the Little Missouri in Montana. This herd, through sales and losses, had been reduced to a fraction of its original size. By 1890, Pierre

Wiboux had built up his W Bar outfit to the extent that he was running forty thousand head of cattle on his Montana range, and branding an average of ten thousand calves yearly. He was recognized as the largest cattleman in eastern Montana at that time.

To the east, across the Little Missouri in the western edge of North Dakota, about twenty-five miles from Pierre Wiboux's W Bar headquarters, another young Frenchman, the Marquis de Mores, who had married the daughter of a wealthy New York banker, also made his start in the cattle business, the same year Wiboux established his W Bar on Beaver Creek.

Marquis de Mores was reported to have been "a very impractical and egotistical young man, with dreams of grandeur and of personal infallibility." He purchased several thousand head of cattle and branded them with the "Y Cross" (no connection with the Y Cross ranch in southeastern Wyoming), then established a townsite at his headquarters on the east bank of the Little Missouri River, along the Northern Pacific Railroad, and named it Medora, after the first name of his wife. He built a large meat-packing plant at Medora, which he visualized as the processing center of what he thought would be his hundreds of thousands of head of cattle. After three years and a few other ventures of a similar nature, his cattle empire collapsed and the Marquis de Mores returned to France a very disillusioned young man. It was understood that the ventures of the Marquis cost his father-in-law over three hundred thousand dollars. Perhaps a title in the family was worth that much to a New York banker at that time.

In that same year of 1883, another young man, the son of a very prominent New York family, destined to become one of the world's best-known and most powerful men, came to the valley of the Little Missouri and established his headquarters on the west side of the river. His range adjoined that of Pierre Wiboux's W Bar outfit, and his cattle ranged in both North Dakota and Montana. This man, Theodore Roosevelt, whom the Indians referred to as "the man with the teeth," was a vigorous, two-fisted, friendly man-in-a-hurry, and, although he came west for his health, he was always in search of excitement and adventure.

This colorful young man established two ranches on the Little Missouri, one branding the "Maltese Cross" and the other using the famous "Elkhorn" brand. Teddy Roosevelt was well liked by his neighbors, and did spend some time working with his roundup wagons; however, he would soon find the hard, grueling work of handling cattle to be too slow and unexciting and he would then be off on one of his big-game hunting expeditions in the high mountain ranges of Wyoming or Montana. Roosevelt did, however, take a considerable interest in the public affairs of this new and undeveloped country, and made several long trips to Miles City to attend some of the cattlemen's meetings.

After a few years of ranch life and with some heavy winter losses of cattle, he liquidated his cattle operations and returned to New York. There he jumped into the political arena with all of his vigor and enthusiasm and pursued his political opponents with all of the zest of a mountain lion hunt in the Big Horns.

Many of the cattlemen (both large and small) from eastern Montana and the western part of the Dakotas, including Pierre Wiboux and Theodore Roosevelt, were active in assisting with the developments which occurred in that part of the high plains country. However, Miles City, the headquarters of the Montana Stockgrowers' Association, continued to be the hub of the activities of the cattle business in the valleys of the Yellowstone and the Little Missouri during the open-range period.

Parade

7 An outfit which became widely known among cattlemen in both Wyoming and Montana during the eighties and nineties was the British-owned 101 outfit, with headquarters at Ames, Nebraska, about forty miles west of Omaha, and operating under the name of the Standard Cattle Company. This cattle company originated in the Panhandle of Texas in the late seventies and shortly afterwards moved to Oklahoma's neutral strip. A few years later, they trailed their herds northward to the headwaters of the Cheyenne and Belle Fourche rivers in Wyoming. The Standard Cattle Company had branded the "JD Connected" while operating in Texas and in the neutral strip, but after moving to Wyoming the "101" became the official brand of the company.

R. M. Allen, the English general manager of the company who had his offices in Ames, Nebraska, had purchased the CO Ranch on the headwaters of the Belle Fourche River, only a short distance west of the beautiful Black Hills of South Dakota and forty miles south of the Devil's Tower, as a headquarters for the 101 outfit before the cattle were trailed northward. As the 101 outfit expanded, it bought the large Shipwheel outfit from Loomis and Andrews, along with several thousand head of cattle. The 101's cattle shipping facilities were greatly improved when, in 1893, the Chicago, Burlington and Quincy extended the railroad into Wyoming and located a railway station and stockyard about four miles from the 101 headquarters. The company named this station Moorcroft, and it became one of the 101 outfit's principal shipping points. Merino (now Upton, Wyoming) and the stockyards at Belle Fourche, South Dakota, on the north side of the Black Hills, were two other major shipping points.

The 101 soon became one of the largest outfits in the Territory of Wyoming, with around sixty thousand head of cattle on the range and with their roundup wagons covering a very large area on both the west and north sides of the Black Hills in Wyoming and South Dakota: including large portions of the watersheds of the Cheyenne River, Little Missouri River, Belle Fourche River and the Little Powder River. The 101 worked in cooperation with and shared territory with other outfits running roundup wagons in that area. Some of these outfits were the T Cross T, owned by Jesse Drickel, with Charlie Cree as one of the wagon bosses; Tom Matthews' T7 outfit; the Spade, with Jeff De France as wagon boss; as well as the AU7; and the Quarter Circle L; the 4W; and the Bar FS. Another outfit that worked in that area occasionally was the Ogallala from the Powder River country, branding the "Keystone."

Doc Long was one of the trail bosses when the 101 trailed their original herds northward to Wyoming. He stayed on with the outfit and became recognized as one of the best wagon bosses in the business. The 101 had several other top wagon bosses and foremen, such as Johnnie Porter and Walter Scott. It soon became known as an outfit that not only knew its business but also took care of its people. When the roundup wagons would pull into headquarters on the Belle Fourche in the fall, the good cow punchers would usually be given winter jobs at Ames, Nebraska, or other places where the outfit had interests; some would be sent to Texas or Oklahoma to get herds shaped up to move north in the spring. The 101 continued to trail in around ten thousand head of southern cattle each year and turn them loose on their range in Wyoming.

In 1891, the company expanded its operations still further and established a Montana headquarters on the Little Beaver (a tributary of the Little Missouri) in the southeastern corner of the territory, near Ekalaka, Montana, where their range adjoined that of the Hash Knife and the Mill Iron. A foreman by the name of Mulcahy was sent north as manager of the Montana operations, with Johnnie Price as one of the wagon bosses. They trailed around eight thousand head of two-year-old Longhorn steers the first year and continued to move in about that many each year. The steers were held there until they were three- and four-year-olds and were then loaded on the Northern Pacific at Fallon, Montana, for shipment to Chicago.

The Standard Cattle Company also had a large cattle feeding operation at Ames, Nebraska, where they owned and leased around nine thousand acres of rich farmland in the Platte River valley and raised corn on this land for their feeding operations. They also owned the town of Ames, except for the general merchandise store. R. M. Allen, the general manager of the company, lived in a twenty-room home in Ames, kept several servants, including a coachman, and lived the life of a wealthy English gentleman.

A large part of their feeding operation was carried on under roof in a gigantic feeding barn, reported to be the largest building of that type in use in the United States at that time. This barn was built of solid oak and had over three thousand individual stalls, with water and feed bunks in each stall and a water flushing system large enough to clean the entire building.

The cattle for this feeding operation were shipped down on the Chicago, Burlington and Quincy Railroad from their 101 open-range operation in Wyoming. In addition to the three thousand head of big steers fed under roof, several thousand head of cattle were always on feed, in open feed lots, at Ames. Each of these feed lots was about forty acres in size, and around five hundred head of cattle were kept on feed in each lot. Cotton cake and other feed was shipped in by the trainload. An operation of this kind required a lot of manpower, and several hundred employees were on the payroll at all times at Ames. Eastern Nebraska lost a very prominent landmark when the big feeding barn burned in 1913.

Another pioneer cattle outfit in the same area was the N Bar, owned by two brothers, H. L. Neuman and E. S. "Zeke" Neuman, operating under the name of the Niobrara Cattle Company, with headquarters, established in 1878, on the Niobrara River, (Indian name for running water), at the mouth of Antelope Creek, about twelve miles east of the site of the present town of Gordon, Nebraska, and about thirty miles southeast of the Pine Ridge Indian Agency in South Dakota. The N Bar cattle ranged principally on the Niobrara and Cheyenne rivers in the country south of the Black Hills.

The Neumans, like many other large operators in the open-range cattle business during that period of time, got their start in the merchandising and freighting business, before the railroads were completed across the continent and while there were isolated areas where merchandise could still be sold at handsome profits.

The first venture of the Neuman brothers in merchandising occurred in 1863, when they bought a wagon train at St. Louis, Missouri, consisting of twenty-one wagons with ninety head of oxen, and Zeke headed for Salt Lake City, Utah, where he sold the merchandise at a very satisfactory profit. Upon his return to St. Louis, the Neuman brothers bought more wagons, oxen, and equipment and expanded for the next four years until the Union Pacific Railroad was completed through to Salt Lake in 1868. Not able to compete with the U. P. Railroad, they closed their freighting business. H. L. Neuman was the inside man in their operations; when they closed out their freighting and merchandising business, he turned his attention to banking. In 1867, he organized a bank in Leavenworth, Kansas, which he operated until 1874, when he moved to St. Louis, Missouri, and started the operation of the National Stockyards Bank.

When the Neuman brothers organized the Niobrara Cattle Company in 1878, H. L. Neuman was made president. In addition to his banking activities, he supervised the accounting and records of the cattle company.

Zeke Neuman, the rugged plainsman, served as vice-president and general manager of the company. Zeke devoted practically all of his time to organizing and supervising what was to become one of the largest open-range cattle outfits in the West. This energetic man rapidly built up the N Bar herds on the Niobrara range by bringing in several trail herds of Longhorn steers from Texas. Billy

Irwin, a top trail boss from Texas, became the first foreman and cattle boss for the N Bar. Within eighteen months, the foreman and his crew of top cow hands had received and branded over forty thousand head of southern dogies and turned them loose on the watersheds of the Niobrara and Cheyenne rivers. Delivery on some of these big steers had been taken in country where there were no branding chutes, and each steer had to be team-roped by cowboys. One cowboy roped the head and the other the heels; the steer was then stretched out and tailed down, branded on one side, turned over, and branded on the other side. The N Bar outfit had a very unusual policy of branding all of their cattle, both large and small, with the N Bar on both sides.

Besides the N Bar, the Evans and Hunter outfit, with Bill Whitaker as ranch foreman, was also running several thousand head of cattle and operating roundup wagons in the same country. Regardless of this, the relationship between the two outfits was always very friendly and cooperative. They signed a joint contract in 1878 with the Pine Ridge Indian Agency, whereby the two big cattle outfits agreed to deliver 250 head of cattle to the Sioux Indians every ten days at the Pine Ridge Agency, and the same number every ten days at the Rosebud Agency. This joint venture worked out quite satisfactorily and proved to be very profitable for both outfits.

During the next five years, the N Bar continued to expand their operations in the Niobrara country, and at the same time they were building up a very fine organization of top wagon bosses and cowboys. Some of the wagon bosses who were working for the outfit were Bennett Irwin (brother of the foreman, Billy Irwin), Perry Parker, Dale Miller, Jim Dahlman and Ed Ross, as well as many other good cowmen. It was recognized, however, that during the same period of time that the N Bar herds were being substantially increased and an efficient organization perfected, major problems for the outfit were developing. These problems were principally due to the very heavy influx of homesteaders who were coming into the northwestern corner of Nebraska along the Niobrara River, with the result that the area available for grazing was rapidly being reduced, and open-range operations under these circumstances were becoming extremely difficult, causing the Neumans to start looking for grass in other parts of the high plains country.

In the spring of 1883, Zeke Neuman established another headquarters for his N Bar outfit on the Powder River, about seventy-five miles south of Miles City and about six miles from the site of the present small town of Broadas, Montana. J. S. Irwin was sent north as manager of the Montana division of the outfit, and within the first year he had trailed in five herds of N Bar steers, with three thousand head of Longhorns in each herd, and turned them loose on the Powder River range.

A couple of years later, with a drought condition developing in some parts of their range country, the N Bar was again running short of grass. They trailed two herds, with twenty-five hundred head of steers in each herd, from the Powder River country to the northwest about three hundred miles, swimming them across the Yellowstone at Terry's Crossing, and turning them loose at the mouth of the Musselshell, a short distance from where they had established a second Montana headquarters for the N Bar on Flat Willow Creek. This location was about twenty-five miles south of the DHS headquarters ranch of the well-known cattleman, Granville Stuart. Some of the other big outfits with cattle then running on the Musselshell and in the Judith Basin were the Quarter Circle C and the Circle

Diamond, owned by Coburn and Seiben, with their headquarters ranch also located on Flat Willow Creek; and the Circle Bar outfit with headquarters on Crooked Creek.

The N Bar outfit sent Johnnie Burgess north as foreman of their new Montana operation on the Musselshell, and George Mitchell as the first wagon boss. Within the next few years, they increased their operations on the Powder River and the Musselshell until they were reported to have around thirty thousand head of cattle on the range in Montana. With combined operations in Nebraska, Wyoming, and Montana, they had over seventy thousand head of cattle.

The Niobrara Cattle Company, like many of the big outfits who were then operating with ranches in more than one state, maintained memberships in the stockgrowers' associations of both Wyoming and Montana. The records of the Wyoming Stockgrowers' Association for the year 1887 show the addresses of the Niobrara Cattle Company as "E. S. Neuman, Vice President and General Manager, Post Office Address, Pine Ridge Indian Agency, South Dakota," and "J. S. Irwin, Foreman, Powder River Range, Post Office Address Miles City, Montana."

The Neumans were seen quite frequently during those years around Cheyenne and Miles City, where they took an active part in the meetings of the stockgrowers' associations and other public affairs.

8 Large fortunes were being made by some of the local independent cattlemen and by members of some of the prominent English and Scottish families who owned interests in some of the British-syndicated cattle companies. It was inevitable, therefore, that Cheyenne and Miles City would become the social and financial centers of the high plains cattle country.

One of the large ranches near Cheyenne which made a substantial contribution to the colorful social atmosphere of the city was the PO horse ranch, located about fifteen miles north of Cheyenne on Lodgepole Creek. This ranch was owned by the Arbuckle brothers of Arbuckle Coffee fame. They ran around six thousand head of good well-bred horses on the fifty thousand acres of grassland. They had purchased it from the Union Pacific Railroad in alternate sections, and, in the process, had gained control of another fifty thousand acres of government land, automatically enclosed when they fenced the perimeter of their purchase.

The Arbuckles built a large and very fine home at their PO ranch on Lodgepole Creek and entertained there quite extensively. Many of their guests were members of the wealthy British families who either lived, or were visiting, in that part of the country. For entertainment for their prominent European guests and friends, they kept a large pack of greyhounds kennelled at the ranch and, from time to time, they would organize wolf hunts in order that their friends might "ride to the hounds" on the plains of Wyoming. Their guests would wear colorful riding habits and carry riding crops, along with all of the other paraphernalia, pomp, and ceremony, that went along with the usual English fox hunt.

When the hunt was under way and some unlucky coyote had been flushed from a willow thicket, the chase would be on. They would be after him in full cry, with the yell of "Tally-ho!" ringing across the Wyoming prairie. This apparently was great sport for the guests, but for the cowboys watching the performance, the whole thing was very amusing and, so far as they were concerned, it was just a lot of foolishness. They couldn't see much purpose in having a pack of twenty greyhounds and a whole crowd of people on horseback chasing one measly little old coyote, when the same result could be obtained by some experienced cowboy setting a steel wolf-trap, baited with a freshly killed rabbit along some cow trail back in the rough country.

As the large cattlemen and merchants continued to prosper, many of them built fine homes on Carey Avenue in Cheyenne. These homes were quite elaborate, costing from thirty to fifty thousand dollars (which would be the equivalent of one hundred fifty thousand dollars today). Most of them were two- and three-story homes of a heavy, Romanesque style of architecture. They were very ornate on the inside, designed with paneled walls, cut-glass chandeliers, and several fireplaces. Beautiful carriages and fine driving teams were stabled in large barns and carriage houses, which were built in the rear of the homes in the same general architectural style. There was always considerable rivalry among the ladies as to which of them had the finest carriage and driving team. Choice of transportation (then as now) was considered in social circles to be an expression of good taste.

Fort D. A. Russell (now Fort Warren), located about five miles northwest of Cheyenne, had originally been established in 1867 as a temporary army outpost to protect the Union Pacific construction crews from Indian raids. It was later designated a permanent military base, and several fine, two-story brick homes were built there as officers' quarters for the high-ranking army officers. These large homes afforded their wives an opportunity to entertain guests from the city and to participate in social functions with the wives of the wealthy cattlemen and merchants of the town. Advantage was also taken of the officers' club at the fort, and of the other clubs in the city. Formal dances and parties were held, attended by guests from some of the most prominent British families visiting the area.

This was the period when culture came to the cattle country. Lending dignity and prestige to Cheyenne was the very fine opera house built in 1882 by Francis E. Warren. After its opening in May of that year, it became the center of theatrical life in Cheyenne and the surrounding area for twenty-five years. Adding spice and luster was the pretentious and palatial ranch home of Harry Olerichs, located on Crow Creek, about eight miles northwest of Cheyenne. This colorful individual lavishly entertained many prominent and wealthy guests from all over the world. He was an extremely polished and skillful host and entertainer. He was also reported to have been a man with extraordinary promotional and sales ability, who operated his ranch as a show place for carrying on his promotional activities and for selling stock in his many ventures. It was said that Olerichs, as a favor, always gave his guests an opportunity to buy some stock in his American Cattle and Stock Company.

Olerichs' talent for showmanship and entertainment was unexcelled. Everything about his home gave the impression of great wealth and good taste. The food was prepared by an excellent French chef and served with the finest of European wines, while an orchestra played soft music in the background. When Harry Olerichs arranged for a party at the opera, his guests would be driven into town (with the ladies in evening dress) in a beautiful, enclosed carriage of the type then being used by the nobility in Europe, drawn by a four-in-hand of perfectly matched, high-reined and high-stepping Hamiltonians. Their bobbed tails were braided and tied up in neat knots with bows of wide ribbon. A liveried coachman sat high on the driver's seat, handling his four beautiful horses with all the skill and grace required. When this beautiful carriage came sweeping down the streets of the big cow town and drew up in front of the opera with all the pomp and circumstance of nobility, cowboys, seeing this display of great wealth and splendor for the first time, were inclined to think that they had either spent too much time at the bar or had stumbled off into another world. It is true that the entire social scene in Cheyenne was perhaps a bit ostentatious, but, after all, these people living in the West always lived fully and played extravagantly. The sky was the limit; they went all out in everything they did.

The famous "Cheyenne Club" was organized by the Wyoming cattlemen in 1880. They built a very fine two-story clubhouse at the corner of 17th Street and Warren. This well built clubhouse had a large dining room, a coffee shop, and a long, hand-carved mahogany bar extending almost across one side of the barroom. In addition, there were several meeting rooms where business meetings could be held. One of these rooms was sufficiently large to be used as a ballroom. Upstairs were overnight accommodations for members of the club, particularly those who lived out of town. There were two long verandas running the full length of two sides of the building; out in front were nineteen hitching posts to accommodate the horses of the members.

This excellent club was originally organized basically as a men's club in cooperation with the Wyoming Stockgrowers' Association. However, with the passing of time and with the increased social activity, it became not only the business center of the city but the social center as well. Many brilliant, formal dances and other social functions were held there with the ladies present and with the officers and their wives from the fort participating. The international nature of the membership of the club gave these affairs an added color and distinction. With its high standards of excellence, it became famous among cattlemen all over the West and among European visitors for its fine food and service, available to members and their guests in a cordial atmosphere of western friendship and goodwill. Phil Dater served as the first president of the club; followed by Charles A. Campbell, and later by Hubert E. Teschemacher, who was often referred to jokingly as "a Harvard man born in Paris, with a British accent." These three did an outstanding job of organizing the club and of creating the atmosphere of friendliness and excellence found therein. Regulations were strictly enforced and membership applications were carefully screened. Membership fees were established at fifty dollars, with annual dues of thirty dollars. Military personnel were not charged membership fees, but paid a fee of thirty dollars every six months.

The annual meeting of the Wyoming Stockgrowers' Association always occasioned a lot of activity around the club. The Stockgrowers' Association was organized in Cheyenne on November 29, 1873 as the Laramie County Stockgrowers' Association. About six years later, at a meeting held in Cheyenne on March 29, 1879, the name was changed to the Wyoming Stockgrowers' Association. The membership dues and fees were established at ten dollars per year, with an additional assessment of one cent per year for each head of cattle running on the open range. The Wyoming association had many original charter members among the Montana cattlemen. (The Montana association had not been formed at that time.) Included in this group were Conrad Kohrs, Joseph Scott, and J. H. Conrad.

The cattlemen's hotel in Cheyenne was the Inter-Ocean, which had its grand opening in September, 1875. In addition to the Cheyenne Club, the facilities of the Inter-Ocean were always used as a meeting place for the three-day sessions of the Wyoming Stockgrowers' Association. In Miles City, after the Montana association was formed in 1884, the famous McQueen Hotel (with its wassail bowl) became recognized as the great cowboy headquarters for

Montana and Dakota cattlemen. The McQueen was also the official headquarters of the Montana Stockgrowers' Association for many years. Most of the meetings of the organization were held there, as well as many beautiful social functions.

The open-range cattle business in the Territories of Montana and Wyoming had, of course, been going through a very prosperous period in the years prior to the formation of the stockgrowers' associations. There had been an abundance of free grass on the range during those years, and, with reasonably mild winters cutting the losses of cattle to a minimum, the big outfits had been making exceptionally good profits. However, a serious problem was beginning to develop, due principally to the surplus money available for investment. With this money available and with a good profit experience, practically all the outfits had been increasing the size of their herds. Then, as this expansion craze continued to gain momentum, it became apparent to cattlemen that an explosive situation had developed. Practically all of the range in the high plains country of the West was being overstocked.

At the annual meetings of both the Montana and Wyoming stockgrowers' associations in 1885, several speeches were made by members, as well as by other informed and interested people, stressing the seriousness of overstocking. However, from the standpoint of the cattlemen, this was still open country, and the only controls on the number of cattle a man could run on the open range was the size of his pocketbook. The result was that the management of each cattle company sized up its operations and made decisions accordingly. With the profits they had been making, few were ready to face the facts. Most determined to continue to play it to the hilt. Some of the big outfits were soon shifting herds to neighboring ranges, only to find they were crowding someone else. In the process, bitter feelings developed. The term *range hog* was beginning to be heard quite frequently in the cattle country.

Most of the big outfits made some effort to keep their herds in a certain general area. Nevertheless, when these great herds of cattle were trailed in and turned loose on the open range, the owners practically lost control of them, except for the yearly workings of the roundup wagons. The result was that cattle running loose in that vast open country without any fences scattered over a big area and would, oftentimes, drift great distances in the course of a year. It took close cooperation between the various cattle outfits and a well-coordinated plan of operation for the roundup wagons to keep the cattle from straying too far from their home ranges. The responsibility for this planning and the coordination of roundup activities soon became one of the major functions of the stockgrowers' association.

This planning was a good-sized undertaking for the roundup committee of the association. The range tally for Wyoming, in 1886, showed an actual count of over eight hundred eighty-nine thousand head of cattle. In Montana, during the same period, the range tally was six hundred sixty-three thousand head, for a total of one million five hundred fifty-two thousand head in the two territories. They applied the cattlemen's rule of thumb, which was based upon past experience, that for every fifteen thousand head of cattle running on the range a roundup wagon with a minimum of twenty cowboys and two hundred head of horses would be needed. Therefore, around one hundred and twenty roundup wagons, with two thousand four hundred cowboys and approximately twenty-four thousand good cow ponies, would be needed to cover the range in the two Territories of Wyoming and Montana during the summer and fall roundup season.

Under the plans developed by the roundup committees of the association, the total area to be covered was divided into districts, with a captain appointed by the committee for each district, who was charged with the responsibility of seeing that his district was properly worked. The records indicate that in 1885 the Territory of Wyoming was divided into thirty-two districts, with a minimum of one wagon assigned to each district. (The larger districts were assigned more than one wagon.) It was necessary, when establishing districts and assigning wagons, to work out a coordinated plan of operation with the stockgrowers' association in the adjoining state or territory. The boundaries of the districts were determined to a great degree by the terrain and particularly by the watersheds and drainage of the different rivers and their tributaries, and by natural barriers such as high mountain ranges. The reason watersheds were important, was that cattle always graze away from water one day and then back to water the next day. Therefore, when roundup wagons were working in a certain area, the circle of riders gathering the herds would always swing out far enough to catch all of the cattle that would normally water at a certain stream and then drift them slowly toward their natural watering place.

The number of roundup wagons that each outfit would be asked to furnish was determined by the number of cattle that they had on the range, how much country that particular outfit was interested in covering, and the type of range country that was to be worked. Small outfits generally formed roundup pools, where each outfit in the pool would furnish cowboys and horses, as well as share in the expense of operating the wagon in proportion to the number of cattle they had on the range. The pool wagons also came under the jurisdiction of the district captains and were assigned their country to cover.

The roundup wagons generally pulled out from headquarters at calf-branding time, around July first, and stayed out for about six weeks. Then they would usually pull back into headquarters for a few days to give the cook an opportunity to restock the chuck wagon, and the blacksmith to make any necessary repairs to the wagon or other equipment, and to give the cowboys time for a fling in town. About August twentieth the wagons would pull out again, this time on beef roundup, which, as the cowboys would say, "lasts until snow flies"; meaning around October fifteenth.

When the roundup wagons were working, the range representatives, referred to as "reps," would be exchanged between the outfits with roundup wagons working adjoining areas. The purpose of the reps was to cut out cattle belonging to the outfits they were representing as they were gathered. These cattle were usually strays that had drifted away from their home range during the year since the last roundups. After they were cut out of the herd, these strays would be carried in the beef herd (which was the herd of cattle being gathered for shipment to market) until the throwback men from the outfit which the reps were representing came out to pick up the strays from the beef herd and drift them back to their own home range.

When a rep went out to throw-in with another wagon, he always took his own bed and string of cow ponies with him, but he was completely subject to the orders of the wagon boss running the outfit. If the rep got out of line, the wagon boss would simply tell him to cut his string and go back to his own outfit. A cowboy under these circumstances would generally find himself out of a job.

9 The efficient and well-organized operation of their roundup wagons was one of the keys to the success of any open-range cattle outfit. It was always an event when the wagons first pulled out from headquarters at calf-branding time in the spring. Working with a roundup wagon, even for an old, seasoned cowpuncher, was always quite interesting and exciting. When the wagons were out, everything was on the move, and danger was always in the air. It was a way of life where anything could happen at any time. Probably the best way to explain the details of a roundup wagon's operation is to describe a typical, two days' experience working with a roundup wagon at the time the wagon first pulls out from headquarters on a calf-branding roundup in the spring of the year.

When the wagon boss gave the signal to pull out, the roundup cook, sitting high on the seat of his chuck wagon, would pop his whip; the leaders would take up the slack, and then, as the wheelers leaned into their collars, the heavily loaded chuck wagon would begin to roll. During the past week, the cook and his helpers, along with the blacksmith, would have been busy getting the chuck wagon ready to pull out on the roundup. New wagon sheets would have been stretched over the wagon bows and anchored in place. The metal tires of the wagon would have been removed from the wheels, heated, shrunk, and reset. A cracked wagon hound at the base of the tongue would have been replaced. Axle grease would have been applied freely to the skeins at the ends of the axles with a wooden paddle. The messbox, sitting crosswise in the back of the chuck wagon, would have been completely stocked with grub and cooking utensils. When the wagon pulled out, there would be plenty of everything. The roundup cook, who was generally a crank, would have seen to that. Good roundup cooks were hard to come by and they generally did not have much trouble getting what they wanted from the ranch foreman when they were loading the wagon.

Trailing along behind the chuck wagon as it pulled out came the bed wagon with the night hawk riding the spring seat and skinning a four-up of rough-broken harness horses. Loaded in the back of the wagon were the bedrolls belonging to the twenty or more cowboys working with the wagon. Also loaded in the bottom of the wagon box was the cook's sheet-iron stove, along with the mess tent, branding irons, and several sacks of spuds and beans. There were a good many cases of canned goods, including condensed milk. No self-respecting cowboy ever milked a cow. Also, there were slabs of sowbelly and two hundred feet of one-inch rope. This rope was for use in setting up the horse corral which was used for holding the horse cavvy when the cowboys were catching out fresh horses. Then, there was a side of freshly tanned leather to be used for repairing the saddles and harness; also, a keg of horseshoes and a can of horseshoe nails. It would be necessary to shoe all of those wild-eyed cow ponies while they were being ridden in this rocky country before the wagon pulled back into headquarters.

Passing the wagons in a cloud of dust as they pulled out came the horse cavvy; two hundred head of good saddle ponies, all fresh and salty after having been on green grass for two months. In the cavvy would be ten horses for each cowboy working with the outfit. Some of these ponies would be hard to ride after not having felt leather for several months. The day wrangler and a couple of kid reps were in the process of moving the cavvy to the noon camp on Spring Creek where the first herd would be worked and where the cowboys would catch out fresh cutting-horses from the cavvy.

Several hours earlier, at the first break of dawn, the wagon boss had moved out with his twenty cowhands to make his first circle drive. When they were a few miles out from headquarters, he divided his cowboys into two groups, one group swinging to the right, led by the wagon boss, and the other group to the left, led by a top hand. As the cowboys made their circles they rode at a lope; horses were not spared. Each man would ride down four horses before the day was over. The wagon boss and the top hand rode the outside of their circles, dropping off cowboys in pairs, who then started combing the country for cattle, shaking them out of the rocks and bushes as they pointed them toward the river valleys below.

Soon cattle could be seen moving over thousands of acres of range land; all headed towards a predetermined roundup ground where the herd would be held and worked. As the drives moved onto the roundup grounds, the horse cavvy could be seen being brought in close to the herd by the horse wrangler. Soon the cowboys were roping out some of their best-trained cow ponies and cutting horses for the working of the herd.

As soon as the cattle were closely bunched, the work got under way. Six top cowhands on cutting horses rode into the herd and, working in pairs, started picking out cows with their calves, working them quietly and easily to the edge of the herd where a few fast, quick moves of the smart cutting horses occurred. The startled cows and calves found themselves headed for the cut being held a few hundred yards from the main herd by a couple of young cowhands. There is nothing more fascinating than watching a good cutting horse work in a herd. He moves with all the skill and grace of a matador, anticipating and countering each move made by the cow and calf.

Almost unnoticed while the herd was being worked, except by the very hungry, the chuck wagon and bed wagon had pulled in a short distance from the herd, and the cook was busy setting up a noon camp. There would be sourdough bread and jerked beef with coffee made quickly over a small open fire. Very little time would be wasted on the noon meal. There was still a lot of hard riding to be done before the day was over and there was no time to be lost.

When all the cows and calves had been peeled out of the herd and were being held in the cut, the rest of the cattle were moved away from the roundup grounds and pointed toward the hills. As they moved out, riders were on both sides of the herd, stringing them out for a brand tally. The owners of the roundup wagon, as well as two of the reps who were working for other outfits, were in the process of taking a roundup count for their records. This would include all of the cattle that were gathered which were wearing the brands of their outfits. As the herd moved out, it was pinched down by riders on both sides until the cattle were passing the tally men in almost single file. When the cowboys who were doing the counting by brands would reach each hundred head of cattle wearing the brand of their outfit, they would tie a knot in one of their bridle reins. When the entire herd had passed, the tally men would count the knots in their reins, add the additional numbers of cattle that had been counted since they had tied the last knot in their reins, and enter the total count in their tally book.

When the wagon boss waved his hat as a signal, cow ponies were immediately running at top speed toward the mess wagon, with cowboys hitting the ground before their horses had stopped running, jerking latigos from the cinch rings, and laying saddles on the ground with blankets on top to dry. Bridles were pulled off and the cow ponies were given a good start, with a pop from the ends of the bridle reins, toward the horse cavvy waiting nearby. The cowboys then took off on a bowlegged lope toward the chuck wagon, each man trying to be first in the grub line. No one ever knew why; there was always plenty of grub to go around at any good roundup chuck wagon. Then, as the cowboys sat cross-legged on the ground with their plates in their laps, some of the old hands started good-naturedly ribbing and rawhiding the greenhorns. They were just taking their measure now and trying them on for size. Later, these youngsters would get the works.

While the noon meal was being eaten, the horse wrangler had driven the cavvy into the rope corral. When the wagon boss yelled "Let's go!" fast action again got under way with the cowboys roping out their fresh circle horses for the afternoon drive. Other horses, broken to harness, were caught out and hitched to the two wagons while the cook and his helper were busy breaking camp. The cook would soon have his wagon rolling again. One old-timer said he would bet the cook would have the wagons at Willow Springs for the night camp in time to bake biscuits if the popper on his whip held out.

The wagon boss sent one old cowpuncher and a couple of green kids to move the cut on out to the next roundup grounds, where they would pick up the cut from the next herd when it was worked later in the day. As soon as the fresh horses were all saddled and ready to go, the wagon boss went up on his horse and led off at a fast lope; his remaining eighteen cowboys rode with him to sweep a wide circle for the afternoon's work. When the drives were all in and the cattle were gathered in a tight herd on the roundup grounds, the change to fresh cutting horses was again quickly made and this second herd was worked as rapidly as possible. The cows and calves cut from this herd were thrown in with the cut from the morning's drive and moved down to Willow Springs, where they would be held by cowboys riding night herd until the calves were branded the next day.

At the same time the big herd was being worked at the roundup grounds, the cook and his helper, along with the night hawk, were busy setting up the night camp at Willow Springs. The mess tent was set up in back of the chuck wagon in such a manner that one end of the tent covered the back end of the wagon, including the mess box. One end of the ridgepole for the tent was then set over a steel pin which had been placed for that purpose on top of the mess box, while the other end of the ridgepole was supported at its outer end by the upright tent pole. The door of the mess box, hinged at the bottom, was dropped down to a level position where it became the cook's working table, and was supported at its outer end by a wooden upright about three and one-half feet in length, which was also hinged to that end of the table. The cook's pot racks, consisting of an iron cross bar about eight feet long and supported on each end by metal tripods, was set up a short distance in front of the mess tent. Pot hooks of various lengths hung down from the crossbar and large iron pots loaded with food were soon hanging by their bails from pot hooks, where they were suspended over an open fire.

The aroma of the cooking food was strong in the air when the hungry cowboys came boiling into camp. There was boiled beef, potatoes, and beans in the iron pots; baking-powder biscuits were browning in a large Dutch oven buried in the coals. The cook reached in with a long iron pot hook and lifted pots of hot food from the fire. Rice pudding and coffee were simmering on the sheet-iron stove inside the mess tent. As soon as the hungry men had hurriedly washed their faces at the spring, they were heaping up their plates with the good food and eating like this would probably be their last chance. At the same time, they were rawhiding the cook because he didn't put more raisins in the rice pudding.

Beds were soon unloaded from the bed wagon and the tongue of the chuck wagon was shoved high into the air and propped up with the neck yoke from the wagon. A rope had been run through the eye in the end of the wagon tongue, and a hind quarter of a beef which had been killed at the ranch the day before was pulled up and swung clear, where it would keep cool and be out of the reach of any night-prowling animals that might be around. Night horses for riding night herd on the cows and calves were also caught out of the cavvy and wagon-wheeled to the bed wagon. The cook and his helper thoroughly checked the canvas wagon covers to be sure they were well tied down and that the supplies were all under cover. It might rain before morning. Then, as darkness began to close in, peace and quiet settled over the cow camp. Cowboys gathered around the open campfire. Some stretched out full length on the ground; others used their bedrolls for back rests. The cowboys spoke quietly, and that particular type of humor known only to cow camps began to unfold.

Old Hoop, so-called because of his bowlegs, opened it up when he said "Dave, that was a pretty good cuttin' horse that you were ridin' out there today. That is, he is a pretty good cuttin' horse if you forget about horses like my old Headlight. Why, that old cuttin' horse of mine is just plain smart. You know, once last fall I sent old Headlight all by himself up to the Chugwater Flats to get a brindle bull that we had missed in the roundup; and I'm telling you for a fact, he not only got the bull, but that old cow pony also had about twenty head of calves that had been fathered by that brindle bull. He had cut them away from their mothers and brought them along to the ranch with the bull."

Dave pulled off one of his boots and then said: "Hoop, you are about the biggest liar that I have ever known. You are damned near as big a liar as old Dinky Moore. Why, I remember when Dinky was runnin' the wagon a couple of years ago. He had us ridin' two circles a day, workin' both herds and then brandin' calves after supper. So when the wagon pulled in on Fox Creek, we boys got together and decided we were all goin' to quit unless Dinky slowed it down. When we got him cornered in his tent and told him what we were goin' to do, he let us have it. He said: 'Work! Hell, you fellows don't know what work is! Why, one time last summer, I trailed fifteen hundred head of yearling heifers all by myself, a hundred and fifty miles from the Greasewood Flats to the Laramie plains. I was five days on the trail, did all of my own cookin', rode my own night herd, wrangled my own horses, and when I got up there, I not only tallied them through the gap and checked the brands, but looked for strays at the same time!' We all got started to laughing; Dinky walked off, and, don't you know, it was two days later before we remembered what we had cornered Dinky about in the first place. By that time it was too late, so we just went on ridin' two circles a day, workin' both of the herds and then brandin' the calves after supper." Some of the cowboys were already unrolling their bedrolls, and soon the only activity around the camp was when the cowboys who were riding night herd came in every two hours to shake out their relief men and crawl under their own tarps.

Morning comes early in a cow camp. The moon still hung high in the sky when the cook started beating on a dishpan with an iron spoon and yelling: "Come and get it before I throw it to the buzzards!" The cook had been up for an hour, frying beef steak and potatoes for breakfast on the sheet-iron stove, and wouldn't be in a very good humor. If any of the young cowboys came straggling in bellyaching about having to get up in the middle of the night, they had better keep out of his way or he was liable to hang a skillet over their heads. When the cowboys finished breakfast, it still wasn't light enough to see to corral the horses. One old hand was grumbling and perhaps exaggerating when he said, "I will bet a month's pay that

I have spent five years of my life just sittin' around a damn cow camp, waitin' for daylight."

The cowboys had set up the rope horse corral the evening before. It consisted of twelve wooden uprights, each about five feet in length, with notches cut in the wood near the top of the upright. These uprights were bolted to movable bases which the cowboys had placed in a circular fashion to form the corral. Stakes were driven through rings around the edges of the bases to hold them rigidly in place. Then the one-inch corral rope which had been brought along for that purpose was dropped into the notches near the top and on the outside of the uprights. The rope was drawn tight, and the corral was complete.

When the horse cavvy was brought in by the night hawk and shoved into the rope corral, the two hundred head of half-wild ponies immediately began churning and milling in the center of the ring. Several cowboys, with loops in their saddle ropes, circled the outside of the rope corral, each looking for the circle horse he wanted to ride that morning. Suddenly, a rope would snake out and the loop would settle neatly over the head and around the neck of the horse the cowboy wanted for his first circle. The reluctant horse would then be half-led and half-dragged out of the milling herd of horses and up to the inside edge of the rope corral. There the cowboy would slip a hackamore or bridle over the horse's head. The corral rope would be temporarily dropped by the men who were handling the big rope, and the horse would be led out over the rope to be saddled.

The roughest and meanest horses in each cowboy's string were always caught out for the morning circle. When the saddling got under way, many of the horses fought with everything they had. Some of them were half-broken broncs, others were just plain outlaws that had never given up their fight against man and his saddle. Some of the roughest ones had to be eared down. One horse lashed out with his front feet and a young cowboy was knocked to the ground, but got up and walked away. When the saddles were in place and cinched down, the competent and crusty wagon boss looked them over, shouted "Let's go!" and the morning's show was on. Some of the circle horses moved off quietly; others hung their heads between their front legs and arched their backs, and the cowboys on top of those ponies were in for a ride. With the cowboys cinching down on his hackamore reins, the pony put on his show: bucking, sunfishing, swapping ends, and using all of the other tricks known only to horseflesh. Two or three of the green cowboys picked themselves up out of the dust. One young rep landed in a cactus patch sitting down while another cowboy got up from the ground displaying extreme pain and holding a dislocated shoulder.

The wagon boss started one cowboy on a fast ride to the nearest town (thirty miles away) for a doctor. The cook turned the young rep over a bedroll and got busy with his tweezers, pulling cactus out of the young cowboy's hindquarters in not a very gentle manner, and grumbling that he couldn't spend all his time on one job. While these things were being done, a couple of cowboys had made a bed for the crippled kid in the back of the bed wagon. Soon afterwards the cook crawled up on his spring seat, and both wagons started rolling on the trail to Lone Tree Creek. The wagon boss gathered up all of his cowboys who were still on horseback and took off on a long lope to make his morning circle. They would only make one drive that day, then work the herd and brand calves at Lone Tree in the afternoon.

When the wagons were pulling in near the big spring on Lone Tree Creek, the cows and calves that had been cut from the three herds during the past two days could be seen being moved slowly out onto the flats near the camp where the calves would be branded later in the day. Wood for the branding fires was being dragged in from a nearby ridge by a couple of cowboys on horseback. They were using their saddle ropes, snubbed to the horns of their saddles, to drag the wood. Good rope horses, to be used for roping calves in the afternoon, were being caught out of the cavvy by the top hands assigned by the wagon boss to do the roping. There were no branding corrals at Lone Tree, so this would be an open-range branding.

The cook soon had his pot racks set up with a good meal cooking over an open fire and, by the time the noon meal had been hurriedly eaten by the cowboys, the branding irons were hot and the branding got under way. Two old hands who were expert ropers rode slowly into the herd; calves were soon coming out on the ends of their ropes and being dragged up close to the branding fires. All calves were branded with the same brand as the mother, regardless of whether the owner of the calf was represented at the branding or not. Other roundup outfits would be doing the same thing. All the calves gathered by the different roundup wagons over the entire open-range country would be branded under this same procedure.

When a roper came to the branding fires with a calf, he would call the brand that was on the calf's mother to the tally man. Then he would flip his rope over a forked post that had been set in the ground to keep the calves from running sidewise and pull the calf up close as two flankers moved in, one on each side. The flankers then quickly threw the calf on his right side; one of them dropped his right knee on the calf's neck and held him down by doubling the calf's left front leg backward. The other flanker caught the calf's hock, sat down behind him and shoved forward on the calf's right leg with his foot.

The rope was flipped off the calf by one of the flankers, and the roper went back to the herd for another calf, building his next loop as he went. Two old hands now moved in, one with a branding iron and the other with a knife. The calf was quickly branded, marked, and turned loose to go bawling back to the herd, looking for its mother.

The wagon boss, who was riding one of his top horses and supervising the branding operations, cocked a weather eye toward the clouds that had been gathering in the southwest all afternoon and said, "Boys, we had better step it up, it's going to rain." Everyone knew what that meant. It is impossible to brand cattle when their hair and hides are wet. The boss sent in another roper. There were now three ropers and six sets of flankers in action. As the tempo of the work increased, everything moved with clocklike precision. The wagon boss sat his big horse in the middle of the churning sea of swirling dust, bawling calves, sweating men, and cows on the prod, as he urged the men on to even greater efforts. The clouds were moving in fast. Just as the first few drops of rain began to fall, the last calf was dragged up to the fire, quickly branded, and the rope flipped off. Riders were already shoving the herd away from the branding grounds and pointing them toward the hills.

Working with the roundup wagons for the big outfits was always a tough and dangerous life, and certainly no place for weaklings. However, for the young man in search of excitement and adventure, it had its compensations. It was not unusual to hear an old cowpuncher say, "It is worth it to be a cowboy."

10

One of the best managed of the big cattle outfits in the business during the open-range period in the West was the giant XIT outfit. With a quarter of a million head of cattle running on the open range in the six states of Texas, Oklahoma, New Mexico, Colorado, Wyoming, and Montana, the XIT, during the peak of its operations, was considered to be the largest cattle outfit in the United States. It had around fifteen roundup wagons working the range, with a minimum of three hundred cowboys on the payroll in the summertime.

Many of these good cowboys had been with the outfit for a long period of years, and liked to stay in the Panhandle, working with the roundup wagons, spending their winters in the line camps in that area. However, with its cattle operations extending from the Panhandle of Texas to the Yellowstone River in Montana, the XIT always had several trail herds moving northwards over the Texas-Montana Cattle Trail during the summer months. Consequently, there were always plenty of opportunities for the cowboys who preferred the hard, wild, rough, and hazardous life of the long trail to go with the trail herds to that big country north of the Arkansas where there were always big rivers to cross, wild stampedes of panicky Longhorns, raids by gangs of outlaws, and other emergencies which might result in the death or serious injury of one or more of the trail drivers.

The origin of the big XIT outfit is one of the most interesting and unusual large business transactions in the history of the Southwest. This deal occurred as a result of action taken by the Texas legislature in 1879 authorizing the construction of a new capitol building at Austin, Texas. The state of Texas was short of cash at that time for this building program; however, they did have a lot of good land in state ownership, and, therefore, the legislature in the same act appropriated 3,050,000 acres of land to be set aside and used to cover the cost of construction of the new capitol building.

Then in January of 1882, a contract was entered into between the state of Texas and a group of prominent Chicago businessmen headed by John V. Farwell, for the construction of this new capitol building; with the contractor agreeing to build the new building to the state's specifications in exchange for the 3,050,000 acres of land.

The fine tract of land involved in this transaction covered a major portion of ten counties in the Panhandle, with the boundaries of this strip of rangeland beginning at the extreme northwest corner of the state and extending southward along the boundary between the states of Texas and New Mexico for a distance of approximately two hundred miles. This rectangular strip of land had an average width of about twenty-seven miles.

The group of Chicago businessmen who acquired this fine block of Texas rangeland had very little knowledge of the cattle business. However, they were experienced businessmen who intended to make a profit on their investment. They realized that they would need a competent organization of experienced cattlemen to carry on a cattle operation of the size necessary to utilize the rangeland.

The group was very fortunate when it obtained the services of A. G. Boyce as general manager. Boyce was a man of exceptional ability who knew the cattle business thoroughly and also knew from experience where to find the necessary foremen, wagon bosses, and other personnel needed to build a big cattle operation of the type the Chicago businessmen had in mind. As a result of his knowledge of the cattle business and his administrative ability, he was general manager of the XIT for eighteen years.

They organized their cattle company under the name of the Capital Syndicate Company, and adopted the "XIT" as the official brand. The letters *XIT* represented the words "Ten in Texas," referring to the ten counties which were owned by the company. It became one of the finest cattle operations in the state of Texas, and was soon stocked to its full capacity of around one hundred and fifty thousand head of grown cattle. An average of fifty thousand head of calves were branded each year.

During the time their herds were being built up to utilize the full capacity of their Texas range, the XIT was moving out over the Tascosa Cattle Trail to Dodge City around twenty thousand head of mature cattle each year; these being loaded out on the Santa Fe Railroad for shipment to eastern livestock markets. However, with their calf crop far exceeding their sales through this outlet, the company was soon faced with the problem of either finding an additional market for many of their young cattle, or of expanding their own operations to handle this increase. As a result, the XIT was soon extending its operations into the adjoining open-range country in the neutral strip of Oklahoma, northeastern New Mexico, and southeastern Colorado, and eventually into the high plains country north of the Arkansas River.

In addition to this expansion, the XIT sold from fifteen to twenty thousand head of Longhorns each year, for about twenty years, to some of the other large cattle outfits operating in the northern high plains country, particularly to the owners of the large British syndicates who were hungry for cattle and willing to pay top prices; especially if the seller would make delivery to their ranges in the territories of Wyoming and Montana. Consequently, the XIT was soon moving from five to ten trail herds of Longhorns north each summer, with their own trail crews, besides the herds which they were regularly moving north to stock their own range.

It was only about three hundred miles from Beaver Springs to Dodge City and this distance could easily be driven, over the Tascosa Cattle Trail, even with a slow-moving herd, in about a month. Consequently it was the policy of the company to hold the mature cattle that were being shipped out to the eastern livestock markets on the good grass in the Beaver Springs area until as late in the summer as possible, in order for these cattle to gain maximum weight, before they were moved out on the trail to Dodge in late August or early September. The several herds of Longhorns which were trailed out, each year, to the northern high plains country were all moved out from Beaver Springs, a day or two apart, during the month of May, then pointed northward, up the Texas-Montana Cattle Trail; with these herds being on the long trail north for three to four months, depending upon where the cattle were to be turned loose on the northern range.

It was desirable to get the herds on the northern range as early in the fall as possible, so that the cattle could settle down and become acclimated to some degree before the heavy snowstorms and bitter winter weather began. It was the responsibility of the trail bosses to move the herds along on the trail as rapidly as possible, but with care that they not lose flesh and go on the range thin and weakened.

Two brothers with the XIT stand out in the history of the West as being two of the greatest trail bosses who ever moved trail herds out of the Texas Panhandle. For almost two decades Ab and John Blocker were in charge of handling and shaping up all of the XIT herds moved in and out from Beaver Springs, whether these trail herds were bound for Dodge City or for the northern plains. The Blockers were credited with moving more cattle to market over the cattle trails during the time they were operating out of Beaver Springs than any other two trail bosses in the business. Eighty-two thousand head were moved by them in one year alone.

It was the responsibility of the Blockers to shape up the herds, organize the trail crews, assign the trail bosses for each herd, and get the herds moving on the trail. The responsibility for each drive would then pass to the trail boss assigned to that particular herd. One of the Blockers would usually be with the last drive to leave the Panhandle. After spending a few days with that herd, he would move on up the trail, checking each drive until he was with the lead herd, where he would be available and could be reached at any time to help handle any unusual problems that might arise.

They would soon pass out of Texas into the neutral strip of Oklahoma. A few days later, after they were across the Cimarron and pointed towards the Arkansas, in wild, virgin territory, the salty old trail boss would shake his outfit down and find out whether he had a trail crew that could be depended upon. The XIT trail bosses could be quite confident that they would have a large percentage of trail drivers who had been over the long trail before and could be depended upon in any crisis. However, there were always the youngsters and greenhorns making their first drive, and who would have to go through some tight spots before they were completely dependable.

In addition to the usual hazards and discomforts such as flood-swollen rivers, spring blizzards, dust storms, stampedes, and horses stepping in prairie dog holes and falling on the riders, there was always the possibility of running into roving bands of renegade Indians off the reservation on a raiding party.

The Indian raiding problem, so far as the trail herds were concerned, became especially serious after the buffalo herds had been almost entirely eliminated from the northern plains by the white buffalo hunters. The Indians had then been confined to small reservations and placed on government food rations which were both inadequate and uncertain of issue. As a result, both large and small bands of half-starved Indians were constantly jumping the reservations in a search for food of any kind, whether it be wild game or the white man's cattle.

Usually, a small party of about fifteen or twenty Indians with a chief would ride in on the flank of the herd under a white flag. The chief then sent word to the trail boss that he wanted a powwow. Situations of this kind were ordinarily not too difficult for an experienced and seasoned trail boss to handle. There was one unknown factor, however, that he always had to keep in mind. Only a small group of Indians might have shown up on the scene, but there might be a thousand or more Cheyenne or Sioux braves with their paint on, waiting over the hill. Of one thing, however, he could be quite certain: these renegade Indians would be more interested in trying to get a few steers to butcher for meat than in trying to steal the herd.

At the beginning of the powwow, carried on mostly in sign language, the chief would probably demand a hundred head of steers, to be cut by him from the lead of the herd. Everyone, including the Indians, knew that the best and fattest steers would always be out in the lead of the herd. After a period of time had passed, with the Indians pressing their demands, the wise trail boss would undoubtedly offer to give them a half dozen sore-footed and crippled steers that very likely wouldn't make the trip anyway, to be cut by him from the drag of the herd. The Indians would probably refuse the offer and ride off into the hills with a great display of anger and a very hostile attitude. If this occurred, the trail boss would double the night guard, with each man carrying a rifle in a saddle scabbard in addition to his six-shooter. The cowboys not on guard duty would sleep with their clothes on, and with their rifles beside their beds. Their night horses would be saddled and tied in close, where they could get into action on short notice.

It was quite well known in the West that the Indians had a very healthy respect for the fighting ability of cowboys and were ordinarily not too anxious to tangle with them. There is the story of the Indian chief who rode into an army outpost and wanted to borrow a cannon. When asked by the commanding officer whether he wanted the cannon to kill soldiers, the chief replied, "No, want cannon to kill cowboys; kill soldiers with a stick."

If nothing unusual occurred during the night, the Indians would be back shortly after daybreak the next morning, with the powwow again getting under way, this time in earnest. In the end, the trail boss would probably settle with the Indians for around ten head of thin and sore-footed steers, to be cut by him from the drag of the herd. The cook and his helper would break camp while the big herd was again being pointed northward up the trail. However, even before the herd was out of sight over the hill, the trail drivers, looking back, would see the Indians chasing their steers across the plains, shooting them down as they ran, and then butchering them on the prairie as though they were buffalo.

During the spring of 1890, one of the greatest expansions of the XIT occurred when the company bought a ranch on the Big Dry, about fifty miles north of Miles City in northern Montana. A. C. Cato, an experienced Texas cattleman, was general manager of the Montana division. Within a few months, four trail herds that had been on the trail for almost four months and had traveled over twelve hundred miles since leaving the Panhandle, came in on the Big Dry with Bill Coats, John Carlos, Ab Owings, and Bob Fudge as trail bosses. These Longhorns were turned loose in the big open on Cedar Creek, between the Yellowstone and the Missouri. Bob Fudge and Rufe Morris, who came in with these first XIT trail herds, stayed on for many years as wagon bosses. With this new operation, the XIT became the largest cattle outfit in the United States, with over a quarter of a million head of cattle in six states.

In the spring of each year, after the snow was gone, the Montana division of the XIT, like all of the other big cattle outfits operating in the northern high plains country, would put a few cowboys back on the payroll for the spring horse roundup. The purpose of this roundup was to gather the saddle horses that had been running on the open range during the past winter, and to get these cow ponies shaped up to go out with the roundup wagons, as a horse cavvy; when the wagons were ready to pull out on the first cattle roundup of the season in late June.

As the horses were gathered, they were brought into headquarters where they were held in a large horse pasture. Some were brought into the corrals each day, where they were shod with new shoes and their tails were thinned out and shortened, a process referred to as pulling their tails. The tails were pulled short in the north country to keep them from dragging in the deep snow and becoming caked with snow and ice. In the Southwest, where snow was no problem but the horseflies were bad, the tails of the saddle ponies were permitted to grow quite long, sometimes until they dragged the ground. The salty ones among the saddle horses would also be topped off. When a saddle pony has had his liberty for six months, running free and wild on the open range, he will oftentimes be reluctant to again submit to the indignity of man's saddle and spurs, and will express his displeasure when he is topped off for the first time in the spring by trying to lay the cowboy in the dust. It was best to get these notions out of his head before the work started.

The XIT roundup wagons operating in Montana would generally pull out from headquarters around the middle of June and stay out on the range almost continuously for the next five months, or until the snow started to fly in early November. During that time, the XIT would load around twenty trainloads of big, double-wintered, four-year-old Longhorns, on the Northern Pacific Railroad, mostly from Fallon, Montana, with these shipments consisting of about twenty thousand head of steers. They were consigned to some of the Livestock Commission firms at the eastern markets.

The beef herds were always handled as quietly as possible when they were being loaded, in order to avoid the loss of weight which occurs from rough handling. A lot of skill and knowledge on the part of the wagon bosses and cowboys was necessary when these big, spooky Longhorns were brought in sight of the loading pens where any unusual disturbance, such as a switch engine blowing off steam or a barking yellow dog, could frighten the wild Longhorns, causing them to break back from the loading pens. A serious stampede of the herd was often the result. When the steers were again rounded up after such a thing had occurred, and were brought back in sight of the loading pens, they would be even more spooky and difficult to handle than before. The cooperation of all the people who lived in the little cow town, especially the ones who owned horses, was needed, before the beef herd could finally be corraled in the loading pens.

The Big Dry and its tributaries covered a lot of good cattle country, lying between the Yellowstone and the Big Missouri. Several other large outfits besides the XIT operated their roundup wagons in that area. One of these was the Hat X, with Hugh Wells as general manager and Glen Hollingsworth as wagon boss. They had their headquarters on Timber Creek near the Big Dry. Another wagon boss for the Hat X was Charlie Bell. The CK outfit, with headquarters on Prairie Creek, sometimes operated two roundup wagons, with Dave Claire as one of their wagon bosses. Frank Weinrich was wagon boss for the Bar Diamond, and Hugh Exum for the Lazy J. The LU Bar, owned by George Baxter, had its headquarters on the Little Dry, with Lawrence Higgins as wagon boss. There were also two good-sized pool outfits operating in that part of Montana; the Buttleman Pool, with Ernest Long as wagon boss, and the Pot Hound Pool, which was operated by several small ranchers from Charlie Creek, with H. A. Miller as the wagon boss.

Although the XIT was the largest outfit operating in the United States, the largest cattle outfit in the world was reportedly the great Three Circle outfit of General Terrazas, which operated just across the border in the Republic of Mexico. Its operations covered most of the three northern Mexican border states of Sonora, Chihuahua, and Coahuila. Terrazas ran close to a half million head of Mexican Longhorns in this good cattle country, which was five hundred miles in length by two hundred miles in width.

It was the colorful vaqueros of General Terrazas' Three Circle outfit who had inspired the famous painting by the great artist of Western American subjects, Frederic Remington, entitled *Coming to the Rodeo*. The rodeo referred to was held while Remington was visiting at the "Hacienda San Jose De Bavicora," owned by his friend Don Gilberto, who originally had been an American cowboy with a love for excitement and adventure and had drifted into the Republic of Mexico, where he later established a vast cattle empire in the state of Chihuahua.

During the visit of Frederic Remington, Don Gilberto, or "Jack" as he was known to his American friends, arranged to hold a big Mexican fiesta, barbeque, rodeo and *baille* for his outfit and for the people from the neighboring *estancias*, including the people from the big Three Circle outfit of General Terrazas.

The Three Circle vaqueros, a well-mounted, wild, and colorful group, came in large numbers from the Llanos and Sierra Madre domain of the great *patrón* General Terrazas.

When these superb horsemen — dressed in terra-cotta-colored buckskins trimmed in white, with highly colored serapes draped from their shoulders or around their waists — came sweeping across the plains in a cloud of dust, they were riding their horses in a devil-may-care fashion. It was their day to play and they were coming to the rodeo with a complete disregard for personal safety.

There would be the excitement and thrills of the hazardous events of the rodeo, and plenty of well-basted red meat from the barbeque pits where the beef, along with a few quarters of venison and a dozen wild turkeys, would have been roasting over the hot coals since the day before. This meat would be served in generous helpings, along with plenty of hot tortillas and frijoles, from the long serving tables set up the day before in the big plaza in front of the hacienda.

There would also be the great patio of the hacienda, with its red, flagstone floors and its large, overhanging balconies, which would be decorated with many strings of bright red peppers suspended from the eaves. In the evening, the wine would be served from large cut glass containers; there would be soft light from many *luminarios* placed on the patio walls, and dancing with beautiful, dark-complexioned, sultry-eyed señoritas with flashing smiles and come-hither looks, while the soft string music would come from the patio. What more could any vaquero from south of the Rio Grande want? It was a *fiesta muy grande*.

Throughout the entire fiesta, even though they were out for fun, the Three Circle vaqueros carried themselves with a quiet dignity, proof that they were quite proud of the fact that they were the people of the great *patrón*, General Terrazas. It was an impression Frederic Remington remembered for the rest of his life.

Terrazas, principally in the eighties and nineties, sold

hundreds of thousands of head of Mexican Longhorn steers to the big cattle outfits in the territories of Wyoming and Montana. These cattle were delivered to the buyers by Terrazas at the border where, after swimming the Rio Grande, they were moved on out through the Paso del Norte and pointed northward on the Texas-Montana Cattle Trail.

There was a story told around cow camps, about a Wyoming cattleman from the Powder River country wiring Terrazas and asking whether he could furnish as many as twenty thousand head of two-year-old steers. Terrazas was reported to have wired back, "Yes, what color?"

While Terrazas was a great cattleman, he was also a great showman who liked to take all of the comforts and niceties of life with him wherever he went. Cap Mossman liked to tell the story of the time that he made a trip down into the Republic of Mexico to buy a string of two-year-old steers that Terrazas was offering for sale, with arrangements having been made in advance by Mossman to meet Terrazas and some of his vaqueros out on the Terrazas range near Montezuma, between Juarez and Chihuahua.

When Terrazas, a small, smiling, and distinguished looking gentleman, with a very definite military bearing, arrived at the designated meeting place, he was traveling in a beautiful Concord stagecoach drawn by six perfectly matched white mules. In addition to the driver, the general was accompanied by two servants in white uniform, who, as soon as the coach was stopped, stepped out and pulled a sliding table from the back of the vehicle, which, without delay, they covered with white linen and then set with a beautiful silver service, cut glass, and fine china.

When the table was ready and everything was in order, the party sat down at the beautifully appointed table set up out there on the Montezuma plains and were served a delicious hot dinner with all of the trimmings, which had been prepared in advance at the general's hacienda and kept warm on the way out over a bed of hot coals, contained in a heavy metal receptacle loaded in the rear boot of the stagecoach. The dinner was also served with the finest of imported wines, brought along in a tub of ice loaded in the front boot of the coach.

Although Cap Mossman did not buy any cattle from Terrazas on that trip, in future years he did handle many thousands of head of Mexican Longhorns wearing the Three Circle brand of Terrazas on his South Dakota leases. The Three Circle brand of Terrazas had the three circles overlapping, and consequently was almost impossible to burn over or alter.

With his many operations under way, General Terrazas, over a period of time, became a very wealthy man. In addition to his great herds of cattle, he also ran thousands of head of horses and mules on his range in northern Mexico, and at one time was reported to be the largest landowner in the Republic of Mexico, where he had also acquired heavy interests in mining and other commercial activities.

The story was told in the border towns that, when the Mexican Central Railroad was built from El Paso across the Rio Grande to Juarez and Chihuahua, General Terrazas approached the promotors of this railroad when the company was being organized and told them that he would be interested in buying some of the stock. When asked how much stock he would like to buy, he said that in dollars or pesos he did not know, but he would put in a cow for every tie and a calf for every spike between El Paso and Chihuahua, a distance of about two hundred and fifty miles.

Regardless of whether or not this story is true, the fact remains that the building of this railroad was extremely important to the cattle operations of General Terrazas.

When this line was completed he could load Mexican Longhorns at any of the many loading pens built by the company where the railroad crossed his range in northern Mexico. From there he could ship them across the border into the United States at El Paso, where the cattle cars would be transferred to the Santa Fe Railroad and routed to Pueblo or Denver, Colorado.

In later years, around the turn of the century, when other railroads running northward from Denver were completed, there was a considerable increase in northbound shipments of cattle by rail, including shipments of the Three Circle, Mexican Longhorns of Terrazas. When the Cheyenne and Northern Railroad, running from Cheyenne northward for about a hundred miles to Wendover, Wyoming, was opened to traffic, cattle shipments could be routed out of El Paso over the Santa Fe Railroad to Denver, and from there north through Cheyenne to Wendover, where they were unloaded and trailed over the Texas-Montana Cattle Trail to the Powder River country or on into Montana.

11 The Powder River and its tributaries drained a vast area of country lying midway between Cheyenne and Miles City in northern Wyoming and southern Montana. It was good cattle country: well grassed, well watered, and well sheltered.

When a young Englishman, Moreton Frewen, first saw this country while on a big-game hunting trip in the Big Horn Mountains of northern Wyoming in 1878 (only two years after the battle of the Little Big Horn), it was virgin cattle country which had been opened to the white man only the year before. The Sioux Indians were then being rapidly confined to their small reservations east of the Black Hills in South Dakota. The buffalo had almost all been killed off in the Powder River country by the buffalo hunters during that period of time and, without any animals of any kind (either wild or domestic) to graze on the prairie, there had grown an abundance of grass which appeared to be inexhaustible. This was a cattleman's paradise.

Moreton Frewen was a tall, handsome and distinguished-looking young man, twenty-five years of age, who came from a very prominent English family. He had a very outgoing personality, was extremely ambitious, and had dreams of becoming an empire builder. Like many of the other young men in Europe, he had heard the stories in the drawing rooms of the best families in England about the fabulous fortunes to be made in the open-range cattle business in the western United States. The previous year he had visited friends of the family in Texas who had cattle interests, and had seen the great herds of Longhorn cattle on the range, some financed with British capital. He heard stories of the many great trail herds being moved north to the high plains country north of the Arkansas over the Texas-Montana Cattle Trail. After seeing the Powder River country, young Frewen decided that this was the land of his dreams. Almost immediately, he started making definite plans for building a vast cattle empire, with his headquarters on the Powder River in northern Wyoming.

The type of cattle operation which he visualized would be as large as, or larger than, any outfit then operating in the West. He quickly realized, however, that an operation such as he had in mind would require far more than the eighty thousand dollars capital which he had. It was obvious that he would need at least a million dollars to carry out his ambitious plans. There was no question in Moreton Frewen's mind as to his ability to raise that kind of money. In his opinion, all that would be needed would be the planning and the groundwork. He would build a showplace, patterned to some degree after the promotional establishments then operating in the Cheyenne area, with the camouflaged purpose of attracting additional foreign capital.

Soon after returning to England from his big-game hunting trip to the Big Horns, Moreton Frewen entered into a partnership with his younger brother, Richard, and both returned to the Powder River country. They started building a very large, two-story house of logs on a slight rise near the junction of the north fork and the middle fork of the Powder River, overlooking the beautiful Big Horn Mountains. This location was about twenty-five miles west of the army outpost of Fort McKinney, also on the Powder River.

The logs for building the house were hauled by several teams of oxen from the nearby mountains, then hewn and laid up in walls by expert workmen. This great log house was approximately sixty feet by seventy feet. The major portion of the first floor was one large room, to be used principally for the entertainment of guests. There was a wide and beautifully designed winding staircase, made from the finest imported hardwood, leading to an upstairs balcony overlooking the big room below, which boasted two massive fireplaces faced with boulders of many colors, hauled from the neaby hills. There were nineteen spacious guest rooms upstairs all beautifully furnished. The woodwork was of the best hardwood. The furnishings were so designed as to give a rustic appearance and were made of the finest materials and built by expert craftsmen; many of the furnishings were beautifully hand-carved.

This massive log house soon became known locally as "Frewen's Castle." There were additional guesthouses built in the area near the big house, and servants' quarters were provided in a separate building. There were also carriage houses for the beautiful Concord coaches, and fine barns for the hot-blooded driving teams that had been imported from Europe. They were to be used for pulling the coaches in transporting their guests the two hundred twenty miles from the closest railway station, that of Rock River on the Union Pacific Railroad. All the materials used in the construction of the big house and other buildings (with the exception of the logs), including hardwood doors, windows, shingles and furnishings, had to be hauled by wagons and teams of oxen the entire distance from the railroad station at Rock River.

When the entire complex was completed in the summer of 1879, it was comparable to the finest of royal hunting lodges to be found anywhere in Europe. Even before their big house was completed, the Frewen brothers were busy mailing out engraved invitations to their many prominent friends and moneyed acquaintances in Europe, inviting them to be the guests of Moreton and Richard Frewen for the fall big-game hunting season in the Big Horn Mountains of northern Wyoming. In these invitations the Frewens stressed the fact that practically all of the different species of big game to be found anywhere on the North American continent were available in large numbers in the Big Horns and the nearby mountain ranges, including mountain lions, grizzly bears, elk, moose, deer, and Big Horn mountain sheep; and that antelope were available by the thousands on the plains near the ranch, as well as a limited number of remaining buffalo.

When the guests began arriving, they were immediately made comfortable in the guest rooms with servants to take care of their every need. Food of the finest quality was prepared by an excellent chef and served in a friendly western atmosphere. Moreton and Richard Frewen devoted their entire time and effort to providing entertainment and other types of activity that would be of interest to their guests. Moreton was a particularly capable host, with a flair for showmanship and a very charming personality, and had the ability to sense the desires of his guests and to provide for them accordingly. Richard was of a more retiring nature, preferring to stay in the background, where he could take care of the details. This made for a very excellent combination of managerial abilities. Big-game hunting expeditions were organized with pack outfits and excellent local guides who knew almost every foot of the mountain country and where the best hunting was to be found. Chefs were taken with the hunting parties and practically all the comforts of home were provided, including portable bathtubs. If any of the guests were not good enough shots with a rifle to kill their own game, that too would be taken care of by the guides.

At the same time the Frewen brothers had been entertaining their guests, they also had started in the cattle business in a very limited way, with Fred G. S. Hesse as their ranch foreman. They had begun to trail in a few small herds, branding them with the "FUF" brand, which they had recently adopted and recorded under the name "Frewen Brothers." After branding, they turned these cattle loose on the good grass along the Powder River near the big house, where they could readily be seen by the guests.

After the hunting parties returned from the mountains to the big house, the trend of the conversation would be turned by Moreton to the great Powder River country and its possibilities. Attention would be called to the fine grass which appeared to be unlimited and was free. He would tell them of his plans for developing a tremendous cattle empire, and would paint a verbal picture of hundreds of thousands of head of cattle running on the open range, wearing his brand, and of the marvelous opportunity to make money. He would even suggest, with the proper degree of hesitancy, that some of them might like to join him in forming a large cattle syndicate, with the idea of expanding the operation still further in the valleys of the Powder River and other nearby streams. He would also call their attention to the proximity of the cattle operations to the marvelous hunting country from which they had just returned, and how convenient it would be for them, as part owners, to return each year for their hunting.

The promotion worked out with a reasonable degree of success and, with the new money coming in, Moreton Frewen began to see his dreams of a great cattle empire starting to come true. However, the rate of growth was too slow to satisfy him, and he began to talk of other promotional methods which might be used and of plans for other lines of activities. Richard Frewen, having a more conservative temperament, did not approve of some of his brother's expansionistic ideas, and, in the spring of 1881, he sold his interest in the Powder River operations to Moreton and returned to the family home in England.

Shortly after Moreton Frewen had obtained entire control of the Powder River operation, he made a business trip to New York City and, while there, met a very prominent sportsman and financier, Leonard Jerome, whose daughter Jennie had married the very prominent Englishman Randolph Churchill, son of the Duke of Marlborough. To this marriage was born a son who became the famous Winston Churchill. Leonard Jerome also had another daughter, Clara, who was living at home. Moreton became acquainted with the beautiful Clara, a romance soon developed, and the young couple was married in April, 1881. By this marriage, the colorful Moreton Frewen then, of course, became the brother-in-law of Randolph Churchill and the uncle of Winston Churchill.

This marriage gave Moreton excellent social standing and prestige with the best of the titled families in England, as well as contact with the friends and business associates of Leonard Jerome in New York. Now, with a lovely hostess in the big house on the Powder River, the scope of Moreton

Frewen's operations increased tremendously. Invitations immediately went out to the titled sportsmen and their ladies in England to visit the Frewen home, which by now had gained a wide and very favorable reputation in England. The type of service and entertainment was changed to include accommodations and entertainment for the ladies. A butler and maids were added to the servant staff. There were now lovely dances in the big room, with orchestras brought in from Cheyenne and Denver to Rock River by rail, then by coach to the ranch. Other guests who attended were from among the army officers at Fort McKinney. A polo field was developed, and polo ponies were trained by an expert trainer employed on a year-round basis. Additional guesthouses were built to accommodate the increasing number of prominent guests.

As the tempo of the entire operation was stepped up, commitments of investment capital from his guests were also increasing; the ambitious goals of Moreton Frewen were in sight. In the early spring of 1882, he again crossed the Atlantic to England, with Mrs. Frewen, where they were entertained by many of the titled families of Europe, including the Duke of Manchester. While there, Moreton Frewen was successful in forming a new syndicate, named the Powder River Cattle Company, with a capitalization of a million and a half dollars. The Duke of Manchester was chairman of the board of directors, and Moreton was president and general manager. All of the assets of the previous syndicate, including those of Moreton Frewen, were purchased by the new syndicate. Moreton took the major portion of his interest in the previous syndicate in stock in the new company. This interest did not, however, represent control of the new syndicate.

One of the brands which had been acquired by the Frewens was the well-known "76" brand, and it was adopted by the board of directors as the official brand. Fred G. S. Hesse, who had become recognized in northern Wyoming as a very competent cattleman, continued in the capacity of foreman of the newly organized 76 outfit. Hesse was well liked by his cattlemen neighbors and had the reputation of being very cooperative in exchanging reps wherever cattle wearing the "76" brand had strayed from their home range. One of these areas was west of the Powder River country, across the Big Horn Mountains, where the Big Horn River, another great tributary of the Yellowstone, drained all of the vast Big Horn Basin country. It was inevitable that cattle from these two great river systems would intermingle to some degree, and reps were exchanged between the big outfits operating in these two river basins.

The first big trail herds of record to have been moved into the Big Horn Basin were those of the Carter Cattle Company, trailed in from Fort Bridger in 1879. These cattle were turned loose on the south fork of the Stinking Water River with the brand "The Bug," a very unusual and interesting brand which later became well known in that part of the country. The headquarters buildings of the Carter outfit were built on Carter Creek, just south of the present town of Cody, Wyoming. Another interesting brand was the "Pitchfork" of Otto Franc, who had established his headquarters ranch on the Greybull River. The Pitchfork outfit was a big operation in northern Wyoming in the eighties. Franc was credited with running around twenty-five thousand head of cattle (mostly Shorthorns) in the Basin during the peak of his operations. John Gleaver was one of his ranch foremen and Roe Avant was one of his wagon bosses. Another large outfit operating in the "Basin" in the eighties was the ML, owned by Henry Lovell, with headquarters on Norwood Creek. The Torrey ranch, branding the "M Bar" and owned by Captain Robert A. Torrey, a retired army officer, was located in the southeastern part of the Basin, with J. S. Price as the very competent foreman. The small ranches on the Shoshone River operated their own wagon, generally known as the Shoshone Pool, and were assigned their own roundup district by the Wyoming Stockgrowers' Association.

Another great showman of that period with ranching interests in the Big Horn Basin, was "Buffalo Bill" Cody. His TE Ranch was located only a short distance from the town of Cody, named in his honor. Cody used this ranch for the winter quarters of his "Buffalo Bill Wild West Shows," and spent a considerable amount of his time at the ranch, particularly during the fall when he went on big-game hunting trips into the nearby mountains with friends and associates.

Some other cattle companies with operations north of the 76 outfit, on down the Powder River and the Tongue, with cattle running over into Montana, who were large enough to run their own roundup wagons were: the very well-known N Bar outfit of the Neuman brothers; and the Mizpah Livestock Company, branding the "LO," with headquarters located on Mizpah Creek about twenty miles southeast of Miles City, and operating under the very able management of John Childress as ranch foreman. Another big outfit was the Hereford Livestock Company, with headquarters on Punkin Creek, a tributary of the Tongue River. They branded the "SL" and operated with C. H. Loud as general manager and Fred Hitzfelt as ranch foreman. Ferdon and Biddle were both old-timers and pioneer cattlemen in the Powder River country, branding the "ROL," with their headquarters a short distance below the mouth of the Little Powder River. The Concord Cattle Company, branding the "Reversed E2," with Nate Spangler as wagon boss, had its headquarters just east of the junction of the Powder River and the Yellowstone, below Miles City. Then there was also the Punkin Creek Pool, composed of a group of small ranchers who ran a good outfit and were assigned their own roundup district.

Within a very short period of time, after returning from England and forming the new syndicate, Moreton Frewen trailed in fifteen large herds from Texas and Oregon, thereby increasing the number of cattle on his Powder River range to over fifty thousand head. His four roundup wagons, with a hundred cowboys and over a thousand head of saddle horses, were now working the range for seventy-five miles in each direction from headquarters. Moreton Frewen soon became recognized as one of the largest cattlemen in the Powder River country.

With a million and a half dollars in available capital (the greater portion of which was in cash), Moreton Frewen moved rapidly in many directions. With his extremely active imagination allowed full sway, many impractical and fantastic schemes soon began to develop. With the great power and social standing with which he was now endowed, his enthusiasm for expansion became boundless. He, like some of the other promoters of big, foreign-owned cattle syndicates, began to develop plans for building his own slaughter houses and meat-packing facilities. It was the belief of cattlemen generally that the large meat-packing companies were making exorbitant profits; and this subject was always discussed by some of the speakers at the meetings of the stockgrowers' associations. Consequently, the idea of a cattleman having his own meat-packing plant, although impractical, became quite popular. The promotors of the big, foreign cattle syndicates also found this idea to be quite usable when they were selling stock in Europe, since it allowed them to show buyers that, through bypassing the big packers and processing their own beef, they were going to tremendously increase the profits.

Moreton proceeded to build his big slaughterhouse and packing facilities at Superior, Wisconsin, on the Great Lakes, with plans for shipping his beef by the shipload, refrigerated, direct to wholesale outlets in England. He even visualized owning his own ships. He established feed lots in eastern Nebraska, where he proposed to feed out some of his cattle on corn before they were shipped to his packing plants at Superior. After having been successful in forming his big syndicate, Moreton Frewen soon became a very egotistical man who had grown to love power and public praise. He now spent a considerable amount of his time around the Cheyenne Club and other public meeting places, where he could expound upon his great development plans and attract public attention and publicity.

Frewen apparently had become so self-centered that he believed his finances were inexhaustible and his ability to raise money was unlimited. However, by 1885, two major problems had developed. First, he was advised by his accountants that, due to his excessive expansion programs and his extravagant promotional and entertainment activities on the Powder River, his cash was completely exhausted. He was also advised by his ranch foreman, Fred Hesse, that due to the overstocking of the range, the grass had become seriously depleted and winter losses were becoming excessive.

Frewen called upon his board of directors for additional cash to meet his current obligations. However, they turned him down and questioned his business judgment, which he considered to be beyond reproach. Angry, and with deep resentment, Frewen caught the fastest ship for England, taking his family and servants with him. Additional clashes with the board of directors occurred in London until, with the pressures continuing to build up, the situation finally reached the point of intolerance, from his standpoint, and Moreton resigned from his position as president. He did not ever again return to the Powder River country. The glamour of the colorful regime of the great showman Moreton Frewen, with his big "castle" and lavish entertainment of the blue-bloods of England, was gone forever from the Powder River country. However, the shadow of this operation remained for many years in that big country.

The management of the Powder River Cattle Company was then transferred to Fred Hesse on a temporary basis. However, the basic problems of the 76 outfit still remained: shortage of cash; shortage of grass, resulting in very heavy death losses in the hard winters; and the butchering of beef and altering of brands by outlaws. These problems were due to continue indefinitely into the future.

South of the 76 was the great CY outfit, founded in 1876 (the same year that the country north of the Platte was opened to the white man) by Joseph M. Carey and his brother, with their fine headquarters ranch, named "Careyhurst," located on the Platte River, about thirty miles east of the site of the present city of Casper, Wyoming. Their good range extended northward to the headwaters of the Powder River, where their cattle intermingled with those of the 76 outfit. The CY cattle also ranged southward and westward to the headwaters of the Platte and over into the Big Horn Basin country. The CY soon became one of the largest locally-owned, open-range cattle outfits in Wyoming. It was reported, at the peak of its operations, to have been running around eighty thousand head of cattle on the open range in central and northern Wyoming.

Joseph M. Carey, who was destined to become one of Wyoming's most distinguished and influential citizens, first came to Wyoming in 1869 as the first district attorney for the Territory of Wyoming. He was appointed to this position by President Grant as a political reward for his having worked diligently the previous year for the election of General Grant to the presidency of the United States. The office of the territorial district attorney was established at Cheyenne, where he served in that capacity for two years until he was appointed justice of the Wyoming territorial supreme court. Young Carey served in both of these important offices with distinction. However, when his term on the supreme court expired, he declined further appointments, having decided to go into the cattle business in partnership with his brother, R. Davis Carey, who continued to live in Philadelphia, Pennsylvania.

The Careys brought in their first herds of Longhorns in the fall of the same year they formed their partnership. They were well financed with eastern capital and built up their herds of CY cattle on the Platte and the headwaters of the Powder River very rapidly, until the CY outfit was soon recognized as one of the most competent and best-managed cattle outfits in the business.

For almost a decade, the CY outfit was very prosperous and successful. However, in the middle eighties, the Ogallala outfit was being forced to move out of western Nebraska by the homesteaders. They moved in on the Powder River with an additional thirty thousand head of Longhorns, making a total for the Ogallala of around sixty thousand head in that area. It then soon became apparent that the range country on the Powder River and the Platte was becoming seriously overstocked and, in general, the range was deteriorating.

There were now four very large outfits operating in the area between the Montana line on the north, the Platte River on the south, the Black Hills on the east and the

Big Horn Mountains on the west, each having over sixty thousand head of cattle running on the open range. These were the 101 outfit, the 76, the CY and the Keystone outfit of the Ogallala. Three of these outfits were foreign syndicates; only the CY was locally owned. In addition to these big companies, there were also quite a large number of medium- and small-sized cattle outfits operating in that part of the country.

Another problem that had become quite serious was cattle rustling. There were many well-sheltered canyons and pockets in the rough country where either small or large bunches of cattle could be hidden out until brands could be altered and had time to heal. Also, it was very easy for rustlers and outlaws to move cattle back and forth across the territorial lines between Montana and Wyoming. There was little law of any kind in this remote area, several hundred miles from the nearest regularly constituted law at Cheyenne or Miles City. The people who lived in this country made their own law, which was always subject to change. The results, oftentimes fatal, depended upon who held the best hand at a particular time, whether it be with cards, in strength of numbers, or with a gun.

12 It was, undoubtedly, perfectly natural that the aspiration of any ambitious cowboy or wagon boss would be to have a little cattle outfit of his own, so it was not surprising when, in the late seventies and early eighties, some of the cowboys who came up north with trail herds saw little valleys along some of the streams in the high plains country which were an answer to a trail driver's dream. It was not difficult for a cowboy to file on a one hundred sixty acre homestead. All he needed was the thirteen dollar filing fee. Material for a log cabin, a barn, and corrals was available in the hills, within a few miles of his homestead. He would need a sharp ax, and some kind of team and wagon for hauling the logs, poles, and fence posts from the hills. When the smart trail driver filed on his homestead, he always picked a valley where there was a stream and, preferably, a good spring for drinking water and some natural meadow. He was not interested in farming the land; he was looking for enough grass and water to run a small bunch of cattle so that he would not have to continue for the rest of his life eating dust on the long trail. Then, just maybe, there was some little girl that he had taken a fancy to who was living in one of the small cow towns back along the trail.

After filing, the big question facing the cowboy was how to get enough cattle to stock his small ranch to make a living. There was an answer to this question, one known to all cattlemen: mavericks, or slicks. A maverick or slick is any unbranded animal that is not following or claimed by its mother and, not having been branded, has a slick hide. The natural, or legitimate, maverick was generally a calf that had become an orphan due to the death of its mother from any one of several causes, including the eating of poison weed or being killed by lightning. Also there were the calves that were missed and therefore not branded at the time of the calf roundups. These calves would be weaned by their mothers when they were about six months old. Not being branded, and not following or claimed by their mothers, it would be impossible to determine the ownership of the unbranded animals under open-range conditions, where cattle wearing many different brands would be running on the same range together.

In the territories of both Wyoming and Montana prior to the year 1884, the maverick was considered to be the property of any man who could get his brand on the animal, providing, of course, that the brand being used was properly registered in the territory where the animal was being branded. All that was needed at that time to claim ownership to a maverick was a long rope and a running iron, which was an iron rod about eighteen inches in length with an iron ring welded on the end. This little branding iron could be carried easily, tied to the skirts of a saddle. The ring on the end of the running iron could always be heated in a small sagebrush fire when it was needed. Any cowboy who was an expert in handling the running iron could fashion almost any kind of a brand simply by turning the ring slowly with the handle as the hot ring was applied. Many of the most prominent and influential men in Wyoming and Montana got their start in the cattle business during that period of time, with the long rope and the running iron, branding mostly legitimate mavericks.

In the West, the term *rustler* applied to anyone who went out and rustled mavericks. The term did not necessarily, at that time, denote anything illegal or improper. As used prior to 1884, it would mean the same thing as rustling some wood. It would depend upon where and under what conditions the wood was to be rustled. Even under the conditions which existed in the West prior to 1884, there was a very narrow line between what was legal, or at least permissable, and what was obviously illegal. The question was, did the calf become a maverick in the natural process of things or did it have some help? In this rugged and broken country, it was quite easy for an ambitious young rancher to hide out small bunches of cows and calves belonging to the big outfits in hidden pockets in the hilly country, where they would be overlooked when the roundup wagons were working in that area. Then, at a later date, he could pick up the calves and brand them after they had been weaned.

Another method of establishing a claim to mavericks when there was some possibility of the rightful owner showing up and claiming the animal and being able to prove his claim, was by making temporary sleepers out of the unbranded animals. This was done by ear-marking the mavericks and then watching to see whether anyone was going to claim them. If not, they would be branded after they had cooled off. The use of hair branding was another method oftentimes used in setting up sleepers. This was done by cutting a brand in the hair of the animal with a pair of shears or small clippers. The hair of course would grow out again in two or three months, and the hair brand would then disappear; but before this would occur, the sleeper would be permanently branded with a regular hot branding iron by the man who had done the hair branding.

There were also, of course, many outright thieves and outlaws operating in the big plains country (as there were over the entire West) who made a business of stealing cattle in large numbers, and who were completely unscrupulous in their methods. Some of these cattle thieves operated by butchering range cattle and selling the meat to small butcher shops or to contractors on public construction, who were interested in buying meat at the lowest possible price and did not ask too many questions.

The thieves butchering other peoples' range cattle would occasionally kill an animal which was wearing their own brand, and then keep the fresh hide hanging on the corral fence where it could be seen by the sheriff or anyone else who should get inquisitive as to where the beef (that the cattle thieves were selling) had come from.

Many of the other outlaws among the big operators in unlawful rustling went in for working over or altering brands. This was done by tracing out and adding to the existing brands with a running iron. In the process, they would create an entirely different brand, which would be registered in the name of one of the outlaws who was doing the altering, or of an associate, who sometimes might not even be in the cattle business. After the altered brands had time to peel (if the work had been properly done), it would become almost impossible to distinguish an altered brand from the original except by butchering the animal and inspecting the inside of the hide. The original brand would always show on the inside when the hide was removed, even when the brand had been altered. In altering brands, the rustler would sometimes use a wet burlap sack under his running iron, which would have the effect, if the work was well done, of making the brand look as though it had been on the animal for a longer period of time.

It was obvious that the cows belonging to the big outfits, who owned almost all of the cattle running on the open range, were the mothers of the greater number of the calves that became mavericks. Practically all of the cattle being butchered by the outlaws and involved where brands were being altered were owned by the big outfits. As these activities increased, coupled with the filing of homesteads on the streams by the small ranchers, many of whom were the former employees of the big outfits, it was inevitable that the situation would soon reach the point where the big cattlemen would begin to consider themselves faced with a double threat to their way of life.

It had long been an axiom and a tradition in the West that "he who controls the water also controls the adjacent range." As the number of filings on water by the small ranchers increased, the big outfits saw the vast empires of government land which they had controlled for many years and had become accustomed to considering as their own slowly being whittled away.

Therefore, it was undoubtedly quite natural, under these circumstances, that the big cattlemen should soon begin to consider the small rancher as being a definite thorn in their sides. This problem, coupled with the losses of mavericks to the cowboys and small ranchers who were using the long rope and the running iron, and also with the additional losses to the thieves and outlaws who were butchering range cattle and altering brands, had continued to build up with tensions and animosities until the big cattlemen became inclined to group all of the small ranchers and the gangs of outlaws together and to consider them all as their enemies.

Fuel was added to the fire at a meeting of the Wyoming Stockgrowers' Association held in Cheyenne on November 9, 1883. A resolution was adopted by the association recommending that all cattle wearing the brands of rustlers, and all stray cattle with brands which were not known to members of the association be considered mavericks. As reported by the *Laramie Sentinel*, "The Association resolved to create a 'black list' of suspected stock thieves, who would be discharged and not hired again by Association members." This action by the association was deeply resented by the small ranchers, as well as by the cowboys and trail drivers working for the big outfits. The resolution had the effect of placing them all in a position where any one of them could be branded as a rustler and a thief, simply by the statement or inference of any member of the association, even though this statement might be based on nothing more than personal animosity. The seeds of resentment and bitterness sown by this action would be reflected in the relationship between big cattlemen and cowboys in the high plains country for many years to come.

With further emphasis upon the pressures which were being brought to bear upon the small ranchers, the territorial legislatures in both Wyoming and Montana (which to a great degree were controlled by the big cattlemen) in 1884 passed so-called "maverick laws" which were sponsored by the stockgrowers' associations in both territories. These laws were heavily weighted to favor the big cattlemen and association members.

Under the Wyoming law, the responsibility for administration and enforcement of the act was vested in the Wyoming Stockgrowers' Association. This law gave the stockgrowers' association complete control over all roundups and set up the procedures for handling mavericks. With this authority vested in them, the association then divided the Territory of Wyoming into thirty-two districts with a captain or supervisor for each district. They then issued a directive that only roundups authorized by the association, and under the jurisdiction of the captains of each district, would be permitted to operate. The directive further provided that all mavericks gathered during the roundup would be sold by the association, and all money derived from the sale would be used by the association for the hiring of cattle detectives to strictly enforce the intent of the act and to apprehend anyone doing anything in violation of the maverick law.

It had been customary in most areas of the West prior to the passing of the maverick laws to divide the mavericks gathered during a roundup among the cattlemen operating in that area, based upon the number of cattle that each of them had running on that particular range, and to brand them accordingly. However, when the maverick law went into effect, the cattlemen who were not members of the association were given no voice or consideration whatever in the disposition of any of the mavericks.

Under this law, as it was administered by the association, it became the practice of the roundup foreman in each district to sell the mavericks which were gathered in the roundups in large lots to members of the association. The records indicate that in 1884 the Wyoming Stockgrowers' Association sold 1,971 head of mavericks to its members for $26,076.15, or an average of about $13.25 per head.

In 1886, the maverick law was amended to provided for the sale of mavericks by the roundup foreman singly or in lots, at his discretion. The law was also further amended to make it unlawful for anyone to brand a maverick at any time except under the supervision of a roundup foreman at an authorized roundup. It was only natural, under these circumstances, that the small ranchers would deeply resent the fact that even their proportion of the mavericks was being sold by the association, and the money used to hire cattle detectives to spy upon them.

The control of the stockgrowers' association membership was maintained through a screening committee, and applicants who did not meet with the approval of this committee were denied membership in the association and were, therefore, without representation. When an application for membership in the association was denied by the committee (and, of course, this could occur due to some personal prejudice or animosity on the part of some member of the association) the applicant would automatically come under a cloud, and, in the minds of many people he would become branded as a suspected thief and outlaw without ever having had recourse to the law. After being barred from membership in the association, there were several things he could not do without violating the maverick law. He could not register or record a brand in the territory without the approval of the stockgrowers' association. He could be black-balled from working with the regularly authorized roundup wagons by the whim of some former employer. If this occurred, he could not then round up his own cattle on the open range, even though he was black-balled from the regular wagons without having violated the maverick law. Also, he could not legally brand a maverick except under supervision, even if he knew beyond a question of a doubt that he was branding his own animal.

Under the strict application of the maverick or "bastard law" as it became known, the activities of the small cattlemen became completely restricted and subject to the exclusive decisions of the stockgrowers' associations. The small cattlemen naturally felt (with justification) that under these circumstances they were being discriminated against as a group and that their individual liberties were being illegally curtailed. There were also many of the medium-sized cattlemen, and a few of the large ones, who were not in accord with some of these high-handed policies and practices. Some of these independent cattlemen were of the opinion that many of the activities of the association and some of its members were in direct conflict with the constitutional rights of the individual cattlemen. They did not propose to become a party to these activities by joining the associations and therefore declined membership.

As the teeth in the maverick law were applied, it became increasingly evident that the big outfits intended to keep their control and to perpetuate themselves in power through the strict application of the tight controls permitted and authorized under the maverick law. It also soon became plain that much of the policy adopted by the stockgrowers' associations had been promulgated in the board of directors' meetings of some of the large British cattle syndicates at their meetings in London. Also, these decisions were then being passed on down to their local managers and foremen in the cattle country of the West "with orders to carry them out." In the eyes of many of the local cattlemen, these foreign owners, who were not even citizens of the United States and who were only interested in grabbing all of the grass they could get, were not entitled to dictate the destiny of the cattle business in the western part of the United States.

Almost all of the small cattlemen had, at one time or another, worked for the big foreign outfits who they now felt had turned against them when they tried to get into business for themselves in what was their own country. This bitterness and resentment continued to build up until the Wyoming territorial legislature, in 1888, amended the maverick law (upon the recommendation of the Wyoming Stockgrowers' Association) to provide for a board of livestock commissioners who would have the jurisdiction over all roundups. However, they still left the Wyoming Stockgrowers' Association in control of the administration and the enforcement of the law. (Montana had wisely created such a board at the time they passed their first maverick law in 1884.) The overall effect of the appointment of the livestock commission in Wyoming resulted in very little change in the administration of the maverick law. Big cattlemen were always appointed as commissioners and they just passed their authority on to the stockgrowers' association, which continued with the same policies and practices that had been in effect in the past. The board of Livestock Commissioners did, however, act as a buffer between the stockgrowers' association and the territorial governor, which gave the dissatisfied members and non-members some place to appeal to and protest to the actions of the association. However, the conditions remained unchanged and the animosities continued to build up until, at some time in the future, they would reach the breaking point and erupt with serious consequences.

One of the areas where the conflict was the greatest between the big cattlemen and the little fellows was in what was known as the Hole-in-the-Wall country, on the headwaters of the Powder River in northern Wyoming. This rugged country was bounded on the west by a range of the Big Horn Mountains, and on the east and south by a high ridge or wall of red sandstone about thirty-five miles in length and impassable except for three narrow gaps or breaks. These gaps were easy for anyone living or camping in the Hole to keep under observation or to defend, if necessary. Flowing northward through the largest of the gaps in the sandstone wall was Buffalo Creek. This gap was known as Red Canyon, and was the gap from which Hole-in-the-Wall got its name. Buffalo Creek flowed from there on northward through a rather wild and broken country, to where it emptied into the middle fork of the Powder River. This Hole-in-the-Wall country was well known as a hideout for cattle thieves, stagecoach robbers and many other types of wanted men. However, not all of the people living in the Hole were outlaws. There were cowboys with small ranches on Buffalo Creek who perhaps did go out through the gaps into the big open country with a long rope and a running iron to pick up a few mavericks. There were also other small ranchers living in the Hole who were strictly law-abiding citizens, and probably wouldn't have branded a maverick even if the animal came to them carrying his own running iron.

There was one thing all of the people who lived in the Hole-in-the-Wall country did have in common and that was they were all independent individuals who did not believe in being pushed around by anyone. It was their opinion that the best way to get along and keep out of trouble was to keep their mouths shut and to attend strictly to their own business and not to be concerned about what the other fellow did for a living. They never asked unnecessary questions, and neither did they answer them. They just figured that what the other fellow did was his business. It was also a well-recognized custom that if a person traveling across the Hole-in-the-Wall country saw some cowboy off in the distance with a small branding fire burning and, if the cowboy who was doing the branding should wave to them to go around, that would be what he meant, and to go around would be the best thing for them to do. Otherwise, a rifle bullet would probably kick up the dust a short distance in front of them, and then, if they still didn't get the general idea, the next shot would undoubtedly come a lot closer.

One cowboy who punched cows in the Powder River country in the eighties was Frank E. Jones (father of the writer), who worked as a cowboy for both the CY and the Ogallala outfits. He said that some of the small ranchers from the Hole-in-the-Wall country who were rustling mavericks and who were black-balled from working with the roundup wagons, would oftentimes ride in and work the drives when the circles had been completed by the roundup crews and while the cattle were strung out, pointed towards the roundup grounds. If they found a slick, they would peel him out of the drive and point him over the hill to where another rustler would probably be holding a small cut of mavericks the two of them had gathered. The cowboys who were working with the wagons for the big cattlemen did not ordinarily do anything about this gathering of mavericks by the small ranchers. In the first place, they did not consider it to be any of their business. The slicks were not wearing the brands of their outfits and the cowboys were not looking for a fight. Then too, they might sometime have a little ranch of their own, up on some creek, and be trying to get a start in the cattle business for themselves. Besides, they considered the enforcement of the maverick law to be the business of the cattle detectives who were employed by the stockgrowers' association for that purpose.

Another surprising thing was that it was not unusual for some of the small ranchers from the Hole-in-the-Wall country and who were black-balled as suspected rustlers to stop at the chuck wagons of the big outfits at mealtime when they happened to be in that part of the country. It was an unwritten law of the range that a hungry man was never denied the privilege of eating at a roundup chuck wagon, regardless of who he was, when he came by at meal time. After the visitors had finished eating, they would wash their dishes, chop wood for the cook, and do any other chores that needed doing, then ride quietly on their way.

An interesting experience for Frank Jones occurred in the late eighties, while he was working as a cowboy with the Ogallala wagons in the Powder River country. When Frank had ridden in at the Ogallala headquarters, at the time he had gone north that spring, he had been riding a nice, clean-limbed, black horse, standing about fifteen and a half hands in height, with two white-stockinged legs and a white star on his forehead. He was also leading an old pack horse carrying his bed and other personal belongings. Frank had become quite attached to his little black saddle horse, which he had named Star and which had cost him about two months' wages. This little black horse was developing into a very fine cutting and rope horse and, needless to say, he was the pride and joy of the young cowboy.

When the roundup wagons pulled out, it was with regret that Frank left his pet horse, Star, along with his pack horse, in a pasture near the Ogallala headquarters. When the wagons pulled back into headquarters after having been out for about two months, the first thing Frank did was ride out to the horse pasture to look for his little black saddle horse. The old pack horse was still there but his good saddle pony, Star, was gone. When he inquired about his horse at headquarters, the horse wrangler at the ranch told him that about ten head of top saddle horses had disappeared from the horse pasture, all at the same time, about two weeks before and no trace of them had been found. He said that it looked like it had been the work of horse thieves. The more Frank brooded over the loss of his pet horse, the more convinced he became that his pony could be found in the Hole-in-the-Wall country. He decided that he was going into the Hole to take a look. He knew that it would not do to go into that country riding an Ogallala horse wearing the "Keystone" brand, so he borrowed a private horse from another Ogallala cowboy. He then packed his bed and a light camping outfit on his pack horse, anchored his rifle scabbard under the right fender of his saddle, and headed for the Hole. He had decided that if anyone in the Hole got inquisitive as to why he was there, he would tell them he was just another cowboy on the dodge, looking for a well-hidden homestead.

Soon after riding through the gap in the red sandstone wall at Red Canyon and starting down Buffalo Creek through the Hole, Frank caught up with another rider going in the same direction. The other rider was a good-looking, young cowboy by the name of Antwine Bush, who had eaten several times at the Ogallala wagon that Frank had been working with. This young cowboy was riding a black horse with a white star on his forehead and with two white-stockinged legs. After the two cowboys had ridden a short distance together, Frank said, "Antwine, that is a good-looking horse that you are ridin'."

Antwine said, "Yes, Frank, he sure is a good cow pony. I think a lot of him."

Frank said, "Well now, Antwine, that is my horse that you are ridin'. I think a lot of him, too, and I want him, right now."

Antwine looked him over very coolly for a moment,

started to make a move, hesitated momentarily, then grinned and said, "Well now. You know, Frank, this could be your horse alright. He just strayed into my ranch one day last summer. I noticed that he had saddle marks, so I caught him up and started ridin' him. Now, if you say that he is your horse, Frank, then just come on over to the ranch and let me get my saddle off him and you can have your pet pony. I still say, though, that he is a mighty good cow pony, and he sure knows how to peel a slick out of a drive. You should try it sometime, Frank."

There was one thing Frank Jones never did find out for sure, and that was how his pet cow pony got into the Hole-in-the-Wall country in the first place. He had his own opinion about Antwine Bush's story; however, there was nothing to be gained by being too inquisitive or in making an issue out of the matter. He had recovered his good black saddle horse and that was what he had gone in after. There was one point upon which Frank Jones was always quite positive, however, and that was that even though his pet horse Star was plenty smart, he didn't find the hole in that red sandstone wall all by himself.

13 One of the first jobs to be held by Frank Jones in Wyoming was skinning six mules on a jerk line, freighting from Fort Laramie to Fort Robinson. This was a round trip distance of about one hundred eighty miles, with the driver making camp each night alongside the wagon trail, except when he was at one of the army outposts. When he was in Fort Laramie, which he considered to be his headquarters, Frank would stay at the old Rustic Hotel. This was a small, one-story log building owned by Joe Wilde, who was the sutler at Fort Laramie. The sutler was an official merchant approved by the army and authorized to sell merchandise to the troops, including tobacco and whisky.

The post of Fort Laramie was first established in 1834 on the banks of the North Platte River, about one-half mile above the mouth of the Laramie River. It was established as a fur-trading post by the well-known pioneer fur trader and trapper William Sublette. The post was first known as Fort William, and it controlled practically all of the fur-trading business in that part of Wyoming for quite a number of years. In 1840, the name of the post was changed to Fort Laramie. The name Laramie was derived from the name of a French-Canadian trapper by the name of Jacques La Ramie, who was the first known white man to thoroughly explore the southeastern part of Wyoming. La Ramie came into that part of the country from Canada before 1830, and established very friendly relations with the Indians. He traded with them for their furs, helped them in time of sickness, and did everything else that would create good will and make him a good neighbor. In turn, the Indians allowed him to build his trapper cabins in locations that suited him, and to trap for beaver on any of the streams in the mountains. However, they warned him not to trap for beaver on the Laramie plains, or any place else in buffalo-hunting country.

The reason for this warning was the fact that the building of dams by the beaver in the flat plains country caused the water to back up and overflow the banks of the streams, where it would then spread out over the bottom lands along the creeks and rivers, creating natural meadows where the buffalo would gather in great numbers. This enabled the Indians to hide in the willow thickets along the streams and kill with bow and arrow, at very short range, whatever buffalo they might need for meat, as well as to obtain the necessary hides to be cured and tanned, then made into clothing, robes, blankets, and other types of shelter. La Ramie observed the restrictions against his trapping on the plains for several years, but as the beaver began to thin out in the mountains, he apparently decided to take a chance, and began setting his traps along the Laramie River, where it crosses the Laramie plains. Shortly afterwards, Jacques La Ramie was found dead in his cabin, where he had been killed with arrows which were said to have been those of the Arapaho.

The post at Fort Laramie first attained military significance in 1848 when troops were stationed there at the beginning of the California gold rush to protect the wagon trains of the gold seekers who were making their way westward. With the passing of time the importance of this military outpost increased tremendously, and in 1875 the army built a one-way bridge across the North Platte River, just below Fort Laramie. This bridge, when completed, permitted vehicular traffic of all kinds to cross at that point, without the hazards of fording the river or the inconvenience of using a ferry. For many years, the Fort Laramie army bridge was the only bridge across the North Platte River between Bridgeport, Nebraska, and Casper, Wyoming, a distance of over two hundred miles. In addition to the use of this bridge by army transport wagons, stagecoaches, chuck wagons, and many other types of vehicles, the bridge was also used extensively by freight wagons, which were moving many types of merchandise and supplies to the army post at Fort Laramie, as well as to other points on both sides of the river.

One day, the young freighter Frank Jones came into Fort Laramie soaking wet, having driven his six mules all day in a cold rain. There was a small, wood-burning stove in his room, and when he came in he threw his wet clothes, including a pair of wet buckskin gloves, down on the floor alongside of the stove. He awoke suddenly during the night, with someone yelling fire and with his room filled with smoke. When he jumped out of bed, the fire was creeping across the floor of his room. He ran for the window, which was closed, broke it out with his head, and jumped. When he went through the window he cut a deep gash in his forehead. The scar from this gash remained with him for the rest of his life. The historic old Rustic Hotel burned to the ground that night, and all that was left of it the next morning was a pile of ashes.

At the time that Frank had pulled into Fort Laramie with his freight wagon on the day of the fire, he had stopped in at the sutler's store and had been paid his monthly wage of seventy-five dollars in currency. When he went out the window, this seventy-five dollars, which was in a billfold, had been left in his room with his clothing. The next day Frank went out and dug around in the ashes and fortunately found his billfold, which still contained the seventy-five dollars, and, although one end of the billfold had been burned off in the fire, enough of the bills remained so that he could turn them in at a bank and get replacements. He also found one of his buckskin gloves in the ashes, which, due to its having been wet, had not burned in the fire but had shrunk up to about one-tenth of its original size and had become hard as a rock, as though it were petrified. What was most surprising was that the little glove had retained its original shape perfectly. Both the burned billfold and the little glove, which are now over eighty years old, are still in the possession of the writer and will eventually be presented to the Wyoming Historical Society, to be placed among the early Wyoming historical relics.

After leaving Fort Laramie, Frank Jones continued to work for several Wyoming cattle outfits over a period of time until, in the summer of 1889, he took the job as foreman for Hi Kelly on the Y Cross Ranch where he remained for the next nine years.

The Y Cross Ranch buildings had been built on Horse Creek, at the mouth of Bear Creek, with fine, large, natural meadows covering several hundred acres, caused to a great degree by the many dams built by the beaver in both streams causing the water to back up and overflow the almost level valley on both sides of the streams. Only a short distance to the east, the Texas-Montana Cattle Trail passed through Horse Creek Gap, and the heavy dust clouds being raised by the trail herds moving up the trail could be seen from the Y Cross ranch house at almost any time of the day.

S. J. Robb, an old-timer in that part of the country, operated a store and supply point for trail herds nearby, with his store and warehouse buildings located only about a quarter of a mile east of the Y Cross ranch house. Robb always carried a good stock of the supplies and merchandise needed by the outfits moving herds up the trail; consequently, the trail cooks would pull in with their chuck wagons at the store, where they would buy enough groceries and other supplies to last them until they would reach the next supply point, which would be several days later. The colorful southern trail drivers, with their clanking spurs and low-slung holsters, would also ride in at the Robb store and buy a supply of Bull Durham tobacco for rolling cigarettes, also plugs of Horseshoe Star and Climax chewing tobacco, as well as clean socks, ammunition, and whatever else they might need. There was always a lot of activity going on around the Robb store, where a growing and inquiring boy, such as the writer was at that time, could learn a lot, not all of it bad.

There were a few other ranches in the valley, in addition to the Y Cross — most of them small — including the homestead of John A. Kessler, which he had filed in 1876 on Bear Creek at the mouth of Fox Creek. This homestead was about five miles upstream from the Y Cross, where there were some other fine natural meadows. John Kessler first came to the Territory of Wyoming in 1868 as a buffalo hunter, furnishing meat to the contractors who at that time were building the Union Pacific Railroad through Wyoming. This energetic young man was probably the first individual to demonstrate the feasibility of irrigation in that part of the country. He dug his irrigation ditch by hand, with a shovel, and without the benefit of a survey, using one of the simplest and most interesting engineering principles known to man: that of just starting to dig at the water level of the stream, and then letting the water follow him down the ditch he was digging, where the water would find its own level, and determine the proper grade. This was a method which the old buffalo hunter had learned from the Indians of the Southwest during his many years on the plains. There was also another small rancher by the name of Cale LaGrange, who had filed on a homestead which was located on Horse Creek, about three miles upstream from the Y Cross ranch. There, in 1889, an official United States post office was established which was named LaGrange. In later years the merchant S. J. Robb moved his store and mercantile business from the Y Cross to the site of the new post office at LaGrange, and a small town began to develop.

One of the other big outfits (in addition to the Y Cross) with many thousands of head of cattle running on the open range in that part of the Goshen Hole country was the big Bridle Bit outfit. It was owned by Sturgis and Goodell, who operated under the name of Union Cattle Company, with their headquarters also located on Horse

Creek, about two miles downstream from the Y Cross. The Bridle Bit outfit was the successor to the great Bay State Cattle Company, which had operated in western Nebraska before the coming of the homesteaders and the passing of the herd law.

One of the major problems for the cattle outfits' operations in southeastern Wyoming, including the Y Cross and the Bridle Bit, after the passing of the herd law in Nebraska, was their Wyoming range cattle drifting across the state line into Nebraska, and there being impounded and subjected to a heavy penalty. In an effort to eliminate this problem, the Wyoming Stockgrowers' Association, in the summer of 1890, built a five-wire drift fence along the Wyoming-Nebraska line, running from the North Platte River southward to the Colorado line, for a total distance of over a hundred miles. The association then established line camps about every twenty miles, where fence riders were stationed who rode the drift fence every other day. One of these line camps was located at the old Crockett ranch, about fifteen miles northeast of LaGrange, and another at the Jim Johnson ranch, which was about twelve miles southeast of LaGrange. This drift fence proved to be very effective in stopping range cattle from drifting across the state line. However, it did not stop the young Wyoming cowboys from drifting across the line, where some of the Nebraska homesteaders had raised a fine crop of good-looking girls.

Frank Jones was one of those young cowboys who strayed across the line and found himself a bride, Carrie Stone, the niece of Ben Stone who, like John L. Jones, older brother of Frank Jones, was one of the pioneer settlers in Banner County, Nebraska. They were married in 1892, and continued to live in the good, solid, log house on the Y Cross ranch until after both my older sister Ethel and I were born. Hi Kelly soon developed a very definite personal interest in his hard-working and ambitious young ranch foreman and helped him in every way possible to get a start for himself. This included allowing him to run some cattle of his own at the ranch without charge. Frank registered his own brand, the "Forty-four Connected," while he was at the Y Cross, and he used this same brand for the next sixty years.

The young foreman was a man who loved to trade, and, with Hi Kelly's approval, he soon had a lively business going at the Y Cross ranch, trading with trail drivers and trail bosses who were moving herds northward up the Texas-Montana Cattle Trail. By the time that these outfits would reach the Y Cross, after having traveled over a thousand miles since leaving Texas, they would always have a good many trail-weary and tender-footed saddle ponies. Frank started trading fresh horses to the trail bosses for some of these beat-out trail ponies. Of course, he always drew plenty of trading difference. He would then turn the trail-weary horses out in the meadows where, within a few weeks, they would become rolling fat. He would then bring them back into the ranch, where he would reset new shoes and have these fat ponies ready to trade to some other outfit that would be going north up the trail. Frank was also a good leather worker and he would trade for broken saddles and harness. Then he would repair them during his spare time, cleaning the leather with saddle soap, and oiling with neat's-foot oil to soften and stain the leather and also to bring out the original color. At the same time that he was doing the repair work, he would be trading good saddles and harness for more broken ones. Frank Jones soon became known up and down the trail as a man who would trade for anything, from a jackknife to a broken-down chuck wagon, if he got enough difference.

In the spring of 1898, Hi Kelly, now a man in his late

sixties, sold all of his cattle and ranching interests for the second time, including the Y Cross, and retired permanently from the cattle business. Frank Jones by this time had accumulated around two hundred head of cattle of his own, in addition to some cash from his trading operations. He now bought a small ranch on Bushnell Creek, about twenty miles south of the Y Cross, and started to realize his lifetime ambition of having a little cattle outfit of his own. The little ranch on the Bushnell, with its small log cabin, built near where a large spring of cold water came boiling up out of the ground, was still on the Texas-Montana Cattle Trail. Bushnell Creek was, of course, the first living water to be reached by the northbound trail herds after they left Pole Creek and had crossed over the high divide country lying between the two streams, which was generally dry country. They would then go in on Bushnell Creek for their first good water in thirty-six hours. The trail bosses would still ride in at the Frank Jones ranch when they were looking for horse trades or when they had some other problems and needed the help of a local man who knew his way around and got along with the other people living in that part of the country, and who also knew of the many problems of the trail drivers from his own personal experiences.

    The small Bushnell Creek cut through a wild and rather rugged, hilly country, where there were large, white sandstone outcroppings, and where the country was covered with a light growth of scrub cedar and pine timber. This, at one time, had been great Indian country. Arrowheads, as well as other relics, evidence of the Indian way of life, were to be found quite easily. One of the first things that my sister and I did after we had moved into the little log cabin, was to start exploring everything within a reasonable distance of the ranch.

Some of the writer's memories as a boy growing up in southeastern Wyoming around the turn of the century are still very vivid. There was the day shortly after we had moved into the little log cabin on Bushnell Creek (with its slab pine floor and dirt roof) when my sister and I were down the creek, about a half mile below the house, hunting for arrowheads to add to our growing collection. We came across an old deserted anthill, which was just covered with Indian beads. We picked up all of the beads that we could find on the surface and took them home with us. The next day we again went down the creek, taking a small shovel with us, and started digging in the same anthill for more beads. Our efforts were meeting with some degree of success when suddenly we hit something hard which was just below the surface of the ground. We dug the object out without too much trouble and found it to be an old rifle with the stock partly rotted off. We continued our diggings and soon came up with some black hair. The hair seemed to be fastened onto something, so we continued to dig until, rather abruptly, we found that the hair was attached to the head of a dead Indian. We had become so thoroughly interested in what we were doing that we had not noticed that the sun had gone down, and darkness was falling. When we suddenly realized what we had found, coupled with the coming of darkness, we became, to state it mildly, quite frightened, and the two of us took off for the house like a couple of scared rabbits.

The next day, our father went down with us to our diggings and explained to us what had happened. He said that the Indian had apparently been killed at or near that spot and had then been buried in a shallow grave by members of his tribe, as was the custom with most of the tribes of Plains Indians at that time. They had buried all of his personal belongings with him, including the rifle and the beads, so that he would have them when he got to the happy hunting grounds. The ants, of course, in building their small mound, had found the beads just under the surface of the ground and had then used them for building material in constructing their mound. We kids very carefully put the rifle back where we had found it, figuring that he might still need it. However, we decided that he could probably get along without the beads, so we kept them and then very carefully covered the grave over again; and as far as I know, the Indian and his rifle are still there.

One of the most vivid memories that I have of those years on the Bushnell is of the day when two young cowboys who were about twenty years of age came by our ranch at noon and stayed for dinner. After they had eaten and were ready to leave, one of these cowboys, who was riding a wild, half-broken bronc, decided that he was going to jump his horse over a pole gate which was in the fence around the horse pasture. When the wild pony tried to make the jump, he caught his front feet on the top pole of the gate, turned over in the air, and came down on top of the young cowboy, killing him instantly with a broken neck. My father, always a handy and sympathetic man in cases of death and sickness, quickly, with the help of the other young cowboy, carried the unfortunate young man into the house and laid him on a blanket on the floor. This was the first dead man that I had ever seen. Soon afterwards, my father went out and found some lumber, and with the help of the other cowboy he began building a rough box. When it was completed, they laid the young cowboy in the box, and loaded it in the back end of a wagon. My father hitched a team to the wagon and started for the young cowboy's home, which was about twenty miles distant, sending the other cowboy on ahead, to tell the relatives of the unfortunate young man what had happened.

One of the big problems in Wyoming at that time was with the packs of grey wolves who were then quite numerous in that part of the country. The grey wolf (not to be confused with his cowardly cousin, the coyote) was quite a large animal. It stood as tall as a yearling steer, and was quite heavily built, weighing several hundred pounds. These large wolves would kill anything that they could get to and hamstring. Their method of attack was for some of the wolf pack to work on the head and the front legs of the animal that they were trying to kill, while the rest of the pack would attempt to cut the tendons in the rear legs. Once the tendons had been cut and the animal was down and helpless, the pack could then take their time about completing the kill. My first experience with grey wolves came during the first winter that we were on the Bushnell. At the time that this experience occurred, my father had been halter-breaking a very fine two-year-old colt in a corral which was some distance from the house. When evening came that day, he decided that he would leave the young horse in the corral, where he could work with him again the next day. However, sometime during that night a pack of grey wolves crawled through the fence into the corral, then hamstrung and killed the colt. When we went out to the corral the next morning, all that was left of this fine young horse was a pile of bones and part of the hide. There was snow on the ground at the time and it was bitter cold, otherwise the wolves, even though they were hungry, would not have been so bold as to have come into the corral to make their kill.

We only had one neighbor living within a ten mile radius from our little ranch on the Bushnell. He was another small rancher, by the name of Nels Sherard, who lived down the creek from us about two miles; and then there were three young cowboys, all brothers by the name of Perry, who were holed up for the winter in an old buffalo hunter's cabin, about three miles up the creek above our ranch. My father rode up the creek and told the Perry boys about the wolves killing his horse. Then one of the Perry boys rode down and picked up Nels Sherard, and all five of them, (including my father) started out on the fresh trail of the grey wolves.

With snow on the ground, the trail was not hard to follow. The tracks indicated that there were five large, full-grown wolves in the pack, all of them being of about the same size. It was obvious from the tracks that the wolves, having gorged themselves on the young horse, were traveling very slowly. After the five cowboys had ridden about five miles, the signs began to indicate that they were getting close to the wolves. They were traveling in open country, and, on topping a low hill they came suddenly upon the animals. It was midwinter and the pelts would be prime. They made a quick decision to rope the wolves, instead of shooting and damaging the hides. Within a few minutes, each of the five cowboys, who were all expert ropers, had a large, snarling, fighting lobo on the end of his rope. Horses are naturally afraid of wolves, and a wild melee resulted, with scared horses hitting the end of the rope and popping the necks of the wolves and at the same time jerking the nooses tight around the throats of the animals. The result was that all of the lobos were soon down in the snow and easy to finish off. When the five cowboys rode back into the ranch, they had five beautiful pelts with the heads still attached. The Perry boys knew how to tan hides and mount heads, so, having nothing else to occupy their time, they agreed to take all five of the prime wolf pelts up to their cabin, where they would cure them out and mount the heads. When they were finished, each of the five cowboys who had gone on the wolf hunt had a beautiful white wolfskin rug, with the head still attached. We had that white rug on the living room floor at the Jones' ranch for many years afterwards.

Southeastern Wyoming, with its heavy growth of good grass and abundance of water, had always been wonderful buffalo country. One of my memories, as a boy riding over that country, is of seeing the great numbers of big buffalo heads with the hide and curly brown hair still attached and covering the head. Lying nearby would be the bones of the animal, bleached white by the summer sun, as proof that here on the Wyoming plains, these great animals had been killed by the thousands by the buffalo hunters, just for their hides. The hunters did not skin out the heads, and of course the hide continued to protect the skull of the dead buffalo from the elements; so, there on the prairie the heads remained, staring toward the sky through sightless eyes, a grim reminder of the slaughter, destruction, and pitiful waste which had occurred here on the prairie.

Also to be seen at that time were the many buffalo wallows on the Wyoming plains. These wallows were depressions in the prairie generally about thirty feet across and three feet deep. They had been started by some old buffalo bull pawing in a soft spot in the ground and throwing the dust into the air, where some of it would then settle on his back and help to keep the flies away. As more buffalo would continue to paw in the same spot for the same reason, a hole in the ground would be started, and as the pawing continued, a large depression would be created which would collect water when it rained. The buffalo would then get into the water and wallow around, collecting mud on their bodies, which would then dry and cake, taking care of their fly problem. In the process, the wallow would continue to be enlarged. Sometimes, if the wallow happened to be in a spot which drained a considerable area of country, the wallow could eventually become large enough to be a good-sized lake, or water hole. There were also the circular paths on the prairie, which were made by the buffalo cows when they would bunch their calves, and then walk circles around them to protect the small calves from the large packs of grey woles. For many years, these circles could be seen on the prairie in the spring of the year, when the green grass was starting. The grass would be a darker shade of green, where these circular paths had been, due to the fertilization which had occurred in the process of the circling.

In 1903, Frank Jones sold the little ranch on the Bushnell Creek and bought the larger Van Alton ranch, where there was a full section of native meadow on Bear Creek, three miles west of the little cow town of LaGrange. There was a four-room log house on the ranch at the time of the purchase, which was later torn down; and an eight-room, two-story house was built among the big cottonwoods, and was painted white. Over a period of years, Frank Jones and his three sons (including the writer) built up a good-sized cattle operation in the area around LaGrange, and in the Goshen Hole country. Down through the years, the white house among the cottonwoods on Bear Creek continued to be the home ranch of the F. E. (Frank) Jones family.

14

There was a period in the early days of the cattle business in the northern high plains country of the West when almost all of the trail herds that were brought into that part of the country from both Texas and Oregon and then turned loose on the open range were composed principally of two-year-old steers. The Texas Longhorn steers, as a type of cattle, were well suited to the open-range kind of operation that was then in existence in that part of the cattle country. After these Longhorn steers were trailed in and had lived through one winter and had become acclimated to the cold north, they became very tough and hard to kill. These southern cattle were also long-legged and rangy and could travel for great distances for grass or water. The principal objectionable feature of the Longhorn was that it was not a particularly good beef animal, due to the fact that it did not take on weight as rapidly or become as fleshy as a more compact breed of cattle.

On the other hand, there were the Shorthorn and Durham breeds of cattle which were trailed in from Oregon. The original stock of these cattle had been brought up the coast by cattle boat to Oregon, from the great herds of these breeds of stock which were then running on the ranges of the large Spanish rancheros in southern California. These Oregon cattle were good beef animals, but they were not good rustlers in hunting for grass or water. This was particularly true of the Durhams. These Oregon cattle were accustomed to the warmer climate of the West Coast, and being shorter legged and of a more docile disposition, they were inclined to stand around under a cut bank, or in some other shelter where they would be out of the cold wind, and starve to death, rather than get out and hit the ridges, in search of spots where the snow had blown off and they could find some open grass.

At a later date, some of the cattlemen who were operating in the northern high plains country began to build up breeding herds, and they also began to experiment with several different breeds of cattle. It was soon learned that when the southern Longhorn cows (which were almost every color of the rainbow) were crossed with a red Shorthorn or Durham bull from Oregon, a calf which would make a good beef animal would be the result. Also it was learned that the red color of the bull would generally predominate in the color markings of the calf, and almost solid colors (which were desirable) would quite often be obtained through this type of cross-breeding.

A few black Aberdeen Angus bulls were also imported from Scotland, and although the black Angus were fine beef and range animals, they never did gain wide acceptance at that time by the cattlemen who were operating under open-range conditions. The principal reason was that when a Longhorn, red Durham, or a Shorthorn cow was crossed with a black Angus bull, all kinds of color combinations would show up on the calves when they were born. So whenever a black bull appeared on the open range, he generally did not remain a bull for very long. In later years, with the enclosed type of ranching, where breeding could be controlled, the black Angus became a very popular type of range cattle in the West.

Another breed of cattle that was imported from Scotland (in very limited numbers) was the Gallaway breed from the Scottish highlands. These animals were a very unusual and interesting type of cattle, generally running to black and brown colors. They were a rather small and short-legged type of animal, with very compactly built bodies and with long, soft, silky, and shaggy hair which hung down in abundance from their rather large heads, which they carried quite high in the air, giving them a very wild and strange appearance. When a cowboy would ride up suddenly on the Gallaways, in the rough hilly country which they liked, he would get the impression, from the way that they would be standing on the top of the hill, with their heads held high, that they were poised and ready to take off at a moment's notice. The Gallaway, like the Angus, did not prove to be a satisfactory type of cattle for the open-range kind of operation.

Some of the cattlemen even experimented with the polled, or hornless, breeds of cattle, but these experiments were soon abandoned, due to the fact that without horns the cows could not protect their calves from the packs of grey wolves and other predatory animals which were on the range at that time in great numbers. It was inevitable that after the buffalo had been killed off the wolves would naturally turn to preying upon the cattle that were running upon the open range, and, of course, the calves and other hornless cattle were the easiest prey. Consequently, it was after the turn of the century, when the grey wolves had been thinned out and most of them killed off, that the practice of dehorning cattle became popular with the cattlemen, and then only due to the fact that in shipping, horned cattle in railway cattlecars were inclined to bruise each other. This was particularly true with the Longhorn cattle, which oftentimes had horn spreads of over eight feet. As a result of this bruising, the meat-packing plants would penalize horned cattle, sometimes cutting the price that they would pay for horned cattle on the hoof as much as two dollars per hundred pounds below the price of dehorned cattle.

An event which had a very definite bearing upon the development of the cattle business in southeastern Wyoming was the coming of the Union Pacific Railroad to that part of the territory in 1866. One of the greatest effects of the railroad upon the cattle industry was caused by the fact that, under the provisions of the Pacific Railway Act of 1862, the Union Pacific Railroad Company was given a grant of ten sections of land as a subsidy for every mile of track laid in Wyoming, as an inducement to the company to build the railroad. This act was later amended in 1864 to provide for an increase to twenty sections of land to be granted for every mile of track laid by the company. The act further provided that the grant would cover alternate sections, or the uneven numbered sections, in a strip of land, which would be forty miles in width, with twenty miles of the strip to be on each side of the railroad. When the railroad was completed across the Territory of Wyoming in 1869, it was determined that the land grant to the Union Pacific Railroad Company, in the Territory of Wyoming, amounted to 4,582,520 acres.

The big impact of this railroad land upon the cattle business in southeastern Wyoming came when, in 1884, the Union Pacific Railroad Company, in a money-raising program, began to liquidate its land holdings in Wyoming by offering the land for sale in large tracts, at an average price of around one dollar per acre. One of these sales was to George Baxter, for thirty thousand acres of good rangeland lying northeast of Cheyenne. Another sale was of one hundred twenty-five thousand acres to Francis E. Warren, in the same general area. Then there were the two big sales: one to the Wyoming Central Land and Improvement Company, of a half-million acres, and another to the Swan Land and Cattle Company, of five hundred forty-nine thousand acres. All of these sales of railroad land were, of course, in alternate sections.

A man who came to southeastern Wyoming at about the same time as the Union Pacific Railroad and who, like Joseph M. Carey, was destined to become a power in the livestock industry, as well as in the public and political future of the territory, was Francis E. Warren. Born at Hinsdale, Massachusetts, on June 20, 1844, Francis Warren was the son of a very prominent pioneer New England family. His great-grandfather was General Joseph Warren, who was killed at the battle of Bunker Hill during the Revolutionary War. Young Francis E. Warren had served with the northern armies during the War Between the States, and had been awarded the Congressional Medal of Honor for exceptional bravery during the war. He came to Cheyenne in 1868, shortly after having been discharged from the Union Army at the end of the war. His arrival in Cheyenne was only about one year after the Union Pacific Railroad had first reached that point. Soon after coming to this frontier cow town, young Warren went to work as a clerk in a general merchandise store owned by A. R. Converse. He made rapid progress, and within a few years he became a partner in the ownership of the business. Later, he acquired sole ownership of this retail store and shortly afterwards founded the Warren Mercantile Company, which operated in both the wholesale and the retail fields. Within a few years, "Warren's" became the largest mercantile establishment in southeastern Wyoming, supplying almost all of the other retail stores in that part of the territory as well as most of the large livestock outfits.

In the early eighties, Francis Warren also branched out into the livestock business. When the Union Pacific Railroad Company offered its land for sale in Wyoming, Warren purchased one hundred twenty-five thousand acres near Cheyenne, where he began operating under the name of the Warren Livestock Company. This very competent young man expanded his livestock operations in both cattle and sheep very rapidly, until, within a few years after purchasing the railroad land, he was reported to have been the largest sheep-raiser in the Territory of Wyoming. He had around ninety thousand head of sheep, twenty-five hundred head of Angora goats, two thousand head of horses, and twenty-five hundred head of fine cattle running on the range in southeastern Wyoming. He was also elected president of the Cheyenne Electric Light Company, and vice-president of the First National Bank of Cheyenne. In addition to his business and ranching activities, Francis Warren was also a very public-spirited young man who devoted a considerable amount of his time to public affairs. He became mayor of the city of Cheyenne, and shortly afterwards, on February 27, 1885, President Arthur appointed him governor of the Territory of Wyoming, where he served with distinction in that capacity.

Around the turn of the century, the lovely and charming Helen Warren, daughter of Francis E. Warren, was married at Cheyenne to the dashing young cavalry Lieutenant John J. Pershing, who was then stationed at Fort D. A. Russell (now Fort Warren) near Cheyenne. This very capable young cavalry officer advanced in rank very rapidly, and it so happened that he was stationed at the Presidio, an army post, near San Francisco in California when the great San Francisco earthquake, with its tremendous loss of lives, struck in the Bay area. As a result, it was here that the great tragedy in the life of the army officer John J. Pershing occurred; at that time, trouble was brewing on the Mexican border and General Pershing had left the Presidio shortly before the earthquake struck, on an assignment to the border area; Mrs. Helen Pershing and the four children, three girls and a boy, remained at the Presidio. After the effects of the earthquake had subsided, it was found that Mrs. Helen Pershing and the three little girls had all lost their lives in the great disaster and that only the small son, Francis Warren Pershing, had survived.

Some time later, when Pancho Villa crossed the border from old Mexico into the United States and raided the town of Columbus, New Mexico, in 1915, General John J. "Black Jack" Pershing was placed in command of a punitive expedition to cross the border into the interior of the Republic of Mexico in hot pursuit of the Mexican outlaw; however, by the time this expedition was authorized, organized, and under way, Pancho Villa and his band had vanished into the rugged Sierra Madre.

Two years later, in 1917, when the United States became

involved in World War One with Germany, General John Pershing was named the commanding general of the American Expeditionary Force in France, an assignment which he carried through to completion with credit to himself, as well as to the forces which he commanded.

At the same time that these events were occurring, Francis E. Warren was serving in the United States Senate as the senior senator from Wyoming, where, over a period of almost half of a century of service in that capacity, he gained very wide recognition as a great statesman in world affairs.

The man who was undoubtedly the greatest American-born organizer and promoter of large cattle companies operating at that time exclusively on the northern high plains was Alex Swan, who had been born in Pennsylvania, moved to Iowa when he was only a boy, and moved to the Territory of Wyoming in the early seventies. Swan's major move in the cattle business occurred when he organized the Scottish-owned Swan Land and Cattle Company in 1883, with offices in Edinburgh, Scotland, and a capitalization of three million dollars. His first move was when he purchased the first, large Hi Kelly cattle empire with ranches on the Chugwater, the Sybille, and the Laramie plains, with operations extending into the Goshen Hole country. In 1884, this ambitious man acquired an additional five hundred forty-nine thousand acres of railroad land, which was located principally in Albany and Carbon counties. This purchase, coupled with the ownership of the previous Hi Kelly holdings, and with the large areas of open-range government land which these purchases controlled, gave Alex Swan a tremendous cattle empire in southeastern Wyoming.

At the time that Alex Swan reached the peak of his career, about 1885, he was a tall, broad-shouldered man, around forty-five years of age, with keen, blue eyes, dark blond hair greying at the temples, and a very magnetic personality. This man reflected power wherever he went. In fact, he was the type of man who, under different circumstances, could have been a great national leader. Alex Swan had raised many millions of dollars for his various ventures in both the United States and Europe. In addition to being president of the Swan Land and Cattle Company, he was president of the First National Bank in Cheyenne, and president of the Wyoming Hereford Company. He was also credited with being the man who had organized the Omaha Stockyards Company, and was on the board of directors of many other organizations. Alex Swan was considered by most of the people who knew him to be a man of mature judgement, very skillfull and eloquent in dealing with other men, and resourceful in handling his many business enterprises.

At the peak of his operations in the cattle business, Alex Swan was reported to have been running around one hundred twenty-five thousand head of cattle on his vast cattle empire, with his six roundup wagons covering an area in southeastern Wyoming that was around two hundred miles in length, with an average width of one hundred miles, extending from Ogallala, Nebraska on the east, to Fort Steele on the west, and from the Colorado line on the south, to the North Platte River on the north. This area, which was mostly open-range country, included the greater part of what is now the five counties of Laramie, Goshen, Platte, Carbon, and Albany in southeastern Wyoming. It is apparent that, as Swan continued to expand his many operations, he was probably stretching his credit to the breaking point. In later years he ran into serious financial reverses and was subjected to very severe criticism by some of his associates and others with whom he had business dealings. It is obvious, however, that, at least in the beginning, this energetic man was sincere and believed in what he was doing. His problems were undoubtedly a result of his being vain and overly ambitious.

Probably the greatest contribution that Alex Swan made to the development of the West occurred when he founded the Wyoming Hereford Ranch in 1883, on a large block of fine railroad land. With the ranch headquarters located on Crow Creek, about eight miles east of Cheyenne, this ranch soon became recognized as the showplace for fine cattle in the Territory of Wyoming. The Wyoming Hereford Ranch was located in a very fine valley, with some of the best quality grass to be found anywhere in Wyoming, and with an abundance of good natural meadows along Crow Creek. The first registered Herefords to be imported by Alex Swan and brought to the Wyoming Hereford Ranch came from Herefordshire, England. Included in this shipment was one bull registered under the name of the Mighty Rudolph and costing thirty-five hundred dollars in England. (A bull of this quality would probably bring over a hundred thousand dollars on today's market.) This bull proved to be a sensational prizewinner at the American Livestock Show and at other livestock shows over the country. The Mighty Rudolph was established as the principle herd bull at the Wyoming Hereford Ranch, and he became the sire of a long line of prizewinning Herefords. Within a period of three years after the founding of the Wyoming Hereford Ranch, Alex Swan had imported around two hundred twenty-five head of registered Herefords from England. Based to a great degree upon the show record of the Mighty Rudolph, the young, registered Hereford bulls which were raised at the ranch were in strong demand by cattlemen from all over the country.

The coming of the Hereford breed of cattle to the high plains country was the answer to the cattleman's dream. This breed had all of the necessary qualifications for an ideal open-range type of cattle. They were beautifully marked, with red bodies and white faces; they were also full of vitality and were natural-born rustlers. In addition, they were an excellent quality of beef animal; being compact in build, they took on weight quite rapidly. Also, when going over the block, they dressed out to the satisfaction of the meat packers, and for that reason they were in strong demand and commanded top prices when they were shipped to market.

Very satisfactory results were also obtained by crossing the Hereford bulls with Shorthorn cows; a very rugged and heavy-boned type of animal resulted from this crossbreeding. The colors ran to red bodies and red-and-white faces, referred to as "brockle-face." In recent years, with the enclosed type of ranching, very satisfactory results were obtained by crossbreeding Hereford with black Angus, resulting in a calf of very high quality, with a black body and white face.

As the popularity of the Hereford breed continued to increase the demand for Hereford bulls, the Wyoming Hereford Ranch further expanded its operation until, within a few years, this great, registered-Hereford ranch, with its sixty thousand acres of fine rangeland, with ten thousand acres under irrigation and all in native hay, was running around twenty-five hundred head of registered Herefords, and had become recognized as being the largest strictly registered-Hereford ranch in the United States, or probably in the world. This ranch continued to maintain that position during a great part of the next eighty years. There were other ranches where more Herefords were run, but with the herds consisting of both registered and commercial cattle.

The Wyoming Hereford Ranch has naturally had problems from time to time, and there have been several changes in ownership. However, down through the years, the Hereford has proved to be a winner, and the size and quality of the herd at the Wyoming Hereford Ranch has been continuously maintained and is still going strong today.

Had it not been for the sale of the railroad land in large blocks by the Union Pacific Railroad Company, which permitted the fencing of a large tract of fine land that was then partially deeded and could be cut up into small pastures by cross-fencing in such a manner as to permit the handling of controlled breeding of registered cattle, there would be a question of whether a ranch of this size, running strictly registered cattle, could have been started at that time in that part of the cattle country.

15 In the period before the completion of the railroad networks in the West, which did not occur until around the turn of the century, the stagecoach was the principal method of public transportation in the high plains country. The well-recognized stagecoach of quality at that time was the Concord, which was built in Concord, New Hampshire, by the firm of Abbot and Downing, master craftsmen in the building of fine stagecoaches. Each coach was custom-built of the finest material available. They were designed and built to withstand the extremely rough usage to which they were subjected when being drawn at a high rate of speed over the rough and unimproved wagon trails that then existed in the West.

Abbot and Downing were people who took great pride in the excellence of their design and workmanship. Every consideration was given to the building of a coach that would give the passengers, who were traveling over long distances, the greatest possible comfort. To assist in accomplishing this purpose, the stagecoaches were so designed that the bodies were suspended, or cradled, between the two ends of the running gear, or chassis, upon several thicknesses, or plies, of very heavy and wide leather belting, called thoroughbraces. These were attached to mounts on each end of the running gear. This type of construction had the effect of leaving the body suspended in the chassis and supported by the thoroughbraces. With this method of suspension, the bodies were permitted to swing freely and to move up and down or sidewise, with the result that the road shocks to which the wheels and chassis of the coach were subjected when passing over the rocks and ruts of the very primitive and hazardous wagon roads were to a great degree absorbed, and unnecessary discomfort to the passengers was thereby avoided.

In the construction of the coaches, two triangular-shaped receptacles, which were called boots and were generally made from buffalo bull hides, were built into each stagecoach. These boots, with padlocked covers, were used for the storage of mail sacks and express and passenger baggage. One of the boots was mounted under the driver's seat, and the other in the rear end of the coach. As many as a dozen large buffalo bull hides were used in making the boots and thoroughbraces for each stagecoach. The finest of white ash was used for building the body frame, and the very best of hardwoods were used throughout in the construction of the running gear, including black cherry for making the wheel hubs. Very little metal was used in any part of the stagecoach, in order to hold down the weight of the vehicle as much as possible. The coaches were beautifully and artistically finished on the outside, with quite ornate woodcarvings and scroll work. Each coach had an individual name, such as "Sybille," engraved in the woodwork. There were also ornamental paintings on the bodies and doors, and harmonizing colors were used in painting the running gear and wheels of the vehicle. In fact, the best of the Concord stagecoaches were almost as elaborate as the finest of railway Pullman cars.

The six-horse Concord stagecoaches were built to accommodate nine passengers inside the coach, on leather-covered and upholstered seats. There were two additional seats, mounted over the front boot, alongside the driver, with two other large seats on top of the coach, inside the railing, which would accommodate six passengers; making a total of seventeen passengers when the vehicle was fully loaded. When the stagecoaches were on the move, the heavy trunks belonging to the passengers were either strapped to the rear boot or carried inside the railing on top of the loaded coach. These Concord stagecoaches were shipped to buyers all over the world, at an average price (fully equipped) of approximately eighteen hundred dollars each, F.O.B. Concord, New Hampshire. Many of the buyers of Concord stagecoaches bought their harness from James R. Hill, a famous leather worker and harness maker, who also had his shops in Concord and who would arrange to have the harness shipped with the coaches.

The large stagecoach lines served a very basic need in the northern high plains country, as well as in other areas of the West. First, and perhaps foremost, was their carrying of the U.S. mail to the isolated cow towns and army outposts scattered over this sparsely settled country. Almost all of the stagecoach lines obtained a contract from the U.S. Post Office Department, with a subsidy for carrying the mail. These mail contracts took care of a major portion of their operating costs. In addition, they had the revenue from the handling of express and from the transportation of passengers, who were always moving about over this vast country for one reason or another. These included traveling men; gamblers; dance hall girls; miners; and, of course, cowboys, with their sacked saddles loaded on top of the coach, who would be moving from one ranch, or job, to another.

Probably the best known stagecoach line in the country north of the Arkansas was the Cheyenne and Black Hills Stage and Express Lines, which ran from Cheyenne, Wyoming (by way of Fort Laramie) to Custer and Deadwood, South Dakota. This stagecoach line was organized and activated in 1875, about one year after Lt. Col. George A. Custer was first authorized by the army to make his so-called military reconnaissance into the Black Hills of South Dakota in 1874. On that expedition, Colonel Custer was accompanied by several professional gold-miners. When he returned in August of that year, official reports were made that gold in substantial quantities had been found on French Creek near the site of the present town of Custer, South Dakota. After this report was made public, even though the country north of the Platte was still closed to the white man by the treaty of 1868 with the Indians, it was generally anticipated that this treaty would be broken, due to the public clamor and newspaper comment, as well as to the political pressures which were being exerted by people who had been bitten by the Black Hills gold bug and who were not inclined to give any consideration whatever to the previously recognized rights of the Indian in that area.

Almost immediately after the reports of the gold strike in the Black Hills had been made public, excited people began to gather in the towns along the Union Pacific Railroad. While it was recognized that the Black Hills area was still forbidden territory, many of these people were willing to take their chances of being scalped by the Indians, and were seeking transportation into this fabulous gold country. The Union Pacific was the closest railroad to the Black Hills, with Cheyenne, Wyoming, and Sidney, Nebraska each about two hundred forty miles from Custer City on French Creek.

Within a very short period of time, strong competition began building up between these two towns for official recognition as the point of departure for mail and stagecoach routes to the Black Hills, and also for recognition as outfitting points for gold miners. During the period of time that this competition was under way, the *Cheyenne Leader*, in May of 1875, printed fifty thousand copies of a special edition for national distribution, which claimed that Cheyenne was the natural gateway to the Black Hills country. The completion of the new military bridge, with its three spans of one hundred fifty feet each, across the North Platte River at Fort Laramie, in 1875, was a big help to Cheyenne in getting recognition for the Cheyenne, Fort Laramie, and Custer City stagecoach route. Another major event that occurred in Cheyenne in that year which helped the booming little city to increase its prestige was the opening, in September of 1875, of the very modern Inter-Ocean Hotel. Another important factor was the fact that Cheyenne was in a direct line between the Colorado gold fields, which were already operating in the Rocky Mountains south of Cheyenne, and the new strike northward in the Black Hills of South Dakota. Of course, many of the Colorado miners were anxious to try their luck in the new fields, and therefore, Cheyenne became the principle outfitting point for these northbound Colorado gold miners.

Many of the Colorado miners bound for the Black Hills were moving across country with their own teams, wagons, and other equipment. Some of these people, instead of using the route by way of Fort Laramie, went northeast from Cheyenne to a point where they crossed Pole Creek at the Warren Ranch headquarters. After leaving Pole Creek, they continued in a northeasterly direction until they crossed Horse Creek at the little cow town of LaGrange. They then moved on down Horse Creek until they crossed over a divide and came down into the North Platte River valley, where they either forded or ferried the wagons across the river at about the same point as the crossing of the Texas-Montana Cattle Trail. When they left the Platte river valley, they would be in Indian country, closed to the white man. As they continued northward, they would be traveling at their own risk. At a point near Rawhide Butte on Rawhide Creek, their trail would join the Cheyenne, Fort Laramie, and Custer City trail.

There were other prospective miners with their own transportation who took the trail running north from Sidney, Nebraska, which was known as the Sidney Trail. On this trail, they crossed the North Platte River on the Camp Clark toll bridge (near where the town of Bridgeport, Nebraska, is now located) then continued northward into the Black Hills country where the gold strike had been made on French Creek.

In addition to all of these people with their own transportation, there were also thousands of eager prospective gold miners with only a pick, a shovel, and a gold pan, who were just as anxious to get to the diggings where they too could make their fortunes. They were the ones who were fighting for any kind of transportation that they could get, especially seats on stagecoaches. There was one thing that these people all had in common, regardless of how they were traveling, and that was a feverish sense of urgency. They would kill, or take their chances on being killed, just for a chance to get their hands on some of that gold on French Creek.

The first stagecoach line from Cheyenne to the Black Hills was started by Frank Yates, a trader from the Red Cloud Indian Agency on the Sioux reservation in South Dakota who had taken a mail contract in January of 1876 to carry the mail from Cheyenne to the Red Cloud and Spotted Tail agencies, which were located on the south edge of the Black Hills. The first stagecoach for the new line pulled out from in front of the Inter-Ocean Hotel on February 3, 1876.

About a week later, on February 12, Yates sold his line to the firm of Gilmer, Salisbury, and Patrick, who were experienced stagecoach line operators, and assigned his contracts for carrying the mail to them. Jack Gilmer, the senior partner in the new firm, had been, at one time, associated with the firm of Russel, Majors, and Waddell, and also with Wells Fargo. Then, in 1869, he had purchased the stage line which ran from points in Utah to Helena, Montana, and several other lines in those states, in partnership with Salisbury and Patrick, before buying the Cheyenne-Black Hills line.

This new line was set up to operate under the name of the Cheyenne and Black Hills Stage and Express line. As soon as the purchase was completed, the management announced that within two weeks stagecoaches would leave Cheyenne daily, travel day and night, and reach Custer City on the third day after leaving Cheyenne. The new firm also brought in Luke Vorhees (an associate of the owners from Utah) as superintendent and part owner of the new line. Vorhees was an experienced frontiersman and an old-timer in that part of the country. He had been born in Belvidere, New Jersey in 1835, came west in 1857, where he worked as a buffalo hunter in Kansas for a couple of years. He then joined the gold rush to Colorado in 1859, and continued in the gold mining business until 1871, when he bought a herd of Longhorns in Texas and trailed them to a ranch which he had established in Utah. A few months later, he also became associated with the firm of Gilmer, Salisbury, and Patrick.

Soon after coming to Cheyenne and taking over his duties as superintendent of the Cheyenne and Black Hills Stage and Express line, and completing the checking of the livestock and equipment which had been purchased with the line, Vorhees placed an order with Abbot and Downing in Concord, New Hampshire for thirty additional six-horse Concord stagecoaches. At the same time, he ordered ninety sets of new harness, with collars, from James R. Hill, to be shipped with the coaches. He also made a trip to eastern horse markets and bought an additional six hundred head of harness-broke Percheron and Belgian stage horses of the best quality, in matched pairs, and shipped them to Cheyenne. Each of the horses was named and numbered. A harness (including the collar) was fitted to each horse and stamped with the same number as the animal.

In addition to stagecoaches, the Cheyenne and Black Hills Stage and Express line also operated wagon trains hauling freight from Cheyenne to Custer City. Some of these wagon trains were drawn by oxen and driven by bullwhackers, while others were drawn by several teams of mules driven with a jerk-line. Many different types of material and equipment were hauled by these freight outfits, including medical supplies, mining equipment, saw mills, hay and grain for the stage stops, as well as some third-class passengers. It took seventeen days to go through from Cheyenne to Custer City with bull teams, while the mules made the trip in nine days. The average freight charge from Cheyenne to Custer City was five dollars for each one hundred pounds of weight.

The organizing of a major stagecoach and freight line outfit of the size of the Cheyenne and Black Hills Stage and Express line required the very close attention and supervision of the superintendent while this work was under way. There was the building of the necessary stage stops, with barns and other facilities, as well as the distribution of livestock, with hay and grain, where they were needed; also, numerous classifications of personnel were required. These included division agents, stagecoach drivers, stock tenders, blacksmiths, freight wagon drivers, station masters, cooks, and shotgun guards. Also, there was the necessity of providing dining rooms and other facilities at the principal stage stops for the convenience and comfort of the stagecoach passengers. It was necessary that all of these details be properly handled, in order for the management to be in a position to give the type of service that was expected from a major stagecoach line operation.

Competent stagecoach drivers, who could handle a six-line team with safety for the passengers and still move the coaches over the road rapidly enough to keep a tough time schedule, were especially hard to find and were very much in demand. When the stagecoaches were on the road, the horses would generally be moving at a long trot; however, occasionally, when the road ahead was reasonably smooth, the driver would pop his long whip and bring his six-horse team to a gallop for a short period of time. The stagecoach driver's whip (which was his only piece of personally owned equipment) was generally on a five-foot stock, with an eighteen-foot lash, and a leather popper on the end. The pop (like the sound of a shot from a rifle) would generally be all that would be needed to get the desired results. Skill on the part of the driver in handling his six-line team under any conditions and at any speed, without losing control of the horses and endangering the lives of his passengers, was an absolute requirement for any driver who worked for a major stagecoach line. The run, or drive, which would be made by a stagecoach driver at one time, would generally be from forty to sixty miles, depending upon the terrain and upon the location of the principal stage stops. Changes of horses would be provided for each stagecoach at stage stops about every fifteen miles. The stock tender at each stop would have the fresh teams harnessed and ready to go when the stagecoach pulled in. The change would be very quickly made, with seven minutes allowed in the time schedule for each of these changes.

In addition to the six-horse coaches, Abbot and Downing also built a light, four-horse coach with canvas sides and with only the driver's seat set over the front boot. These light stagecoaches were generally used on branch lines which ran to the outlying cow towns and isolated ranching communities, where the traffic was light and the roads getting in and out were especially rough and rugged to travel. Another vehicle which was also built by Abbot and Downing was the little two-horse jerkie with an express body. These were used by the stage lines for many purposes, including that of transportation for the blacksmith who went up and down the line with his small forge and fuel loaded in the express body. He would shoe horses and repair broken equipment of all kinds for the stagecoach line.

Tickets for the run from Cheyenne to Fort Laramie or

Custer City could be purchased in advance at the offices of the stagecoach line in the Inter-Ocean Hotel. The regular fares from Cheyenne to Custer City were: first class, $20; second class, $15; third class, $10. There was always a flurry of excitement around the Inter-Ocean when the Custer City stagecoach came down the street, drawn by six perfectly matched and beautifully groomed horses. The driver would swing his team up in front of the hotel with a flourish, lightly apply his brakes, and bring the coach to a stop exactly in front of the front steps of the hotel. The stageline owners, who were always public-relations conscious, kept some of their best teams and equipment on the Cheyenne end of the run, where they would attract public attention. When the loading of the passengers and their luggage got under way, very close attention was always given to good weight distribution and balance of the coach. Otherwise, there would be danger of turning the coach over in the rough going. Buffalo robes and coats were also provided, when they were needed, for the comfort of the people who would be riding outside on the front boot or in the seats on top of the stagecoach. After the coach was fully loaded, the driver would climb back up on his seat, pick up his lines, and speak to his leaders, holding them lightly in check, until he had his swing team and wheelers leaning into their collars. He would then release his brake and slack off on the leaders, and the six-horse team and the stagecoach would be swinging gracefully out into the street on their way to the new El Dorado at Custer City on French Creek.

After leaving Cheyenne, the eighteen-mile run to the stage stop at Pole Creek (which was operated by Fred Schwartz) would be made very quickly. A change to fresh horses would be made at this station, and they would again be on their way to the next regular stop at the Horse

Creek station; which was located twenty-eight miles north of Cheyenne and was operated, for a period of time, by Mike Fagan. This particular stage station was later moved about three miles north, to the Bard Ranch on Little Bear, where Isaac Bard had a small cattle ranch and also operated the Little Bear post office. The next stop on the run was located thirty-eight miles north of Cheyenne on Big Bear Creek, at a station called Bear Springs. The ranch where this station was located raised a good supply of both hay and grain and was a favorite stopping point for freight wagons, as well as for stagecoaches.

When the coach left Bear Springs and moved on down the stage trail for an additional twelve miles, making a total of fifty-two miles that they would have traveled since leaving Cheyenne that morning, over what had been a gentle rolling and well-grassed country (where there had also been a fifteen hundred foot drop in elevation), the stage trail which they were following would begin to gradually drop down into the snug little Chugwater valley, with its green meadows and cottonwood trees. Then, after traveling for a very short distance, the stagecoach would roll up in front of the stage station at the Hi Kelly ranch, where the passengers would be given thirty minutes to stretch their legs and eat their lunch.

There was a small hotel with a dining room and a bar in the little cow town of Chugwater which was run by an old-timer named John (Portugee) Phillips, where good meals were served to all comers. This was the end of the run for the driver. He would stop over at the Phillips Hotel for about twenty-four hours, then pick up another stagecoach (the next day) which would be going in the opposite direction, and take it on into Cheyenne.

When the stagecoach pulled out on the trail again with a new driver and fresh horses, it would follow the wagon trail down the Chugwater valley to the first temporary stop, about ten miles distant, where there was a small post office, named Chimney Rock, near the site of the present town of Slater, Wyoming. After the mail sacks had been unloaded at this post office, the coach would move on down the trail for another four miles to the regular stage station at the John Hutton ranch, where another change of horses would be made. This stage station was called Bordeaux and it was here that another well-known wagon trail, known as the Bozeman Trail, forked off, bearing to the northwest to Fort Fetterman and on into Montana. As the coach moved on down the Chugwater valley on the Fort Laramie trail, its next stop would be at a station known as Eagle Nest. From this station, it would be only seventeen miles into Fort Laramie in the valley of the Platte. Upon their arrival there, the stagecoach passengers would have traveled ninety-two miles since leaving Cheyenne that morning.

Fort Laramie was considered to be the most important point on the stage line. It was not only important from the standpoint of the number of passengers and the quantity of freight and express moving between Fort Laramie and Cheyenne, but perhaps more importantly, because the fort, being located midway between Cheyenne and Custer City, afforded a very high degree of protection to the traffic moving over the stage line from stagecoach robbers, as well as from Indian raiding parties. The stagecoaches were not ordinarily provided with military escorts unless the situation was particularly dangerous, or if they should be carrying a military payroll. However, the fact that army patrols were in the field most of the time who knew the schedules of the stagecoaches, had the effect of acting as a deterrent, so far as outlaws and Indian raiding parties were concerned.

When the coach pulled out of Fort Laramie for its next run to Spring Creek, there would be a new driver handling the lines on the six-up of fresh horses. There would also be a considerable change in the passenger list, due to the fact that many of the passengers who came from Cheyenne had Fort Laramie as a destination. Also, there would be others who had stopped for an overnight rest at the old Rustic Hotel and who would then catch another northbound stage the next day. In addition, there were the new passengers on board who had taken the stagecoach at Fort Laramie and who were bound for the gold diggings on French Creek, with a get-rich-quick gleam in their eyes. After a quick change of horses at the Spring Creek station, the coach would again be rolling on the twelve-mile run to the famous Rawhide Butte station, which was located on the fine little Rawhide Creek, only about a mile from the old landmark of the Rawhide Buttes.

This was buffalo country; here on Rawhide Creek had been a favorite camping spot of the Indians for hundreds of years, before the coming of the white man. In this good grass country they had hunted the buffalo for meat in the summertime; then, when cold weather came, they had moved their lodges back into the edge of the Black Hills, where there was plenty of wood and good spring water, as well as fine shelter and protection from the bitter cold winds and blizzards of the northern winters.

As the coach traveled the rough trail from the Rawhide Buttes to the Running Water station, which was sixteen miles to the north, the stage trail ran almost parallel to the Texas-Montana Cattle Trail, and the passengers could look out of the windows of the stagecoach and see the dust clouds being raised by the trail herds moving northward to the Powder River and the Yellowstone.

The Running Water station was located at Silver Cliff,

which was only about a mile west of the site of the present nice little city of Lusk, Wyoming. Since the stagecoach had left Cheyenne, it had been traveling almost due north. However, about three miles after leaving the Running Water station, the stage trail turned to the northeast, for an additional eleven miles, before it reached the Hat Creek station, where a good stock of supplies of all kinds was carried to take care of any emergency. This station was operated by Jack Bowman, who was considered to be one of the best station masters on the line.

Almost immediately after leaving the Hat Creek station, the topography of the country through which they would be traveling would change very abruptly, from a well-grassed rolling plain to a very rugged, wild, and dangerous type of terrain, which was well-suited to stagecoach holdups by outlaws, as well as to attacks by Indian raiding parties. As a matter of fact, many holdups and raids did occur on this section of the Custer City trail over a period of several years. When the stagecoach had traveled for about fifteen miles after leaving the Hat Creek station, it would pull up at the Harding Ranch station, on a nice little stream called Indian Creek, where regular meals were served and overnight accommodations were available.

A small dugout fort with portholes on all sides, where a small party could defend themselves against great odds in the event of an Indian attack, had been built at the Harding Ranch. Also, army patrols oftentimes were camped on Indian Creek while they were patrolling this very dangerous section of the stage trail. The next regular stop for the stagecoaches was at the Prairie Springs station, followed by the Cheyenne River stage stop, where overnight accommodations were available. This station was used quite extensively by freight wagons, as well as by stagecoaches. The next important stop on the Custer City trail was the Red

Canyon station, which had been built near the mouth of Red Canyon. Here, there was another stretch of very dangerous road, which the army regularly patrolled from Camp Collier, which was only a short distance from the stage station. When the stagecoach pulled out again, it would be in the well-known and treacherous Red Canyon, which was a narrow gorge with high canyon walls rising abruptly from the canyon floor to a height of as much as a thousand feet.

Many stagecoach holdups were pulled off in Red Canyon; also, several small parties of miners were killed in this canyon — their wagons burned and their livestock run off by Indian raiding parties, while the miners were trying to get in or out from the gold fields on French Creek. Army patrols operating in the area usually warned the miners not to attempt to go through this canyon in parties of less than ten, though some of them still tried to do so. As the stagecoach moved on up Red Canyon, the next station where they would stop was known as Spring on the Hill, followed by another station called Spring on the Right. Eight miles beyond this latter station, the stage trail broke out into a beautiful little area known as Pleasant Valley. From here on in, for the next nine miles to Custer City, the stage road was considered to be quite safe.

By the time that the stagecoach pulled up in front of the little log Occidental Hotel in Custer City, the passengers would have travelled a total distance of approximately two hundred forty-six miles since leaving Cheyenne. When they pulled in, the coach would barely have stopped before the new tenderfoot miners would be out and rushing madly up and down French Creek, in search of gold nuggets. Most of these people were doomed to disappointment in their gold mining activities. Successful gold-mining is generally accomplished by a combination of two things: know-how, and luck; though the greatest factor is know-how.

The most difficult period in the operation of the Cheyenne and Black Hills Stage and Express line came in April, May, and June of 1876. Early in the spring of that year it became apparent that the Indians were going to make a major effort to regain and hold their good hunting grounds in the Powder River country, as well as their winter home and shelter in the Black Hills of South Dakota. Both of these areas had, of course, been granted to them under the Indian treaty which had been signed with the United States government in 1868; and it was soon obvious from the moves that the Indians were making that they did not intend to yield this country to the invasion of the white man without a fight to the finish. Reports and rumors were beginning to come into Cheyenne and Miles City during the early spring months of 1876 of very heavy concentrations of warriors, mostly Cheyenne and Sioux, along the Tongue, Powder, and Big Horn rivers in northern Wyoming and southern Montana; also, that they were assembling under the very able leadership of several prominent and well-known Indian chiefs, including Sitting Bull and Crazy Horse. It was said that these wise old Indian chiefs were admonishing their followers to concentrate in large numbers in well-chosen and well-protected areas of the country and not to get scattered out, where they could be cut to pieces by small army patrols.

From the activities that were occurring, it was soon apparent that the overall strategy of the Indian chiefs was to draw the army troops as far away from their bases as possible, where it would be difficult for them to get supplies and reinforcements, and then to make the white man fight on a battleground of Indian choosing. It also shortly became obvious that, in addition to the major battle strategy of the chiefs, the Indians also had very definite plans for cutting the lines of communication and supply to the approximately ten thousand gold miners and other white people who were concentrated around Custer City in the Black Hills. They would completely isolate them in that area by burning the stage stations of the Cheyenne and Black Hills Stage and Express line, and by attacking the miner groups, wagon trains, stagecoaches, and other traffic that were moving on the Cheyenne and Black Hills Stage trail.

As the spring of 1876 opened up, major military operations by the army got under way, with the result that, during the next few months, several major battles were fought with the Indians in the high plains country. Among these engagements was the Battle of the Little Big Horn, where the impetuous Colonel George A. Custer, in June of that year, rode headlong (without proper reconnaissance) into a pocket in the hills which was occupied by several thousand well-equipped and well-led Indian warriors. Custer lost his entire command of two hundred fifty-six officers and men.

As the Indians continued in their efforts to isolate the white people in the Black Hills, they burned the stage station at Rawhide Butte to the ground in the spring of 1876, followed a few weeks later by the burning of the stage stations at both the Hat Creek Ranch and at Running Water Creek. Also, while these raids were under way, H. E. "Stuttering" Brown, who was in charge of the northern division of the Cheyenne and Black Hills Stage and Express line for Luke Vorhees, was shot and badly wounded, about eighteen miles northeast of the Hat Creek station, while he and two of his men were making a night run with a light coach to the Indian Creek station. Brown, an excellent division superintendent, died the next day from his wounds.

The Indian raiding parties swept as far south as Chugwater, where they threatened to burn the stage station at the Hi Kelly ranch. However, probably due to the longstanding agreements with Hi Kelly which had never been broken by either party, they did not burn that station. Hi Kelly was in Cheyenne at the time that this raid occurred. When he learned that the Indian war party was threatening to burn the stage station at his ranch, he made a fast ride to Chugwater, changing horses three times. When he finally rode in at his ranch, the Indian raiding party had already left, but had taken twenty head of his best horses, which he later recovered.

During the next few months, the Indians continued their pressures upon the stage line, with numerous raids against the stage stations and stagecoaches, in their effort to completely block traffic on the line. One of these attacks was made on a southbound stagecoach shortly after it had pulled out from the Indian Creek station. C. H. Cameron, an excellent old-time driver, was on the boot skinning the six-up when the attack occurred. He made a run for it, with the Indians firing from cover alongside the road, and with the four passengers inside of the coach returning the rifle fire. The Indians finally succeeded in blocking the trail, which forced Cameron and his passengers to take to the rocks. The entire party finally succeeded in making their way to the Hat Creek station under cover of darkness that night. However, one of the passengers who had been on the stagecoach had been shot through the cheek while the running battle had been under way. When an army patrol went out the next day to where the fight had occurred, they found that the stagecoach had been burned and completely destroyed and that the stage horses had been run off by the Indians.

As the Indian raids continued to gain momentum, the situation for the white people in the Black Hills was becoming extremely critical. With Custer City almost completely isolated, the people in that area were running out of needed food and medical supplies, as well as many other necessary items. In the period following the death of division superintendent H. E. Brown, Luke Vorhees was spending practically all of his time at the Hat Creek station and at Custer City where he personally took charge of directing the efforts of his people in trying to keep the traffic moving on the stagecoach line.

As the situation continued to become more desperate, territorial Governor Thayer of Wyoming requested additional troops from Commanding General Crook, to be used for patrol duty and as military escort in the movement of essential transportation for relief of the people who were isolated in the Black Hills country of South Dakota. General Crook was in need of all of the available troops under his command for carrying on the campaign in the field against the Sioux and Cheyenne, in the Big Horn and Powder River country. However, he did assign ten troops of cavalry and three companies of infantry to keeping the lines of communication and supply open from the Hat Creek station to Custer City.

Some of the gold miners in the Black Hills, in fear of their lives, abandoned their mining claims and attempted to get back to safety across the Platte River; some of them made it, while others did not. Luke Vorhees reported that while he was making a fast ride from Custer City to the Cheyenne River stage station, he came across the burned wagons and scalped bodies of the Metz group of gold miners who had been attempting to get out of the hills. Two of that party, who were wounded, escaped, but died later from their wounds at the Red Canyon stage station. During this same period, several stage line employees were killed by the Indians; including Charlie Clark, a stage driver who was ambushed and killed north of Fort Laramie. Another driver, by the name of Tate, was also killed near the Rawhide Butte station. Regardless of the hazards that were involved, the stagecoaches continued to go through, in very limited numbers, handling only mail and absolutely essential passenger traffic, and then only with a strong military escort. In June of 1876, Luke Vorhees moved his division agent, named Moulton, from the Custer City office to Fort Laramie, with instructions to the young man to organize an expedition of seventy-five freight wagons, and to bring it into Custer City with the most seriously needed supplies. This long wagon train, after many difficulties, finally made it through, under heavy military escort, to the hungry people in Custer City.

While these events were occurring in the Black Hills country, the campaign against the Indians in the Big Horn and the Powder River country to the north was moving very rapidly toward a conclusion. The temporary successes which had been gained by the Indians in the Battle of the Little Big Horn were of short duration. General Nelson A. Miles, operating from his base as Fort Keough on the Yellowstone, was in direct command of the army outposts and troops in the area south of the Yellowstone; while Commanding General George Crook, with his headquarters in Omaha, was in the field, operating from Fort Laramie and the Pine Ridge Agency in South Dakota, in direct command of the troops operating north of the Platte. The overall effect of the troop movements was to create a giant nutcracker type of campaign: hinged in the west on the Big Horn mountains and in the east on the Black Hills. As these operations gained force and momentum, the Indians soon realized that they were caught in a trap, and as a result, the Sioux began streaming eastward in large numbers to their reduced and restricted reservation located east of the Black Hills.

The organized resistance of the Indians was completely broken when Congress passed an appropriation act on August 15, 1876, which provided, in part, as follows:

> While said band is engaged in hostilities against the white people and hereafter there shall be no appropriation made for the subsistence of said Indians; unless they first agree to relinquish all right and claim to any country outside the boundaries of the permanent reservation established by the treaty of Eighteen Hundred and Sixty-Eight for said Indians and also so much of their permanent reservation as lies west of the one hundred and third meridian of longitude.

The last sentence of this quote, pertaining to that portion of the permanent reservation which "lies west of the one hundred and third meridian of longitude," was the pertinent portion of this act so far as the Indians were concerned, as this was the portion of their reservation which was in controversy at that time.

With the back of the Indian resistance broken, activity in the Black Hills country gained momentum very rapidly. The burned stage stations of the Cheyenne and Black Hills Stage and Express line were quickly rebuilt, and heavy movement of both passengers and freight traffic was soon under way, with stagecoaches moving on a daily schedule. Also during the period of time that the conflict with the Indians had been in the process of reaching its peak, changes had been occurring in the gold-mining activities in the Black Hills country. Some of the miners from Custer City and on French Creek had been reaching out during this period and prospecting many of the streams and gulches further to the north, with the result that a very rich strike was made at Deadwood Gulch. This strike gave every indication of being quite extensive and far richer than anything that had been found elsewhere in the Black Hills. Interest in French Creek soon began to die down as the big rush to the new strike at Deadwood gained momentum. The Deadwood strike proved to be all that had been anticipated and became one of the great gold strikes of all time. By the late summer of 1876, over a half-million dollars in gold dust and nuggets had been brought out by the Cheyenne and Black Hills Stage and Express line, in addition to the gold which had been carried out by individuals.

Luke Vorhees moved quickly in extending the operations of his stagecoach line for the additional fifty miles from Custer City northward to Deadwood, in order to furnish service to the new mining camp at that location. Five additional stage stations, built on this new stretch of stage trail, were located at Spring Creek, Mountain City, Reynolds Ranch, Rapid Creek, and Deadwood. The total distance from Cheyenne to Deadwood (including the additional mileage involved in this extension) then became approximately three hundred ten miles. Several other changes and additions to the stage trails which ran north and east from the Hat Creek station, that were regularly used by the Cheyenne and Black Hills Stage and Express line (or as it became commonly called, the Cheyenne and Deadwood Stagecoach line), were made over a period of several years, as the need developed. One of the alternate routes opened up ran almost due north from the Hat Creek station, skirting along the west side of the Black Hills and then cutting through the north edge of the hills to the mining camp at Deadwood Gulch. Additional stage stations were established northward from the Hat Creek station, along this new route, at Lance Creek, Cheyenne

River, Beaver Creek, Cold Springs, and Whitewood. This alternate route, which did not pass through Custer City, was considerably shorter than the old route, with a total estimated distance from Cheyenne to Deadwood of approximately two hundred sixty-eight miles.

The production of gold in the Deadwood area continued to increase very rapidly until, within a short period, it was running at an annual rate of approximately three million dollars a year. With this tremendous increase in production, and with practically all of this gold being shipped out by the Cheyenne and Deadwood Stagecoach line, robberies and stagecoach holdups on the stage line became an almost weekly occurrence. One of the most daring of these stagecoach holdups occurred only two and a half miles out of Deadwood when Johnnie Slaughter, who was considered to be one of the best six-line drivers on the line, was knocked from the driver's seat by a shotgun blast from one of the five masked outlaws. Johnnie died instantly, with fourteen buckshot through his body. One of the passengers, by the name of Walter Dar, was also wounded but later recovered. About a week later, Ed Moran from Cheyenne was also held up and robbed of two hundred dollars in gold dust, only five miles out from Deadwood, on the same stage road.

With the robberies of stagecoaches increasing, Luke Vorhees doubled the shotgun guards on all stagecoaches going out of the Black Hills which were carrying gold shipments, and took all other reasonable precautions for the safety of his passengers. Also, as a protection for the gold shipments that were being handled by his line, he ordered two specially built armored Concord stagecoaches from Abbott and Downing with instructions that these coaches be heavily reinforced and lined with bullet-proof steel plate on the inside walls, but not on the ceiling.

Two portholes were also provided on each side of the vehicle, which could be used by the guards riding on the inside of the coach for firing at stage robbers on the outside. Strong boxes, or small vaults, which were almost impossible to remove, and could only be unlocked at origin or destination of the stagecoach were also built into these armored vehicles while they were under construction at the factory. The first of these armored vehicles to be delivered was named the Monitor. These armored coaches were used strictly for the movement of gold or other highly important and valuable material and no passengers were allowed in these vehicles under any circumstances.

The first robbery of one of these armored stagecoaches occurred on September 26, 1878, at the Canyon Springs station on Beaver Creek, near the site of what was later known as the Cold Springs Ranch station. Gene Burnett was on the boot, handling the lines on the six-horse team that was pulling the coach, while Gale Hill was riding shotgun on the seat beside him; Eugene Smith, Scott Davis and Hugh Campbell were guards riding inside of the coach. They pulled up and stopped about twenty feet from the log barn at the station. The robbers had already ridden into the station a couple of hours before the arrival of the stagecoach, had surprised, bound, and gagged Bill Miner, the stock tender, and had then proceeded to pull the chinking from between the logs of the barn, in order to make openings that they could use as loop-holes for firing on the stagecoach when it arrived.

As the armored stagecoach pulled up and came to a stop, Gale Hill, the shotgun guard, jumped down from the boot with his shotgun in his hand to help with the change to fresh horses. Almost immediately, heavy rifle fire was opened on the stagecoach by the masked outlaws hidden inside the barn. Hill was instantly wounded through the left arm and chest, but he managed to crawl to cover, from where he returned the fire of the stage robbers, wounding two of them, one seriously. Soon afterwards, one of the masked holdup men managed to get on top of the barn, where he found some cover and began to fire down through the unarmored roof of the stagecoach, wounding Gene Smith, one of the guards. Scott Davis and Hugh Campbell, the other two guards inside the stagecoach, upon finding that they were exposed to the rifle fire, decided to abandon the vehicle by opening the door of the coach on the opposite side from the barn, then firing as they ran, making a run for some trees which were about fifty yards away. Scott Davis made the cover of the trees; Campbell did not. He was killed instantly by two rifle bullets when he was only part of the way to cover. Scott Davis, using the trees for cover, managed to escape and made his way on foot to the Ben Eagar ranch, a stopping point for stagecoach guards, where he knew that help would be available.

Davis found three other guards who were off duty at the ranch, and they all returned to the Canyon Springs station together, where they found the driver and all of the guards who were still alive lashed to trees. Even though these men were all wounded, except one, they had all been lashed securely to the trees and abandoned there by the stage robbers, who had left shortly before the arrival of the guards. They also found that the robbers, who had worked with sledge hammers and large cold chisels, had succeeded, after about two hours of steady work, in breaking into the strong box. They had then escaped with the contents, amounting to about twenty-seven thousand dollars in gold bullion, in addition to a substantial quantity of jewelry. About two-thirds of the gold bullion was eventually recovered. Two of the robbers who were involved in the stagecoach holdup were later identified, and another one of them was reported to have died from his wounds.

This rugged country lying east and north of the Hat Creek station, even with the taking of all possible precautions by the stageline, continued to be a very dangerous country for stagecoach operations. Robberies of passengers and strong boxes continued to some degree over the entire decade that the Cheyenne and Black Hills Stage and Express line was in business.

In the fall of 1877, Gilmer, Salisbury, and Patrick added to their stage line holdings when they acquired the Western Stage lines, which had been operating for sometime out of Sidney, Nebraska, over the Sidney Trail, to the Black Hills of South Dakota. As soon as this deal was closed, the purchasers moved in additional livestock and equipment, with Luke Vorhees taking charge. They then continued to operate both stagecoaches and freight wagons over both of these lines for several years afterwards.

During the following year, Vorhees also opened up another new section of stage trail, with additional stage stations, which was fifty miles in length, running eastward from the Rawhide Butte station to a station on the Sidney Trail in South Dakota which became known as the Horse Head station. This new stretch of stage trail served as a connecting link between all of the stage trails which were being used by the two stage lines, and tied the entire system together. This addition to the stage trails gave Vorhees the opportunity of routing some of the stagecoach traffic going northward from Cheyenne by way of the Rawhide Butte station, and from there eastward to the connection with the Sidney Trail at the Horse Head station.

From this station at Horse Head, the traffic moving on

the Sidney Trail continued northward along the east edge of the Black Hills through Buffalo Gap and the new little town of Rapid City to Deadwood Gulch. In future years, almost all of the company's stagecoach traffic was routed over this trail, which ran through open country most of the way and where the stagecoaches were not so vulnerable to stage holdups and robberies as on the other routes. The total distance from Cheyenne to Deadwood over this route was approximately two hundred seventy miles.

In May of 1883, Russell Thorpe, Sr., an experienced stage line operator, became the owner of the Cheyenne and Black Hills Stage and Express line when he purchased the entire operation, including all livestock and equipment, from Gilmer, Salisbury, and Patrick. In addition to these stage lines, Thorpe also owned a good-sized ranching operation on Rawhide Creek, near Rawhide Buttes, where he continued to maintain his headquarters and to direct the operations of the stagecoach line from that point.

However, with the completion of the Chicago and Northwestern Railroad to Chadron, Nebraska, and Rapid City, South Dakota, in 1886, and also with the completion of the Cheyenne and Northern Railroad from Cheyenne to Chugwater, Wyoming in 1887, the usefulness of the Cheyenne and Black Hills Stage and Express lines was ended. The last stagecoach to make the run over this line left from the Inter-Ocean Hotel on February 19, 1887. The Cheyenne Deadwood Stagecoach line had then completed ten years of continuous service to the many people in that area, as well as to the rapidly developing activities of many kinds which were occurring in the northern high plains country of the West.

The last time the writer had an opportunity to visit with Luke Vorhees was in 1919. This courageous man passed away six years later, at the age of ninety. It was not always so that the man in the West who lived dangerously died young.

16 A man who gained wide recognition in the West was John Clay, well known as a very practical man, and still with something of the artist, dreamer, and poet about him. His writings were brilliant and reflected the depth of his character and his understanding of people and their motivations. He had a very unusual talent for using words and left a remarkable record of his observations and accomplishments in his great book, *My Life on the Range*.

John Clay was born in the southeast of Scotland, near

the small town of Kelso, where his father, John Clay, Sr., was a very influential and prosperous farmer and stockgrower. Young Clay was born with a love of life and a spirit of adventure. In 1874, at the age of twenty-two, he made a pleasure trip to Canada and the United States and was immediately attracted by the feeling of freedom and liberty which he sensed in what he referred to as "the champagne air" of the high country. The magnitude and apparent opportunities of this vast cattle country appealed to him greatly; without hesitation he decided that here was his future.

After returning to Scotland and completing his very fine education, John Clay again crossed the Atlantic and became associated with the Bow Park Farms, breeders of registered Shorthorn cattle and Clydesdale horses, at Brantford, Ontario, Canada. There he was assistant manager for a period of time. He soon became widely recognized among the Scottish cattlemen with interests in Canada and the United States as being a young man of integrity, with unusual ability as an administrator, and with the capacity and knowledge to appraise and pass judgement upon livestock operations, due, in some degree, to his having been raised in the livestock business in Scotland.

In the spring of 1882, young Clay was employed by W. J. Menzies, one of the leading Scottish financiers, with investments in the cattle business in the United States, to make a thorough "inspection, analysis, appraisal and report" on the Chowchilla Ranch property, which was located near the town of Merced in the San Joaquin Valley of California and consisted of about one hundred fifteen thousand acres of land and fifteen thousand head of cattle. When this appraisal and report were completed, Mr. Menzies and his associates exercised their option to purchase this fine property and then employed young Clay as general manager.

This venture proved to be a very satisfactory and profitable one for the investors; they sold this property about twenty-five years later for approximately three times the original purchase price. The value of this property today would be fabulous.

Later in the same spring of 1882, another large group of Scottish investors arranged with Mr. Menzies for John Clay to take time off from the Chowchilla operation for the purpose of making an inspection and report on the holdings and operations of a large cattle company being syndicated under the name of the Cattle Ranch and Land Company. The headquarters of this outfit, branding the "YL," was located on Kiowa Creek, in the neutral strip of Oklahoma, about ninety miles south of Dodge City, Kansas. The young man spent several weeks riding over this property and inspecting the cattle, which ranged over a large area of country from the neutral strip of Oklahoma into the Panhandle of Texas. When this inspection was completed and John Clay filed his report, he raised several questions on some phases of the operations of this outfit. However, the purchasers were anxious to finalize their deal, and regardless of the questions and criticisms which Clay had raised in his analysis, the purchasers decided to complete their syndicate and the deal was consummated shortly afterwards, with a small block of stock in the syndicate going to John Clay as compensation for his work in making the inspection, appraisal, and reports. Young Clay then returned to California to finalize the Chowchilla deal for the Menzies group and to organize the operation of that large cattle outfit.

During the early eighties, the Scottish and English investors desired to increase their holdings in the open-range cattle business in the United States. This desire was most intense at that time because many of them believed that this fascinating business was a bonanza which could not fail. They were anxious to get fast action, and under these circumstances the services of John Clay, as a recognized authority and expert in the field of analysis and appraisal of cattle operations, became very much in demand. In July of 1882, while he was still busy in California in getting the Chowchilla Ranch operations organized, he received a cablegram from W. J. Menzies, one of the principal owners of the Chowchilla, requesting that he leave immediately for Rawlins, Wyoming, to inspect the 71 Quarter-Circle cattle outfit, which was operating on the Sweetwater in central Wyoming. Menzies also advised him in the cablegram that John T. Stewart from Council Bluffs, Iowa, who was the present owner of the 71 Quarter-Circle outfit, would meet him in Rawlins and arrange to show him the property. The instructions in the cablegram further stated that the book count of John T. Stewart would be acceptable as a basis for settlement, and therefore an actual tally of the cattle would not be required. Clay was specifically instructed to report only on the quality and value of the cattle and deeded land and upon the condition of the range. There had been two years of good moisture in the Sweetwater country in the period immediately prior to this inspection, and Clay found the range to be in excellent condition, with plenty of water in the creeks and water holes. He also found that the cattle were principally a good grade of Oregon Shorthorns, in very good flesh.

John Stewart, who was apparently a very shrewd businessman, had negotiated his deal with the Scottish prospective purchasers on a book-count basis, and also had chosen the perfect time for the inspection of the property. The Sweetwater valley is ordinarily a rather bleak and windswept country, not too well suited to an open-range type of cattle operation. However, during wet years there is always a good growth of fine quality grass and under these circumstances the country shows up particularly well; during the month of August the weather is always warm. When summer rains occur there is adequate water, which results in the cattle being in good condition and ready for market. The very nice and well-improved headquarters ranch of the 71 Quarter-Circle was located near Three Crossings above Devil's Gate on the Sweetwater River, and was located in a very attractive setting. John Clay was quite favorably impressed with what he had seen and therefore his report upon the operation was favorable, covering the items in the cablegram that he had been instructed to report upon. The Scottish group then completed the organization of their syndicate, under the name of the Wyoming Cattle Ranch Company and the deal was finalized shortly after the report was received in London.

Book counts prior to the 71 Quarter-Circle deal, had been quite generally recognized and accepted by British interests in the purchasing of American open-range cattle companies. These book counts had been used almost exclusively by the promoters of British cattle syndicates, in the preparation of their prospectus for presentation to prospective investors, when cattle companies were being organized.

The owners of big cattle outfits in the United States selling to British interests were probably fairly honest. However, in many instances the allowances which were set upon their books for death losses were not adequate to cover the heavy losses which frequently occurred during some of the extremely hard winters in the northern high plains country, with the result that the actual roundup count, when it was taken at a later date by the purchaser, oftentimes did not show more than fifty percent of the cattle that were paid for, based on the book count.

Questions of misrepresentation in the book count were raised by the purchasers of the 71 Quarter-Circle outfit at a later date, against John T. Stewart, with the result that this matter was in controversy for several months. However, John Clay did not take any position in this dispute or accept any responsibility for any discrepancies that may have existed in the cattle counts, due to the fact that his instructions in the cablegram had been explicit that the book count was being accepted and that an actual count was not required.

Late summer of 1882 found young John Clay on board ship bound for Scotland in connection with the formation of still another cattle company, which was being organized by the firm of Gordon, Pringle, Dallas, and Company, and which was to be syndicated under the name of Western Ranches, Limited. W. J. Menzies, who was one of the heavy investors in the Chowchilla Ranch in California, was also to be one of the investors in this new syndicate, which was being organized for the purpose of absorbing the holdings of Dan Clark and Duncan Plumb, owners of cattle ranching interests in the area lying north of the Black Hills, along the Belle Fourche River in South Dakota. The brand that was to be used by this new syndicate was the "VVV," or "Triple V" as it was oftentimes called. There was also another large British-owned cattle company operating in the same general area, on the Belle Fourche, under the name of the Prairie Cattle Company, which was partially owned by Mr. Gordon, of Gordon, Pringle, and Dallas.

When the negotiations in Edinburgh were completed, Robert Pringle, a promising young Edinburgh attorney who had been appointed by the Scottish group of investors to handle the legal details of setting up the new syndicate, came back to the United States on the same ocean liner with

John Clay, who, in addition to his other extensive management responsibilities for the Menzies group of investors, had also been authorized to make an inspection and report on this new venture and then to become finanical agent for the syndicate. Therefore, almost immediately after arriving back in the United States, these two young men left for the Belle Fourche country. In making this trip, they took a ferryboat across the Missouri River at Pierre, South Dakota. Then from there they traveled by six-horse stagecoach for a distance of two hundred fifty miles, going by way of Rapid City to Deadwood, where they were met by Dan Clark, one of the sellers of the cattle outfit being purchased.

The beautiful Belle Fourche country, with its well-grassed, rolling hills, as seen by these two young Scotsmen in 1882, was certainly the answer to a cattleman's dream. The great herds of buffalo had practically all been killed off by the buffalo hunters and not enough cattle had been brought into the Belle Fourche country at that time to have any great effect upon the heavy stands of buffalo grass and blue stem which grew in abundance everywhere. There were also the hundreds of cottonwoods and the heavy willow thickets which were growing along the many streams, to furnish shelter for the cattle. Many deer, antelope, and other types of wild game were to be seen almost everywhere that they went. John Clay was very much impressed with the open-range possibilities of the Belle Fourche country, and his report to the Scottish group of investors was very favorable.

The inspection trip had been a very enjoyable one for both of the young Scots. However, when they returned to Pierre by stagecoach, after having been gone for almost three weeks, they found that the Missouri River had become partially frozen over during their absence, and that the ferry was not operating. After some delay at the river crossing, they finally arranged for a small, flat-bottomed boat, which they pushed ahead of them on the ice until they came to the open channel. There they climbed into the boat and shoved off from the ice into the water by using the oars for that purpose. They rowed across the channel to the opposite side, where they broke the thin ice ahead of them with the oars until they reached a point where the ice was sufficiently firm to support their weight. They then pulled the boat up on the ice and skidded it to shore and left it there. A few days after making the crossing of the river, Robert Pringle left for Scotland and shortly afterwards, the organization of the Western Ranches, Limited, cattle outfit was completed.

Later in the fall of that same year, which had already been very eventful for him, John Clay also was asked to take over the active management of the 71 Quarter-Circle on the Sweetwater, in Wyoming. The young Scot, only thirty years of age, suddenly found himself in the position of having the direct responsibility for the management of three tremendously large cattle outfits having a combined capitalization of many millions of dollars and with tens of thousands of head of cattle on the range. In addition, these operations were scattered from the Missouri River to the Pacific Coast; with the VVV outfit on the Belle Fourche in South Dakota; the 71 Quarter-Circle on the Sweetwater in central Wyoming; and the Chowchilla in the San Joaquin Valley of California. In addition to these responsibilities, this young man was also serving in an advisory capacity for the Cattle Ranch and Land Company (in which he owned an interest) that was operating in the neutral strip of Oklahoma.

Clay found it necessary to spend most of that winter on the Sweetwater in Wyoming, getting the 71 Quarter-Circle reorganized and operating to his satisfaction. He then left in the early spring for Dodge City and began contracting for trail herds of Texas Longhorns to be trailed north for stocking his VVV range in South Dakota. When he had four trail herds, totaling approximately ten thousand head of southern steers, moving up the trail, he then rode a horse from Dodge City, Kansas, to Sidney, Nebraska, and from there he took one of Luke Vorhees' stagecoaches for the two hundred sixty miles to Deadwood. There he had a horse waiting to ride out to the headquarters ranch of his VVV outfit. As these herds of Longhorns began coming in off the trail, they were turned loose along the Belle Fourche River, from where, during the next few months, they ranged to the head of that river and south to the headwaters of the Cheyenne River in eastern Wyoming. These Longhorns did well in that country during that year. The following year, he increased the herds on the Belle Fourche that were wearing the "VVV" brand by another fifteen thousand head of Longhorns, for a total of twenty-five thousand head.

During the next four or five years, John Clay saw many ups and downs in the cattle business, suffering reverses from time to time from droughts, blizzards, and many other causes. However, he soon became recognized in the cattle country as a man with a definite talent for handling large operations under adverse conditions, and as one with the courage to either move ahead or retrench with the companies which were under his control, as conditions at a particular time seemed to indicate. He learned many lessons in the process. One of them was to never buy a herd of cattle on the owner's book count. Another was to never permit any of the companies which were his responsibility to become burdened with debt to the point where, if an exceptionally hard winter came along, the outfit could be wiped out. It was generally recognized by smart cattlemen that if they owned their cattle outright and a few were left after the storm, it was then always possible to pick up the pieces and start over again.

Early in the spring of 1887, John Clay was approached by the British shareholders of the gigantic Swan Land and Cattle Company — whose offices were in Edinburgh, Scotland, and their operating headquarters in Chugwater, Wyoming, in an effort to get him to assume management control of their operation in addition to his other responsibilities.

Alex Swan, who had been the organizer, president, and general manager of the great Swan Land and Cattle Company, had become involved in very serious financial difficulties. His great cattle empire was collapsing in the period that followed the very hard winter of '86-'87. As a result of this situation, he had been relieved of the presidency and of the active management of the company, by the British shareholders of the syndicate.

After giving this offer thorough consideration and discussing it with the Scottish directors of the other cattle companies which were his responsibility (where there was apparently some degree of overlapping financial interest) John Clay finally agreed to accept this added responsibility, but with the distinct understanding that he would have the right to resign, or the company would have the right to terminate his services, at any time by the giving of one year's notice in writing.

The book count shown by the records of the Swan Land and Cattle Company, or Two-Bar outfit as it was locally known, for the year 1886 was 113,625 head of cattle. However, when an actual count was made in 1888, it was found that less than half that number of cattle wearing the "Two-Bar" brand were actually running on the Two-Bar range in southeastern Wyoming. Undoubtedly, a large portion of this discrepancy in numbers was due to the extremely heavy losses which had been suffered in the two previous extraordinarily hard winters. Regardless of the reasons for this situation, when the books were balanced to conform to actual count and the necessary heavy capital adjustments and write-offs were taken, the Swan Land and Cattle Company was on very thin ice and in an extremely difficult cash position.

John Clay was a man who could make harsh decisions when in his opinion, actions of that kind were necessary in order to salvage an outfit that was in financial distress. Therefore, soon after taking over as general manager of the Swan Land and Cattle Company, the new general manager made several personnel changes in the organization, including making Al Bowie local manager of the outfit, with his headquarters to be at the old Hi Kelly ranch at Chugwater. He named Ed Banks, an excellent cowman, as cattle boss of the outfit. In addition, he gave orders that the herd was to be stabilized at around forty thousand head of cattle, which the available Two-Bar range was capable of handling. The new general manager also effected other economies in methods of operation, with the result that reasonable profits could be anticipated during average years on this operation.

When he was in the Cheyenne area, John Clay maintained his headquarters in rooms at the Cheyenne Club, where he could easily be reached by other cattlemen or by his associates in the other cattle companies which were his responsibility. He also became quite active in the affairs of the Wyoming Stockgrowers' Association, and at the annual meeting of the association in 1890 he was elected president of that organization. He continued to serve with distinction in that office for the next six years. John Clay was, of course, very articulate and an excellent public speaker, with a fine sense of humor, and he was a very effective and well-liked presiding officer. He also worked out a very close and cordial relationship with the Montana Stockgrowers' Association, and in this connection visited Miles City on many occasions.

As he moved around over the high plains country, carrying on his many activities, John Clay frequently used the stagecoach lines as a means of transportation, particularly those lines running northward from Cheyenne, including the Cheyenne and Black Hills Stage and Express line. He also used another line which ran from Cheyenne northward to Bordeaux, over the same route as the Cheyenne Black Hills Stage line, then from Bordeaux northwest into Montana, over what was known as the Bozeman Trail. This trail had stage stations at Douglas, Fort Fetterman, Antelope Springs, the Powder River crossing, Fort Kearney, and the little cow town of Buffalo, Wyoming. At Buffalo, connections were made with other stagecoach lines which ran to Miles City and other points in the Territory of Montana.

Another stagecoach line which John Clay also frequently used was one which ran from Miles City, on the Yellowstone, to Belle Fourche and Deadwood. This stagecoach line had been activated during the period of time when the great gold rush to Deadwood was at its peak and many gold miners from around Virginia City (in western Montana) were wild to get to the new gold diggings in the Black Hills of South Dakota. Two of the stage stations on this line were located at Powderville and Stoneville, in Montana, with another station at the little cow town of Belle Fourche, South Dakota, the latter only a short distance from the headquarters ranch of the VVV outfit. From there the line ran into Deadwood.

In the late eighties, John Clay founded the Clay Robinson Livestock Commission Company, with principal offices in Chicago, but with branch offices in the exchange buildings of practically every major livestock market in the United States. This company always had some of the best livestock salesmen and feeder buyers operating for them in the stockyards.

The Clay Robinson firm was later succeeded by the livestock commission firm of John Clay and Company. During the same period of time that these firms were operating in the livestock commission business, John Clay was also representing several large money interests in Scotland, in addition to financial concerns in Chicago and other eastern cities which were interested in making large loans to responsible cattlemen in the West. The interest rate at that time on this type of loan was ten percent per annum, compounded every ninety days and the entire principle was to be paid within one year.

This very versatile man was then operating in every phase of the cattle business; from the production of cattle to financing and marketing, not only of his own cattle operations, but of many other cattle outfits as well which were scattered all the way from the Missouri River livestock market to the San Joaquin Valley in California. All of these operations were dovetailed together and supporting each other.

As this dynamic man traveled over the area, in connection with his many operations and interests he became known to almost all of the cattlemen in every corner of the big cattle country. John Clay was not a man large in stature. However, with his tremendous mental capacity and physical stamina, he soon became recognized as a big man with courage and integrity, who sat high in the saddle in the cattle business, over the entire country, as well as in his dealings with other cattlemen.

John Clay was a masterful writer and storyteller, and, in spite of his other activities, he found time to write articles for *Breeders' Gazette,* which was the most popular and widely read cattlemen's publication printed at that time. These articles were always sprinkled with a touch of wisdom and with a breadth of expression which were a part of the gift of this unusual man. John Clay was also president and chairman of the board of directors of the Stockgrowers' National Bank in Cheyenne. This bank was just what the name implied, the stockgrowers' bank. (This writer did business at this bank for many years.) John Clay was a good banker and a good friend to the cattlemen with whom he came in contact.

This fine gentleman bowed out of this life in Chicago on March 17, 1934, at the age of eighty-three years. His activities, and the things that he built while he lived, as well as the writings which he left behind, are a part of the great heritage of the West.

17 Not within the memory of any cattleman living in that part of the country had there been such vicious blizzards as those that hit the northern high plains country in the winter of '86-'87. These blizzards followed what had been an exceptionally hot and dry summer over the entire area lying north of the Arkansas. In many parts of this vast country, the precipitation had been less than two inches for the first nine months of the year. With this extremely severe drought, almost all of the water holes and many of the small streams had completely dried up during the summer. Prairie fires had broken out in the dry grass and run wild in many parts of the cattle country, burning off hundreds of thousands of acres of good rangeland. As a result of these drought conditions, the cattle had gathered in great numbers along the large rivers, such as the Missouri and the Yellowstone, where water was still available. All of the grass within grazing distance of these rivers was grazed off so closely by the thousands of cattle that were concentrated there that many of them were dying from starvation.

Adding to the drought problem was the excessive overstocking of the range which had been occurring during recent years. Many of the big cattle outfits had been borrowing money and buying additional cattle by the thousands in a wild scramble to increase their earnings. There were many new outfits moving into the country from the south with large herds of Longhorns and turning them loose on what was already an overstocked range. In addition to these problems, the prices being paid for cattle at the livestock markets had dropped quite drastically within the year, causing many of the outfits to hold over cattle that otherwise would have been shipped out to market. Also, there were the hundreds of thousands of sheep that had been coming into the northern high plains country in constantly increasing numbers over a period of years until they had become a major factor in depleting the available grass over the entire range country. With the combination of all of these conditions which had developed on the open range, the losses from the death of cattle would have been extremely heavy, even during a normal winter.

It was on November 22, 1886, that the first Arctic blizzard of that terrible winter came howling in from the north in all of its fury and struck the northern high plains country. Old-timers who had lived in that country for many years and who had seen many hard winters said that when this blizzard struck they knew that there was serious trouble ahead. As this great storm swept southward across the Yellowstone into the Powder River country, across the Platte and on to the Arkansas, it caught many herds of young southern cattle that had been trailed in from Texas and turned loose on the open range in this high country only a couple of months before the coming of this great storm. These southern yearlings were of course accustomed to the warm southern climate and had not had an opportunity to become acclimated to the cold of the northern winter. When the terrific blizzard struck, with its icy snow driven by extremely high and cold northern winds and with very low temperatures, these thin-blooded southern yearlings did not have a chance; they just curled up and died. The older cattle were also drifting blindly before the storm, with no visibility, and were drifting over cliffs and cut banks and piling up in the deep ravines, arroyos, small streams, and rivers, where they too died by the thousands.

The cowboys in the line camps were completely helpless to do anything about the problem of the drifting cattle. The great blizzard was so vicious and blinding that, even to get from their log cabin to their small barns to feed their winter horses or to bring in wood for their fires, they found it necessary to tie saddle ropes to the outside latches on the cabin doors so that they could follow the ropes on their return and find their ways back to their cabins. They also kept shovels inside so that they could dig their way out if the cabin should become completely buried in the snow.

In its November 27 issue, five days after the beginning of the storm, the *Glendive Montana Times* reported as follows: "The great storm continues and far exceeds anything of record heretofore." Two days later the storm let up, after having pounded the high plains country steadily for over a week. Drifts were thirty feet deep in many places, and the entire cattle country was completely isolated. This terrific storm had cut a swath a thousand miles in length and four hundred miles in width, extending all of the way from the Canadian border southward across Montana, Wyoming, and western Nebraska to the Arkansas. It even extended to some degree into the Panhandle of Texas. There was no grass available anywhere for the starving cattle that had survived. Every blade of grass was completely covered over by the deep and heavily crusted snow. It was impossible to estimate what the losses had been at this time; thousands of cattle were still buried in snow and ice in the deep drifts and dry washes, as well as in the streams and rivers of the watersheds.

During the early part of December there were a few intermittent thaws which caused some of the ridges and rough country to become partially bare and exposed. However, due to the drought which had existed during the summer, and to the overstocked condition of the range, even with these few bare spots, there was still very little feed available for the starving cattle.

On December 23, another very drastic change occurred in the weather when the temperature dropped to thirty-nine degrees below zero. On Christmas day, the thermometers stood at forty-one degrees below. These temperature levels continued on the northern plains for the next three weeks and then, on January 9, with the temperature standing at forty-two degrees below zero, another killer blizzard struck which was far more vicious than the first one, due to the intensely cold weather.

As the icy blasts of hard-driven snow from this new storm hit the thin, weakened cattle, they again began drifting before the storm. This time, with the heavy snow and bitter cold, the snow and ice caked and froze over the eyes of the animals as they drifted, completely blinding them. Many of the weak cattle went down in the snow as they drifted, blinded and helpless in this terrible storm. Under the feet of the other cattle coming from behind, they were soon trampled into the deep snow and drifts. Their bodies would then completely disappear from sight as they became covered by the heavily drifting snow. The stronger cattle would keep going, driven on by the terrific blizzard and bitter cold to their own destruction. They too would find their graves, as they piled up by the thousands upon the bodies of the cattle dead from the previous storm, buried and frozen in the snow. There were a few of the animals that were fortunate enough to drift into sheltered pockets in the hills, or into willow thickets or other shelter along the streams; some of these cattle survived the storm.

The great blizzard finally lifted, after having lasted for ten days, with temperatures that had been running around forty degrees below zero during most of that time. Death and desolation were to be seen everywhere. Only a few live cattle were to be found; they were some of the big, double-wintered Longhorn steers and dry cows that had gone into the winter in good flesh, and for which reason they had managed to survive. However, these few remaining cattle were now just living racks of skin and bones. The streams and rivers were choked with snow and ice and the bodies of the great herds of cattle.

The wild animals had also suffered severely in the storm, particularly the deer, elk, and antelope. After the storms lifted, their bodies were also to be found in large numbers. Only the grey wolves, mountain lions, and other predatory animals had fared well from the effects of the storm; as they lived upon the dead cattle and game, they just had one big feast after another. Even the bald eagles came down from the mountain peaks to feast upon the dead animals. These predatory animals still had a good supply of beef and venison "on ice," enough to last them until spring.

When the storm subsided, the depth of the snow on the ground over the entire vast northern high plains country ran from two feet in some areas to four feet in others. The creeks and rivers were frozen solid to a depth of four feet or more in most localities, and there was no water available for the cattle that were still alive. Horses will paw in the crusted snow to obtain feed and will eat snow if no water is available — cattle will not; therefore, the lack of water was probably almost as great a factor in the death of cattle as the almost total lack of feed.

When the storm broke, there was one thing that the cowboys in the line camps could do to help the starving cattle, and that was to chop holes through the four feet of ice along the streams and rivers wherever water was available underneath, and then try to keep it open. However, in the bitter cold, below-zero weather, within thirty minutes after the water was opened up it would be frozen over again. As the cowboys began to move slowly around the country, through the deep snow after the storm had subsided, they found that where there had been any standing timber, the starving cattle had eaten all of the bark from the trees as far up as they could reach. Also, they had gnawed the willows in the willow thickets along the stream almost to the ground; they had then lain down among the remaining small stumps and died by the thousands from starvation. Many of the starving cattle drifted into the little cow towns where they sought shelter behind the buildings and tried to eat anything they could find, including some of the black tar paper covering the outside of some of the old shacks in the towns. There they were found in great numbers, where they had died in the streets and behind the buildings.

Most of the big cattlemen who lived in Cheyenne and Miles City, or the other big cow towns over the country, tried whenever possible, while the blizzards were under way, to make their ways through the storms and deep drifts to meeting places like the Cheyenne Club and the McQueen Hotel in Miles City, in a search for information on the extent of the storms.

As reports began to come in on the ferocity of the blizzards and the conditions on the range, it became obvious to the cattlemen that the loss of cattle had been tremendous, far exceeding any winter losses that had previously occurred in that part of the country. It also became apparent to them that, when spring opened and the roundup wagons could be pulled out and actual roundup counts made, a day of reckoning would be at hand; most of them would be broke and out of the cattle business.

It was also quite generally recognized among cattlemen that the great blizzards were a blessing in disguise for those excessive and padded book counts of the number of cattle they were supposed to have on the range. This was particularly true for some of the big foreign outfits, who had bought their original herds on a book count and had never reconciled these book counts with actual roundup counts made on the range at a later date.

The shareholders and creditors of the big British syndicates would now never know, nor be able to prove, whether there were actual discrepancies in their cattle counts, or the cause of those discrepancies where they did exist. It is probable that, if an investigation of some of these shortages had been made before the storms, there would have been instances wherein misrepresentation and thefts could have been involved.

The prize bartender comment, which has lived down through the years in the cattle country, was made by Luke Murrin, who was tending bar at the Cheyenne Club at the time of the blizzards of '86-'87, when he said: "Cheer up, boys! Don't worry about the cattle; just keep the books warm, boys, just keep the books warm."

As reports of the diastrous effects of the great blizzards began to circulate over the United States and Europe, in areas where investors and creditors had interests in the cattle business, in the West, it was of course natural that inquiries would begin to come in from these people seeking information on how their particular interests had been affected by the storms. The most famous of the replies to these inquiries was made by Charlie "Kid" Russell, a young cowboy who at that time was spending the winter with another cowboy in a line camp in the Judith Basin of Montana, where they were looking after about ten thousand head of Texas Longhorn steers that had been trailed in from Texas late in the fall and turned loose on the Judith River.

When these cowboys received a letter from the owners of the steers, after the January blizzard, asking about the condition of their cattle, Charlie Russell drew a sketch on a piece of cardboard, which the cowboys then mailed to the owners. This sketch showed just one lone Longhorn steer, a living skeleton or rack of hide and bones, as he stood upon a bare spot on what was otherwise a snow-covered ridge. The big thin steer, with all of his ribs showing, stood poised, with a hump in his back, his head lowered, and his feet braced outward to support his body. At the same time, he was trying desperately to defend himself against a large pack of snarling grey wolves that had him completely surrounded, with two wolves coming in from behind the big steer as he stood at bay, in an attempt to hamstring him by cutting the tendons in his hind legs. The sketch was captioned, "The Last of Ten Thousand."

For many years afterwards, copies of this remarkable and vivid sketch were to be found hanging from the walls, or over the bars, in almost every saloon west of the Missouri River. In later years, this Montana cowboy became recognized all over the world as the greatest cowboy artist of all time for his action paintings of cowboy life, as seen through the eyes of a working cowboy. These paintings are still very much in demand, and command fabulous prices in art galleries all over the world.

During the month of February, 1887, the temperatures continued very cold. Then on March 2 of that year, another very drastic change occurred in the weather, with a rise of about fifty degrees in the temperature and with a chinook wind blowing out of the west. Within hours, the chinooks were rapidly cutting the great drifts and heavy packs of frozen snow. Soon, the dry washes, draws, creeks, and ravines became raging torrents, carrying the bodies of the dead cattle that had accumulated in these depressions down to the rivers by the thousands. Also, the snow which had been piled deep in the Big Horns, Black Hills, and other mountain ranges was cutting loose, adding to the tremendous volume of water going down the big rivers until they were all at flood stage. As these conditions continued, a continual stream of the bodies of dead cattle could be seen for several days as they floated in increasing numbers down the Big Horn, Missouri, Yellowstone, and all the other streams and rivers in the high plains country of the West.

As the people who lived in the small cow towns along

these rivers watched from the banks of the flood-swollen streams, they were seeing the hopes and dreams of many people going down the big rivers with the bodies of the dead cattle, without hope of recovery. Included, of course, were the fortunes of many of the greedy foreign investors, as well as the dreams and aspirations of some of the over-ambitious cattlemen who had been seeking power and recognition through the building of great cattle empires, which had resulted in the overstocking of the range without any measures having been taken to provide protection for the cattle from the extremely bitter weather of the northern winters.

It had taken the white buffalo hunters several years to destroy the greater number of the great buffalo herds. The same thing had been accomplished by the elements with the cattle herds within a matter of weeks. The Indian was probably right when he said, "The great white father, in his anger at the cattleman's greed, was just showing him who had the big medicine."

When the snow went off the following spring and the roundup wagons pulled out on the range to gather the remnants of the once great herds of Longhorns, it was found that some of the cattle had drifted in the great blizzards for distances of as much as three hundred miles from their original home range. Under these circumstances, it was necessary for the different outfits to exchange reps with the throw-back men then combining their drives as they moved the cattle slowly back to their home range.

Then, as the roundup tallies began to come in to the headquarters of the different outfits from the wagons working different parts of the range, it was found that the losses from the storms were staggering. For instance, in the big, open country lying between the Missouri and the Yellowstone, losses had been especially heavy. Some of the outfits operating in that area reported losses as high as ninety percent of their herds. The average loss for the Missouri, Yellowstone, Big Horn, and Powder River watersheds was about seventy percent; and losses on the Sweetwater and the Laramie plains were almost as heavy. Southward, on the watersheds of the Arkansas and the Platte, including the Goshen Hole country, the loss ratio dropped considerably, with losses in those areas running only about fifty percent.

Among the losses reported by individual outfits was that of Conrad Kohrs, who went into the winter with thirty-five thousand head of cattle running north of the Yellowstone. When the wagons worked that part of the country in the spring, they found only three thousand head of Kohrs' cattle still alive, indicating a loss of ninety percent of his herd. Granville Stuart reported losses of sixty-six percent in the Judith Basin of Montana. The Hash Knife outfit of Hughes and Simpson, with sixty-five thousand head of Longhorns running on the Little Missouri, gathered only sixteen thousand head of their herds, for a loss of seventy-five percent. In the Powder River country of Wyoming, the 76 outfit, which had been founded by Moreton Frewen, liquidated with a very heavy loss to their shareholders.

In general, the smaller ranchers over the country fared the best, with their average losses running only about twenty percent. This difference in loss ratio was due principally to the fact that the little fellows had some land under fence, where the cattle could be held and prevented from drifting for great distances, and also where the water could be kept open. In addition, most of these small ranchers had a limited amount of native hay which they had cut from the natural meadows on their own property along the streams, which was available for feed during the blizzards.

In the very turbulent period which followed what was referred to as the "big die-off," it was, of course, inevitable that major changes would occur in the methods of handling cattle throughout the West. Money was scared: many of the shareholders of the big British syndicates and some of the lending institutions and banks with loans on cattle became panicky and demanded immediate liquidation of their holdings. In most instances, these were the very same people who had been the most anxious to get into the cattle business, with loans and investments, when it looked like a bonanza. Now, these same people were the most demanding and unreasonable in seeking to recover their losses. However, the bubble had burst, and their money had already gone down the rivers.

The cattlemen who found themselves in a position of being forced by their shareholders, or creditors, to liquidate the remnants of their once great herds, upon what was already a depressed market for feeder cattle due to a short corn crop in the corn-producing states of the east, were flat broke and soon out of business. Some of the big outfits did not even attempt to gather the remnants of their herds. Instead, they just looked around for a buyer who was willing to gamble and sold the brand, with all of the cattle that the buyer could find wearing that brand, for whatever they could get, and then just faded out of the picture. This was particularly true with most of the foreign investors and cattlemen who found themselves in trouble. It is also true that there was very little sympathy on the part of the local cattlemen for the foreign outfits that were forced out of the cattle business. This was due to the fact that these foreign outfits had been operating in the West without the owners even having been citizens of the United States. They had moved in hundreds of trail herds without any particular regard for the overstocked conditions which were developing. Consequently, from the viewpoints of the local cattlemen, these foreign outfits had been the greatest contributing factor to the disaster which had occurred.

When the repercussions from the big die-off had subsided, it was recognized that the winter of '86-'87 had very definitely rung down the curtain on the wild and hazardous methods of operation that had prevailed during the past phase of the open-range cattle business, in which great herds of cattle were bet against the whims of the weather in the north country, without any provision whatever having been made for the control and feeding of the animals during these extremely vicious blizzards and unusually hard winters. John Clay, in some of his widely publicized articles, said that the open-range type of operation which had been carried on up until that time had been on a very hollow foundation.

It was recognized in the cattle country that a few of the creditors who had been financing some of the cattlemen proved to be wise and cool-headed men — when they realized that if they were to force immediate liquidation of the cattlemen's remaining assets they could only hope to recover a very small portion of their loans and investments. In most instances, men of this type stayed with the cattlemen who were their partners and customers and who had the desire, courage, and determination to carry on and try to work out of a difficult situation. At the same time, they were changing their methods of operation to where they would be in a position, in the future, to provide feed and protection for their cattle during blizzards and exceptionally hard winters. In most instances where the creditors had shown this consideration for the cattlemen, they eventually recovered their loans in full and also retained the good will and friendship of the cattlemen in the process.

In the end, it was quite obvious to everyone that, regardless of the losses which had occurred during the winter, nature, through the elements, had adjusted the number of cattle on the range to fit the grass, the overstocked situation being taken care of in the process. In addition, the snows which had fallen during the winter would provide adequate moisture over the entire northern high plains country, and the range would soon come back to normal.

These courageous people of the West had not lost hope. They knew that, with the coming of spring, the meadow larks and whippoorwills would return to the meadows and that later, when fall came, the tall grass would again wave heavily in the wind while the leaves on the cottonwood trees would again be changing to a golden color — a true and dependable gold for everyone to see, enjoy, and possess.

18

There are always some people with confidence in themselves and faith in the future who, after any great disaster, will rise up out of the rubble and wreckage, take a good hard look around at the damage which has occurred, and then start slowly picking up the pieces and putting them back together again. At the same time, they are using the experience which has been gained from the disaster for the purpose of establishing new guidelines, for the laying of a solid foundation of a new structure that will withstand a similar disaster in the future.

Many of the pioneer cattlemen among both the large and

small operators in the country north of the Arkansas were men of this type. They had known when they came here that it would take a lot of fortitude and a life of trial and hardship to make a success of the cattle business in this new and rugged country. They had suffered many previous reverses since coming here, although none as severe as this one, from other blizzards, droughts, and depressions. There also had been serious trouble with both Indian raiding parties and outlaws. These men had seen other men killed in gunfights, as well as in carrying on the hazardous work that was a part of their way of life.

As a result of their experiences, they had become toughened and hardened by the vigorous and dangerous life that they lived, to the point that survival in the cattle business — regardless of the measures and actions which might be necessary to accomplish this purpose — was the most important thing in their lives. Those men who remained in the cattle business were there because that was their life and they intended to stay. They would fight, and if necessary they would die, here in this high plains country, for the survival of themselves, their families, and their way of life.

With many of the big outfits now out of business, there were hundreds of cowboys scattered over the high plains country who were also out of jobs. These men were of much the same temperament as the cattlemen who still remained in the cattle business. Also, these cowboys were determined to stay with the only kind of work that they knew, as well as the way of life that they loved. They too would make their fight for survival here in this high plains country. There were quite a few of these cowboys, particularly among the ones who had worked as foremen and wagon bosses, who had a few dollars of their own, and some of them were of the opinion that the time had come for them to get into the cattle business for themselves.

There were still plenty of spots along the streams where homesteads could be filed, where there was living water and some native meadows. Then, with the grass coming back on the open range after the deep snows, they were sure that they could make a start on their own. After the blizzards of the winter that had just passed, there were hundreds of unclaimed cattle that had drifted completely out of the country where they belonged running loose on the range. With so many of the big outfits going out of business, some of these stray cattle were practically abandoned by their owners.

As a result of this situation, it soon became apparent that some of the cowboys who had filed on homesteads, were not at all hesitant about using a long rope and a running iron on these abandoned strays. Many of these cowboys took the position, with some justification, that all they were doing was collecting the back wages which were due them when the big foreign outfits went broke.

It also soon became quite obvious that, after the hard winter of '86-'87, if a cattleman wanted to get a new start in the cattle business, or financing for an old operation, he would need to be in a position where he could show the bankers and cattle loan companies that he had the winter grass and sufficient hay to carry the cattle through the winter without excessive losses.

The question with the big outfits was how to corral enough country, get it enclosed and under control, to meet these changing conditions; as well as how to provide the quantity of winter grass and hay which would permit them to continue to run the great herds of cattle in the future that they had been accustomed to running in the past.

In providing this necessary winter grass and feed,

there were other types of filings, in addition to homesteads, which could be used by the cattlemen for the purpose of acquiring a limited amount of additional land for these purposes. One of these methods was through the use of the provisions of the preemption act which was passed by Congress in 1841. Under this act, title could be obtained to 160 acres of government land by "squatting" on the land for a long enough period of time to make a preemption claim valid; after which, the land could be put up for sale. This sale could be requested by the individual who had established residence through squatting on the land for the required length of time. When the land came up for sale, the person with the squatter's right had the first option to buy the land, at a fixed price of $1.25 per acre.

There was also the Timber Culture Act, which was passed by Congress in 1873, or what was generally known as filing a "tree claim." The requirements under this act were that the person making the filing on a maximum of 160 acres was required to plant forty acres of this land in trees, (this requirement was later reduced to ten acres) and to keep these trees growing for eight years. If, at the end of that period of time, when final proof was made, the trees were still growing and in good condition, a patent would then be issued for the 160 acres. However, whether or not the requirements of the act had been met, and final proof was actually made, the person who had made the filing could have kept the land under control and under fence for the entire eight years unless someone had contested their filing in the meantime, on the grounds that the person making the filing was not fulfilling the requirements under the law. However, cattlemen were not inclined, ordinarily, to contest the other fellow's filings, the reason being that all of them generally had done this sort of thing themselves.

The land act which was most helpful to the greater number of cattlemen was the Desert Land Act which was signed into law in 1877. Under this act, filing could be made on up to 640 acres (a full section) of land that could not be cultivated without irrigation. The intent of this act was to bring as much land as possible under irrigation. For this reason, it was required under this law that certain specified portions of the land which was being filed upon must be brought under irrigation within three years from the date of the filing. Also, a payment of twenty-five cents an acre was required at the time of the filing; at the end of the three year period, when final proof was made, an additional one dollar an acre was required. It was also required that proof be made, within the three year period and by the person making the filing, that water had actually been delivered to that portion of the land which had been designated for irrigation at the time that the filing had been made. Residence on the land was not required (under the Desert Land Act) in order to obtain a patent for the land, providing that all of the other provisions of the act had been complied with.

Upon the filing of desert land claims, application was then made to the state, or territory, for water rights from the natural flow of the streams from which the water was to be drawn. An appropriation of water for the beneficial use of the lands to be irrigated was then determined by the state, and priorities for the use of water from the streams by the various known users was established, based upon the date when the appropriation of water was granted by the state.

The filings of these desert land claims were generally made on land lying in the valleys, along the small streams and rivers, where water could easily be diverted from these streams to small irrigation ditches by very low diversion dams built in the streams with the use of rocks, brush, logs and other available material. In addition, the water was sometimes moved, in ditches, to other low-lying valleys in the area by taking advantage of the drop in elevation which generally occurs along streams. When this water was applied to the rich, virgin bottomland in these valleys in sufficient quantities, fine natural meadows of native hay would develop very rapidly. Then, in the fall, after the hay had been cut and stacked, these meadows would make a second growth and provide very fine winter pasture for cattle.

By using all of the filing entries permitted under the four land acts, one person could file on a total of 1,120 acres of land, which was generally adequate to furnish winter pasture and sufficient feed for a small rancher who was running not more than three hundred head of cattle. However, for the large cattlemen who had been accustomed to running tens of thousands of head of cattle, these requirements were an entirely different matter. As a result, it soon became apparent that the needs of the big cattlemen and the requirements of the land laws were in conflict.

For instance, there was a provision in all of the acts covering the filing on government land which required that the person making the filing must sign an affidavit, when making final proof, which stated that the entry had been made for the purpose of actual settlement and cultivation of the land and not directly for the benefit of anyone else.

Regardless of these requirements in the law, the big cattlemen, with their pressing need for getting large blocks of land enclosed in order to survive and to continue their type of operation, were using all of the possible means that they could find to bypass or get around these restrictions and requirements in the land laws which pertained to the filing of homesteads, and other types of claims on government land, including arranging for filing on land in their area by their relatives and friends, as well as by some of their cowboys, foremen, and other people who had been in their employ over a period of years. They even, in some instances, arranged for filings on land by their cooks and housekeepers.

These filings were oftentimes made in such a manner as to enclose large areas of government land under their fences, in the process. One method which was widely used was to make the filings on a string of forties, instead of in a block. With this type of filing, very few entries were needed in order to accomplish the purpose of establishing a "color of title" in the land, which would permit the fencing of the outside perimeter of a large area, and make the fencing of the area legally justified. In addition, the Desert Land Act was used quite extensively by the big cattlemen as a means of bringing large tracts of land under their control. Due to the fact that under the provisions of this act filings could be made on 640 acres (or a full section) of land, with no residence on the land being required when making final proof, the names of non-residents were sometimes used by the big cattlemen in filing under this act.

It was also possible, under the Desert Land Act, for the big cattlemen to put together great blocks of many thousands of acres of land under one irrigation development plan, by having surveys made of the large, proposed developments, then submitting these plans, which were approved by the state and left on file with the land office, at the same time that the filings were being made by the individuals under whose names the entries on the many sections of land in the big irrigation development plan were being made. As a result, regardless of the feasibility of the irrigation system (as it was planned) or the availability of water to actually irrigate the land, a color of title was established which permitted the legal fencing of all or any part of this large block of land. Consequently, if, in the future, an irrigation system for this land was not actually built and the land which had been designated under the plan was not actually brought under irrigation within the period of time provided for under the law, the filings would then expire, and the land would revert to the federal government. Regardless of this fact, the fences would already be in place around this large tract of land and would generally remain there for a long period of time after the filings had expired.

One of the most controversial cases of this nature was that of the Goshen Hole Ditching Company, which was the successor to the Union Cattle Company (or Bridle Bit outfit) that had gone bankrupt following the hard winter of '86-'87. Thomas Sturgis of Cheyenne was president of both of these companies, which held extensive holdings of land in the Goshen Hole and Horse Creek country of southeastern Wyoming.

In the summer of 1887, both the Union Cattle Company and the Goshen Hole Ditching Company were charged by the commissioner of the United States General Land Office with having fifty-five desert land claims filed on land in southeastern Wyoming for their own benefit. These filings covered the greater part of fifty-five sections of land, for a total of approximately thirty-five thousand acres. Also, these Desert Act claims were, for the most part, filed by people who were non-residents of Wyoming and who at that time were living in the states of New York, New Jersey, and Massachusetts. Only seven of the individuals who made the filings had ever seen the land upon which their filings were being made. This group of filings covered a strip of land thirty-five miles in length; with the filings and entries made in such a manner as to enclose a considerable amount of additional government land. As a pretense of having developed an irrigation system, and in an attempt to make final proof of having fulfilled the requirements of the law, these people plowed a single furrow thirty-five miles in length and attempted to use this furrow as proof of irrigation of this land. In December of 1888, following this attempt at making final proof, the Cheyenne land office recommended the cancellation of fifty-one of the fifty-five filings. However, this case was still pending before the U.S. General Land Office in Washington, D.C., in 1890, when there was a change in the national administration. Following this change, the filings were approved, and some of the patents were issued.

It had also, for many years, been common practice among cattlemen in the West, whether they were big cattlemen or small operators, when they acquired ownership of the water in a certain area, to fence all of the government land within grazing distance of this water. This practice was based on the old concept, generally recognized among cattlemen throughout the entire West, that he who controls the water also controls the adjacent range. This practice did not have any legal foundation, as all fences on government land were considered by the federal government to be illegal. However, almost all of the cattlemen, regardless of the sizes of their operations, did have some government land under fence; for instance, the United States Land Commissioner reported in March of 1884 that there were in excess of one hundred twenty-five cattle companies in the Territory of Wyoming alone, with fences on public land. Obviously, the size of a cattleman's ranch (during that period of time) depended, at least to some degree, upon his ability to get control of the water and then to raise the money for buying the posts and wire to build fence.

The federal government, from time to time, with very

little success, attempted to eliminate this unlawful fencing of government land. A quite serious effort along this line was made during Grover Cleveland's first administration when, in 1883, William A. J. Sparks, who was commissioner of the U.S. General Land Office in Washington, D.C., issued orders for the removal of all fences from government land. Suits were also filed in December of that year against Alex Swan, John Hutton, and H. B. Kelly. The cases against these cattlemen were pending in the courts until 1886, when, in response to court orders, these particular cattlemen and a few others removed their fences from government land. However, almost all of the fences on the public domain still remained in place until, with a change in the presidential administration in 1889, Mr. Sparks was retired as the commissioner of the U.S. General Land Office, and the new administration (due, probably, in some degree to the political influence of the cattlemen) was much more lenient and sympathetic with regard to the fences on public land. As a result, some of the fences that had been pulled down were rebuilt, and many new ones went up. This was particularly true after the winter of '86-'87; when the need for controlled winter range became so necessary.

The fencing of winter pastures, of course, reduced the area of the open range to some degree. Regardless of this fact, the total amount of grass and the carrying capacity of the range remained approximately the same. The only difference was that, with the fencing, some of the grass was held back for winter pasture. However, in the process of fencing and enclosing of government land, it was perhaps inevitable that over a period of time these cattlemen would naturally develop a feeling of proprietorship, through long usage, in the land they held inside of their fences. As a result, when anyone attempted to disturb that exclusive usage, even though this was public domain, serious trouble would generally develop. This sentiment and attitude on the part of the cattlemen was to be the cause of many very bitter controversies and conflicts in the future.

It was quite surprising how rapidly things began to come back to normal after the big die-off of '86-'87. By 1890, with confidence returning and with money again becoming available, the herds of cattle on the open range were quickly being rebuilt. Even the sheepmen, who had lost as heavily, were bringing in many new bands of sheep. With the prices of both cattle and sheep increasing on the livestock markets, prosperity was again returning to the high plains country. Trail herds of Longhorns were again coming up the Texas-Montana Cattle Trail from the Panhandle and helping to restock the range. In addition, with railroads now building into the West, many of the cattle were beginning to be shipped in by rail. At the same time, the quality of the herds on the open range was being greatly improved by bringing in more good Hereford and Shorthorn bulls from Europe, as well as from registered breeding herds in the eastern part of the United States.

With more small ranches now running cattle on the open range, the number of pool wagons in operation had naturally increased. In addition, when both the large outfits and the pool wagons were on the fall roundups, they now gathered all of the cattle (except the big steers and dry cows), and moved them into winter pastures. Later in the winter, if the weather got real rough and the grass on the open range became completely covered over with deep and crusted snow, the strong cattle that had been left on the open range would sometimes be picked up and fed temporarily until there was a break in the weather.

Even the little cow towns were beginning to come back to life, with the cowboys again riding into town in search of fun and excitement and at the same time freely spending their money at the saloons and honky-tonks with very little regard for the future. There were fistfights and gunfights as the cowboys blew off steam in their usual reckless and devil-may-care, fun-loving way of life. These boys were always ready for a fight or a frolic; and the merchants in the cow towns were beginning to realize that they were becoming more dependent for business upon the rapidly increasing number of small ranchers, rather than upon the big outfits who generally bought most of their supplies direct from the wholesale companies. As a consequence, when a conflict would develop between the big cattlemen and the small ranchers, the local merchants were inclined to side with the little fellows.

While all of these changes were occurring in the West, many of the big cattlemen who still had credit or who could raise additional money by borrowing on their remaining assets were in the process of rebuilding their own herds by buying the remnants of some of the outfits that were forced out of the cattle business by the hard winter, or who had become discouraged by the heavy losses that they had taken and had decided to get out of this high-risk and dangerous business. One of the remaining cattlemen who had moved quickly to take advantage of this distress situation was the Frenchman, Pierre Wibaux. When this courageous and dynamic young cattleman returned from France, where he had raised several hundred thousand dollars in new capital, he began immediately to buy the remnants of several large herds as quickly as possible. He had reached the well-found conclusion that these remaining cattle, with the strength and vitality to have survived the winter that had just passed, would surely live though any other that might occur in the future. One of his first moves was in the spring of 1887, when he bought the eighteen thousand head remnant of the once great

Running Water Land and Cattle Company. Later, in the same summer, he also picked up the fifteen thousand head remnant of the Hunter and Evans outfit, which consisted mostly of big steers. In addition, he succeeded in buying the brands and remnants of several other outfits at very attractive prices. His average cost on these cattle ran around twenty dollars a head. When, in the fall of the same year, he shipped these big steers out to market, they brought an average of about forty dollars a head, doubling his investment in just a few months.

The following spring, Wibaux continued his buying program; he bought the remainder of the famous Hash Knife outfit and the remnant of the Powder River Cattle Company, followed later the same year by the purchase of the Green Mountain Ranching Company of Forsythe, Montana. Altogether, during this two year period, this cattleman probably handled around two hundred thousand head of cattle. With cattle prices increasing steadily during that period, Wibaux made a substantial fortune on those two years of operations.

Another very resourceful Montana cattleman who was not easily discouraged by financial reverses was John T. Murphy, owner of the big 79 outfit. Even though his losses in the big, open country lying between the Yellowstone and the Missouri rivers were extremely heavy, he still had other extensive remaining assets which were not greatly disturbed by the hard winter. With his usual courage and self-confidence, Murphy almost immediately started picking up some of the remnants of the herds whose owners were in financial distress. He also began to move in additional trail herds of Texas Longhorns to restock his range.

Conrad Kohrs (the former butcher from Virginia City), who was operating in the same general area as Murphy, had also dropped a half-million dollars when ninety percent of his cattle had gone down the Yellowstone or had curled up and died from the effects of the storms. However, Kohrs also had adequate financial reserves and the courage to make a new start in the cattle business, which was his life. As a consequence, he also soon began rebuilding his great empire in central Montana.

John Clay, who was one of the few British cattlemen remaining in the business after the winter of '86-'87, was also hard hit, having lost about half of his VVV cattle, which were running in the Belle Fourche range in South Dakota. However, with his remarkable vision and stamina, as well as sources of new capital, he was soon in the process of moving in additional trail herds from Texas to restock his good South Dakota range. Southward from the VVV outfit, on the headwaters of the Platte in Wyoming, the CY outfit, owned by Joseph M. Carey and associates, had also taken about a fifty percent loss on their herds. However, with his strong family financial connections in the east, Joseph M. Carey was in a position to raise a sufficient amount of money to rebuild his herds, and also to develop large hay meadows along the Platte to the point where he was never again in a position of not having adequate hay and good winter pasture to carry his herds through a tough winter.

Perhaps the most fortunate of the big cattlemen was H. B. "Hi" Kelly, who had sold out his holdings in the cattle business in 1884 to the Swan Land and Cattle Company. As a consequence, he was sitting on the sidelines, with plenty of money in the bank, during the winter of '86-'87. Kelly thought that he had retired from the cattle business. However, when some of the good cattle outfits were offered for sale at bargain prices following the hard winter of '86-'87, he could not resist the temptation, and, in the summer of 1888, he again jumped back into the business. He bought the remnants of four outfits on Horse Creek, in the southeastern part of Wyoming, including the Y Cross ranch with its fine native hay meadows. At the same time that these changes were occurring, almost all of the other big cattlemen who were still in business and who were rebuilding their outfits and restocking their ranges were making all possible provisions for adequate winter pasture and hay, even to the point of shipping in some hay by rail and storing it for an emergency.

Many of the cowboys who had been cowpunchers for the big outfits were now successful cattlemen in their own right, and quite proud of what they had accomplished. Some of them were running their own wagons, while a few of them were feeling their oats to the point that they even jumped the fence and joined the stockgrowers' association. Curtains were also beginning to appear at the windows of many of the new log cabins that had gone up along the creeks, a sure sign that there would be another crop of young cowboys coming along before many years. There was even an occasional schoolhouse, and some of the cow towns had gone so far as to build a church and hire a preacher.

19 In the years which immediately followed the hard winter of '86-'87, the many conflicts which had been smouldering for several years between the big cattlemen and the little fellows began to break out into the open. These conflicts and animosities were caused to a great degree by the constantly increasing number of cowboys who had been going into the cattle business on their own and filing on some of the best water and meadows in the high plains country of the West; while, at the same time, they were also fencing in additional government land which had always been open range that had been used almost exclusively, in the past, by the big cattlemen.

The lines which became drawn between the big cattlemen and the small ranchers were quite well defined by whether or not the particular cattlemen were members of the stockgrowers' association. If a cattleman was a member of this organization, he was then, in the eyes of the majority of the other members, a good, law-abiding citizen; an assumption which was certainly subject to question. If, on the other hand, he was not a member, he was then in a position where, regardless of his reason for not having a membership, his actions were subject to question by the big cattlemen who were. At the meetings of both the Wyoming and Montana associations in 1887, several of the cattlemen who were present at these meetings complained bitterly that many of the small ranchers who were not members were stealing their cattle by the thousands. Some of these cattlemen even contended that their losses to the rustlers were becoming greater than the losses which were caused by rough winter weather. Some of the more impetuous of the younger cattlemen demanded at the meetings that the stockgrowers' association take immediate and drastic action to eliminate the rustlers.

It was certainly true that a very lawless period in the history of the West did develop in the period which immediately followed the hard winter of '86-'87. Many of the cowboys who were out of jobs and with no money became drifters. Some of the more reckless and wild ones turned outlaw, with mavericking and outright stealing becoming their way of life. As a result, the operations of this outlaw element did become quite extensive. Regardless of this fact, the little fellows were not all rustlers and they deeply resented being so considered by the big cattlemen who constituted the membership of the stockgrowers' associations.

As it appeared to the small ranchers, the big outfits tried to hog the range, controlled the roundups, dominated the legislature, and claimed all of the mavericks. Also, with the powers which had been granted to the stockgrowers' association under the maverick law, the big cattlemen had taken the law into their own hands and they had become very vindictive as well as dictatorial. Furthermore, the big cattlemen were taking all of the money that was derived from the sale of mavericks and using it to hire professional gunmen and killers as cattle detectives, who were turned loose on the range to eliminate any of the small ranchers who were accused by members of the stockgrowers' association of being cattle rustlers. The little fellows also contended that many of the big cattlemen were accusing some of them of being rustlers without justification and then using these false accusations for the purpose of applying the pressure to try to run them out of the country.

On the other hand, the big cattlemen were very emphatic in their claims that they could not get justice in the courts, where the juries were composed principally of small ranchers and other people from the little cow towns. They also claimed that the judges, who were elected by popular vote, showed favoritism towards the local people who were in the majority at the polls. In addition, the big cattlemen contended that the cattle detectives who were working for the stockgrowers' association could catch a gang of rustlers red-handed, bring them in for trial, and, regardless of the evidence, the local newspapers would side with the defendants, and the judge and jury would then find the rustlers not guilty and turn them loose. As a result of the losses to the rustlers which they were taking, and of what appeared to be their lack of success in getting convictions in the courts, the big cattlemen finally decided that they were justified in taking extreme measures in coping with the rustler situation. Therefore, they proceeded with plans for setting up an organization to accomplish this purpose.

The majority of these cattlemen, among both the large and small operators, were strong and fearless men, with the courage of their convictions, who would take whatever steps they considered necessary to protect their own best interests. There were, however, many very willful and unscrupulous men of both sides (in addition to the outlaws) who believed in taking what they wanted, regardless of who got hurt in the process. These were, of course, the men who (to a great degree) were responsible for bringing these conflicts to the point where bloodshed between the two groups became inevitable. The basic cause of these conflicts was due to the powers which had been granted to the stockgrowers' association under the maverick laws to determine what was acceptable practice and what was not acceptable so far as the cattle business was concerned.

In the process of carrying out the plan which had been developed for the elimination of the rustlers from the range, small groups or committees of big cattlemen, not officially recognized as committees of the stockgrowers' association, were designated to determine, wherever charges of cattle rustling were reported by members of the association, who was guilty of being a cattle rustler and who was not guilty. The methods of operation which were adopted by these committees and which became known as "cattlemen's law" were extremely cold-blooded and ruthless. Under this plan, with responsibility for determining the guilt and penalties of the small ranchers, or others, who were accused of being cattle thieves resting with the members of the committee, they automatically became judge, jury, and executioner.

It was perhaps inevitable, under the circumstances, that rustler accusations were used in some instances by a few of the more arrogant and unscrupulous of the big cattlemen as justification for killing some small ranchers, or individuals, who, in their opinion, were encroaching upon their range. As a result, the cattleman's law was sometimes warped to fit a particular cattleman's purpose.

As the rustler elimination campaign gained headway, with the pressures building upon the part of the more radical and ruthless of its membership, the officers of the stockgrowers' association reluctantly changed their policy with regard to the type of men to be employed as cattle detectives: from the strictly law enforcement type of officers, to men who were not at all hesitant to use a gun to whatever degree the big cattlemen should consider necessary to accomplish the objective of eliminating the rustler from the range. These cattle detectives, regardless of their qualifications, had the legal authority to make arrests, and to take any steps necessary to enforce the maverick law.

The methods adopted by the committee of big cattlemen provided that when an individual was tagged by a cattle detective, or by a member of the stockgrowers' association as a rustler, he was then warned to either cease his "illegal" operations or get out of the country. If the suspect did not comply, he would then get a rifle bullet, "fired through a window by a person or persons unknown," or he would be dry gulched from ambush. In any event, there would be no witnesses, and if there should be any questions asked, the killer would have the weight and influence of the stockgrowers' association behind him, which was considered to be adequate.

With this program under way, the Wyoming Stockgrowers' Association increased the number of its inspectors and detectives working the range from one, in 1874, to twenty-one in 1885. N. K. Boswell, who was considered to be a ruthless, shotgun-carrying officer who had been sheriff of Albany County, was appointed as chief of detectives with his headquarters in Cheyenne — while Frank Canton, who had served two terms as sheriff of Johnson County and who was reported to be a cold-eyed killer, was appointed chief of the detectives in northern Wyoming.

There is no question that the limited scope of the regularly constituted territorial law of both Wyoming and Montana, at that time, as well as the scarcity of regularly elected or appointed local law enforcement officers, did create a situation where law enforcement over the entire area was very weak, ineffective, and incapable of coping with, or combatting, the strong forces of lawlessness during these critical years.

Under these circumstances, cooperation between the local law enforcement officers and the detectives of the stockgrowers' association was certainly highly desirable. Instead, serious conflicts continued to develop between these two groups, with each accusing the other of lack of cooperation, resulting in extreme bitterness between all of these officers, to the point where very serious law enforcement problems, and conflicts between cattlemen, would develop in the future.

Shortly after the rustler elimination campaign got under way, several cases of dry gulching occurred in the Goshen Hole country of southeastern Wyoming. One of these cases occurred when a small rancher was arrested by the sheriff upon information furnished to him by a detective in the employment of the Wyoming Stockgrowers' Association. When the case was brought to trial the small rancher was acquitted by the jury on the grounds of insufficient evidence and released from custody. The accused then filed suit for $25,000 damages against the cattleman who was the owner of the calf that he had been accused of stealing. This suit was based upon defamation of character and other alleged damages. However, shortly after the filing of the suit, this small rancher was found one morning shot through the heart from ambush as he walked from his cabin to his corral.

In instances where an ambush of this kind was being carried out, the killer would come in under cover of darkness, then lie in hiding until his victim would come out of the house in the morning. After firing the shot he would slip away quietly, over a well-planned escape route, before anyone else showed up and realized what had happened.

During the summer of 1880, another dry gulching occurred in the same general area of the Goshen Hole, when goateed Ben Morrison, who at the time was a detective for the Wyoming Stockgrowers' Association, shot and killed a small rancher by the name of J. J. McGinnis while camped at the Sam Yoder draw, located about fifteen miles northwest of the Y Cross ranch. (This draw later became known as McGinnis Gulch.) Morrison had arrested McGinnis on the charge of cattle stealing and was taking him to Cheyenne for trial when this shooting occurred. Morrison claimed that his prisoner was trying to escape when he shot him. However, there has always been some question in the minds of many of the people who lived in that part of the country as to the justification for this shooting. Two soldiers, who were camped nearby when the shooting occurred said afterwards that, in their opinion, the shooting was a plain case of murder.

When Morrison arrived back in Cheyenne after the killing, he filed the following report with his office: "Feb. 13 left to arrest J. J. McGinnis, captured him in Fort Laramie. On the trip to Cheyenne he attempted to escape and met his death, arrived in Cheyenne on Feb. 20." A coroner's jury which met on the case concluded that McGinnis had actually been trying to escape when he was shot by Morrison. Regardless of this decision, Mrs. McGinnis filed charges with a grand jury against Morrison. She failed to get an indictment, and this ended the McGinnis case.

Over on the Sweetwater in central Wyoming, a shot was fired one night which was intended for D. H. Andrews, foreman for John Clay of the 71 Quarter-Circle. This shot had apparently been fired by one of a large gang of rustlers and outlaws who had been operating in that area at that time. Fortunately for the foreman, the bullet missed its mark. Andrews, who was a very fine ranch foreman, was not a gunfighter, and did not consider himself to be competent to cope with the very serious rustler problem which had developed in the Sweetwater country. Therefore, following this attempt upon his life, he asked John Clay to find someone else to take over as foreman of the big 71 Quarter-Circle.

George Henderson was the man who was sent in by John Clay in the fall of 1887 to relieve Andrews. This man had for several years been in the employment of the Pinkerton Detective Agency. He was recognized as a very capable and experienced lawman, as well as a good ranch foreman. Henderson moved quickly to reverse the action with the outlaw gangs by leading some of his cowboys in raids upon their camps, with the result that most of these outlaws soon left the valley of the Sweetwater for other parts where the climate was healthier for their type of operation and where the pickings were easier. However, in the fall of 1890, Henderson was shot and killed by one of these same outlaws while at a small ranch located only a short distance from the 71 Quarter-Circle headquarters, which was also only a short distance above what was known as Three Crossings on the Sweetwater. The man who killed Henderson was captured, tried, and sentenced to twenty years in the penitentiary. However, he soon escaped and was never recaptured, although he was reported to have been seen afterwards, on several occasions, in different parts of the cattle country.

One of the most revolting hangings in the history of the West also occurred on the Sweetwater. A woman by the name of Ella Watson, who was known on the Sweetwater as "Cattle Kate," and Jim Averell, a neighbor, were hanged as cattle rustlers by a small group of local cattlemen. Both Ella Watson and Averell had filed on homesteads in the Sweetwater valley, near Independence Rock, about fifty miles southwest of Casper, on range which had been used for many years by A. J. Bothwell, a large cattleman who operated in that part of the country. Averell, a man of about thirty-five years of age, was a surveyor by profession, and had devoted most of his time to locating other small ranchers on homesteads and other land filings in the Sweetwater valley. This activity on the part of Averell did not, of course, create kindly feelings toward him on the part of the big cattlemen who were operating in that area. Averell had also written letters to the Casper newspapers (which were published), in which he stated that three large cattlemen had been trying to hog over a hundred miles of meadows along the Sweetwater for their exclusive use, and had been trying to keep everyone else out of that area.

Ella Watson (or Cattle Kate) was a rather husky, well-built, blonde woman, about twenty-seven years of age, who was supposed to have been a woman of questionable virtue; in fact, it was reported that she had been a prostitute. How much of this story was true, and how much was propaganda spread for the purpose of justifying the hangings, is a question that still remains unanswered. To say the least, hanging is certainly a pretty stiff penalty for being a prostitute, especially during that period of time when prostitution was legalized in most of the towns in that part of the country. In addition, the big cattlemen claimed that Jim Averell and Cattle Kate were not only living together but also working together, rustling cattle from the big outfits. Furthermore, it was claimed by a few of the people on the Sweetwater that some of the cowboys and drifters who were "friends" of Cattle Kate were going out on the open range and branding mavericks for her, in exchange for her favors. It is quite possible that some of the other women who were living in the Sweetwater valley, and who considered their morals to be beyond reproach, had a lot to do with stirring up the gossip and public sentiment which resulted in the hangings.

The records indicate that during the period of time that this controversy was developing, Jim Averell had made application each year, for five years, to the Carbon County Brand Committee (composed principally of big cattlemen), for the registration of a brand in his own name, and that each time the application had been denied. Under the provisions of the maverick law, it was required that any person must have a registered brand in order to legally brand livestock. If the brand was not registered, the livestock could be confiscated by the Wyoming Stockgrowers'

Association and sold as mavericks. Averell claimed that the only reason for the rejection of his application was that the big cattlemen were using the denial of a brand registration as a means of applying the pressure to try to run him out of the country. In December of 1888, Ella Watson had also applied to the brand committee for registration of a brand, and this application had likewise been denied.

Calls were made upon both Jim Averell and Ella Watson in the spring of 1889, by representatives of the big cattlemen in the area, with demands that they both abandon their homesteads and leave the territory immediately, or suffer the consequences. They both rejected these demands, refused to leave the country, and defied the cattlemen in no uncertain terms. It was on the afternoon of July 20, 1889, following the calls by the cattlemen, that seven heavily armed and masked men rode up to the log cabin of Jim Averell, where they also found Ella Watson. The riders immediately disarmed and bound both of the homesteaders and then proceeded to hold a mock trial, wherein they found them both guilty of cattle rustling and sentenced them to death by hanging. The prisoners were then taken out under a tree, where the hangman's knot was tied in the ropes and the nooses were fitted around the necks of the two homesteaders. Both ropes were then thrown over the same limb of a tree; when their horses were led out from under them, they were left hanging side by side, until officers came out from town later and cut them down.

Some of the cattlemen who were reported to have participated in the hangings said afterwards that Jim Averell broke down and cried for mercy, but that Ella Watson, the only woman ever to be hanged in Wyoming, legally or illegally, went to her death with a very calm and courageous attitude, her head held high and with not the slightest evidence of fear. It was also reported later that Jim Averell and Ella Watson were probably married, but that they had used different names so that they could file on two homesteads at the same time.

A coroner's jury was called in Carbon County to hold a hearing on the deaths of the two people who had been lynched. Their verdict was that "Jim Averell and Ella Watson came to their deaths by being hanged by the neck, at the hands of A. J. Bothwell, Tom Sun, John Durbin, R. M. Galbraith, Bob Conner, E. McLain and an unknown man."

The six cattlemen named by this coroner's jury were arrested by Sheriff Frank Hadsell of Carbon County, then later released from custody on bond of five thousand dollars each. This group who had been arrested and charged with the lynching retained three of the most competent and influential attorneys in the Territory of Wyoming — John W. Lacey, John A. Riner, and J. R. Dixon — as counsel to defend all of them in any court action if and when the case against them came to trial. However, when four known witnesses of the lynching failed to show up for a hearing before a grand jury, the charges against the six cattlemen were dismissed. Therefore, no one was ever punished for the lynchings. There were rumors later that the four witnesses had been spirited out of the country by the big cattlemen before the grand jury had convened.

After a few months had passed, the homesteads and other land filings of both Jim Averell and Ella Watson were contested on the grounds of desertion, and the land was filed upon by other individuals. Then, when final proof was made on the land, it was acquired by A. J. Bothwell, one of the cattlemen who had been arrested for the lynchings of Jim Averell and Ella Watson.

There is no record of what became of the cattle that these two individuals were supposed to have owned or to have branded illegally. Under the provisions of the maverick laws, if either of these people actually had illegally branded cattle in their possession then those cattle should have been turned over to the Wyoming Stockgrowers' Association to be sold as mavericks. The fact that there is no record of such a sale having been made by the stockgrowers' association raises the question of whether the two people who were hanged actually did have any illegaly branded cattle in their possession. If so, it would seem that someone must have made off with them, illegally, after the hangings.

There were many other hangings and dry gulchings from ambush over a period of years in the Territory of Wyoming, including the hanging on June 1, 1891 of a small rancher by the name of Tom Waggoner, who lived southwest of Newcastle. Waggoner was supposed to have been guilty of rustling cattle from some of the big outfits who were operating on the headwaters of the Cheyenne River, west of the Black Hills.

There were also (at about the same time as the Waggoner hanging) two other small ranchers, Orley E. Jones and John A. Tisdale, who were dry gulched while they were near their ranches, south of Buffalo. After these killings, Frank Canton, who was cattle detective in that part of the country for the Wyoming Stockgrowers' Association and who at one time had been the sheriff of Johnson County where these ranches were located, was arrested and charged with the killing of John Tisdale. However, the judge, with very little delay, dismissed the case against the cattle detective.

To the north, in the Territory of Montana, the livestock people had also been faced with a very serious cattle-rustling and wholesale horse-stealing problem (even before the hard winter of '86-'87) from outlaw gangs operating along the

Missouri River between the mouths of the Judith River and the Musselshell. This problem had reached its peak in the spring of 1884, when Granville Stuart, a very able and experienced leader of men (later both president and secretary of the Montana Stockgrowers' Association during different periods of time), formed what became known as the Montana Vigilantes. This organization was composed of some of the leading livestock men in central Montana.

These men proceeded to move quickly and decisively in combating this horse-stealing problem. However, as a matter of policy, for their own protection, all of the men who participated in the activities of this organization were sworn to complete secrecy. As a result, very little ever became known of the operations of this organization until many years afterwards, and even then the information which did become available was extremely limited. Very rarely was the name of any man who participated in these activities ever mentioned in any statement that was made public by anyone who knew the facts.

The Montana Vigilantes used a sign, a skull and crossbones and the figures 3-7-77, as a warning to rustlers and horse thieves. This sign was generally tacked to a cabin door or fastened to a pasture gate, with a notice to the party concerned to leave the country immediately, or suffer the consequences. This sign referred to a grave three feet wide, seven feet long, and seventy-seven inches deep and was quite effective in accomplishing its purpose. This group of vigilantes soon gained a wide reputation in the Territory of Montana for following through with their warnings and taking drastic action, and also for being quite cold-blooded and ruthless in carrying out their objectives.

The country along the Missouri River where the outlaws and horse thieves had their hideouts was a rough, rugged, and broken country, with deep canyons running back several miles from the river. Here, stolen horses could be hidden almost indefinitely, until the altered and burned-over brands on the animals had time to heal to where they would give the appearence of being old brands. Scattered in the bottoms along the river were the camps, tents and log cabins of numerous Indian traders, wood choppers, buffalo hunters, and wolfers, with their many different kinds of vehicles and equipment, which they used in the process of making a living. The wood choppers made a few dollars by cutting wood and then piling this fuel at the boat landings along the river, where they could sell it to the occasional paddle-wheeled steamboats which came slowly up the big river. Then Indian traders shipped in rotgut whisky, calico, trinkets and other miscellaneous items of merchandise on the steamboats, which they then traded to the Indians for furs, pelts, stolen horses, or anything else of value that the Indian might offer for trade. Also in the camps along the river were many drifters and outlaws, "on the dodge," who were hiding out from the law in that isolated part of the country. They came in from the mining camps and up the river on steamboats. No questions were ever asked along the river as to where a man came from, or why; they all just attended to their own business, and kept their mouths shut about what went on along the Missouri.

Rocky Point, (which later became known as Wilder) with its Indian trading post, two saloons, a steamboat landing, and a few other questionable places of business, was the supply point for the principal areas along the river, as well as the headquarters for the horse thieves and outlaw gangs who were holed up in the rough country which ran back into the badlands from the river. In their operations, the outlaws would swim many of their stolen horses across the Missouri River at this point, then trail them northward into Canada, where they would be sold to the Canadians to be used for various purposes in that rapidly developing plains country. The gangs of horses thieves would then run stolen Canadian horses back across the line into the United States, where the brands would be altered and the animals would be hidden out in the rough country until the trail had cooled off. The outlaws would then move these stolen horses on southward under cover of darkness, swim them across the Yellowstone in some out-of-the-way place, and sell these horses to some of the small ranchers who were homesteading along the creeks and rivers in southern Montana, or even take them over into the Powder River country in the northern part of the Territory of Wyoming.

The leader, or captain, of the principal gang of these horse thieves, with their hideouts around Rocky Point on the Missouri, was a tall, handsome, and well-educated young man, with striking features and piercing grey eyes, by the name of Jack Stringer, better known as "Stringer Jack." This young man had been a buffalo hunter along the Tongue River and the Yellowstone before the buffalo had thinned out and caused him to look elsewhere for a way of making a living. Jack Stringer was a wild and reckless man, with a daring disposition, who loved to gamble for big stakes and, as a result, (in order to satisfy his craving for money) to play the big games which were to be found in some of the mining camps or in some of the larger cow towns in that part of the country. This young man had organized his gang of horses thieves, with their principal hangout located in the rough country along the Missouri, near the mouth of the Ponchette.

It was in the early part of July, 1884, that the Fort Benton River press reported the stealing of over two hundred head of horses, in one raid, by the Missouri River horse thieves. About the same time reports were also made of stage horses having been stolen from stage stations along the Musselshell. Then, on July 9, the same newspaper reported the stealing of other stage horses from a stage station at Judith Gap. In the same issue, this newspaper reported the lynching of two half-breed Indians, by name of Leo and Narcissa Laventure, at the mouth of the Judith River near the little cow town of Clagget, Montana, for stealing horses from some of the Judith River stockmen.

It was about this same time that William "Floppin Bill" Cantrell, who had been a woodcutter on the Missouri, rode up out of that wild country and reported to Granville Stuart, at his DHS ranch in the Judith Basin, that there was a large gang of about fifteen outlaws who were holding around a hundred head of stolen horses at Bates Point on the north side of the Missouri River, about twenty miles below the mouth of the Musselshell. Without delay, Stuart sent out riders to neighboring ranches, calling an emergency meeting of the vigilantes to meet at his headquarters ranch. At this meeting, plans were carefully made, and a list of names of the horse thieves was prepared from the information which had been furnished to the group by Bill Cantrell.

Pack mules were soon being loaded with beds, cooking equipment, food, extra rifles and ammunition, and all of the other supplies which might be needed for a two week expedition. When the vigilantes rode away from the DHS ranch on July 12, they proceeded to pick up a few additional livestock men as they moved towards the river, until, altogether, there were a total of fourteen cool-headed, dependable, determined, and close-mouthed men, all sworn to absolute secrecy, making the hundred-mile ride to Bates Point, with Bill Cantrell, who knew every foot of the country, as guide. Cantrell, who was later to become the first cattle detective to be hired by the Montana Stockgrowers' Association, guided the party to a point on the river where the saddle horses and pack mules were swum across the Missouri under cover of darkness and were then hidden out in the heavy willow thickets along the stream.

One man was left in charge of the horses and mules, while the rest of the party worked their way on in, quietly, on foot, to where they successfully bypassed the two guards who were on duty. Then, on the morning of July 20, 1884, before daybreak, they completely surrounded the outlaw camp and took cover, without having disturbed any of the outlaws who were in the camp. There was an old woodyard at Bates Point, a log cabin with loopholes on all sides, and a tumbled-down log barn, with a large, pole corral connecting the cabin and the barn. There was also a stack of dry prairie hay in back of the barn while, in a small grove of trees about a hundred yards from the cabin, near the river, there was a large tent, with the framework built from small poles and covered over with wagon sheets.

Living in the cabin at that time was one man, referred to locally as "old man James," with his two sons (who were supposed to have been cousins of Jesse James). All three of these men had been living for some time in the old log cabin at Bates Point. The James boys were a wild pair of youngsters, and they had almost immediately thrown in with the Stringer gang, who were also using the deserted buildings at Bates Point for one of their camps.

On the morning of July 20, when the vigilantes moved in on the river and surrounded the camp at Bates Point, old man James was sleeping in the cabin, along with three other members of the Stringer gang. Sleeping in the big tent down by the river were six other members of the gang: Jack Stringer, Orville Edwards, Silas Nickerson, Dixie Burr, Swift Bill, and Paddy Rose. The two James boys, who were supposed to have been on guard duty, were stationed in some trees a short distance back from the camp.

As daylight began to break in the sky, signs of life began to appear in the log cabin. Smoke, with bright red sparks of fire, could soon be seen coming out of the stovepipe. It was only a few minutes afterwards that old man James came out of the cabin door and walked slowly toward the barn. When he reached the corral gate, two of the vigilantes, hidden in the barn, immediately covered him and ordered him to open the corral gate and let the horses out, which he did. However, he then turned very suddenly, grabbed a rifle which had been standing, unnoticed by the vigilantes, inside the barn door. Keeping the two vigilantes covered with the rifle, old man James started backing slowly toward the open door of the cabin. Once inside, he immediately opened fire on the raiders through one of the loopholes in the side of the cabin.

When the two James boys heard the rifle fire, they came running toward the cabin, shouting as they ran that the camp was surrounded by the vigilantes. They failed to stop and surrender when called upon to do so by the raiders and were cut down by rifle fire as they ran toward the cabin. A few minutes later, rifle fire was belching from all of the loopholes in the walls of the cabin, as well as from the tent, and from the brush down along the river where some of the outlaws who had been sleeping in the tent had taken cover.

The vigilantes were now returning the rifle fire with a vengeance, from cover which had been chosen as providing the best protection available. Jack Stringer, the outlaw leader, made his last stand in a willow thicket located only a short distance from the big tent where he had been sleeping. This young outlaw shot it out with the raiders at short range, until he went down under the heavy rifle and revolver fire.

At this point in the fight, two of the raiders slipped

in and set fire to the haystack alongside the barn. Then, using the smoke from that fire for cover, they moved on in and threw burning hay on top of a trash pile which was alongside the cabin, setting it on fire. As a result, the log cabin, which had been built from pitch pine logs, was also soon burning furiously. Within a very short period of time, the cabin, barn, and corrals, with everything in them, had burned to the ground. None of the outlaws who were in the cabin ever came out alive. They were apparently all either killed by the rifle fire or overcome by the smoke and burned to death in the fire.

It was found after the fight (which had lasted for about two hours) that of the twelve men who had been at the camp when the vigilantes came in that morning, seven were dead. The other five, with three of them wounded, had escaped down the river and were hiding out in the heavy brush and willow thickets along the stream. The vigilantes spent the afternoon trying to flush them out into the open without success.

When, later that same day, the hungry vigilantes started looking for something to eat, they found that almost all of the grub that had been loaded on the pack mules had become water soaked and completely ruined when they swam the mules across the muddy Missouri that morning, on their way into the outlaw camp at Bates Point. While they were standing around discussing their problem, a steamboat was heard coming up the river. Granville Stuart went down to the boat landing and waved to the steamer to pull in to shore. However, when the captain of the boat chose to ignore the signal, all of the vigilantes mounted their horses and rode rapidly up the stream to where they were some distance ahead of the steamer. When it came along again, Stuart waved for a second time for them to pull to shore, this time with emphasis. Finally, when the captain saw the rifles that the riders were carrying across the front of their saddles in a rather threatening manner, he complied and pulled in to where the captain learned from them that all they wanted was his boat could be boarded by the men on horseback. When flour, bacon, coffee, and a few other groceries, he gave the impression of being very much relieved to find that he was not being hijacked and robbed. As a result, he told the group of vigilantes to go on down to the galley and take whatever they needed and that there would be no charge.

Four of the outlaws who had escaped from the Bates Point fight were picked up a few days later at Rocky Point, near Fort Peck on the Missouri, by the military authorities, who also wanted them for stealing government horses. It was then learned that, after having escaped from the Bates Point fight, the four men had built a raft from poles that they had found along the river and had then drifted on the raft down the Missouri to where they were picked up.

Shortly after the four outlaws were captured, United States Deputy Marshal Sam Frishchel deputized two cowboys to go with him to the little town of Poplar, where the four prisoners were being held, to help him bring them back for trial on charges of horsestealing. However, while the marshal and his deputies were camped on the Missouri at the mouth of the Musselshell, a group of riders rode in and forcibly relieved the officers of their prisoners. These riders then took the four prisoners up the river a short distance to two old log cabins that had been built close together. A log was quickly lifted into place, extending from the dirt roof of one cabin to the roof of the other, and all four of the outlaws were then strung up and hanged, side by side, from the one log. The cabins were both then set on fire and burned to the ground. In the process, the bodies of the four outlaws were, of course, cremated.

As a final result of the Bates Point fight, all of the Stringer gang who were in the fight that morning, except Paddy Rose, who escaped out of the country, were either shot or hanged. Altogether, it was estimated that there were at least fifteen, and probably as many as eighteen, suspected outlaws who met their deaths at the hands of these vigilantes along the Missouri, during the month of July, 1884.

On the third day after the Bates Point fight, Granville Stuart left the Missouri River operations of the vigilantes for Helena, Montana, to attend the organization meeting of the Montana Stockgrowers' Association, where he was elected as the first president of that organization. When he left the Missouri to attend this meeting, he assigned the command and the responsibility for the continuing operation of the vigilantes along the Missouri to "Floppin" Bill Cantrell. This group continued to make raids on other small outlaw camps along the river, as well as to gather the many stolen horses that they had found in the area. When this job was completed, the vigilantes had picked up around one hundred sixty-five head of stolen horses along that section of the Missouri; then had trailed them out to the DHS ranch, where the owners of the horses were notified to come to the ranch to claim and pick up their animals.

Some of these horses were from the Powder River country in Wyoming; others were from Canada, including a few branded with an "M P" on their front hooves which belonged to the Canadian mounted police. There were also some stage horses that belonged to one of the Montana stagecoach lines in which Luke Vorhees had an interest.

It was reported that Vorhees went in with the vigilantes at the time of the raid at Bates Point.

With the constantly increasing problem of cattle rustling after the hard winter of '86-'87, the Montana Vigilantes were again activated. As a result, they continued to work closely with the cattle detectives of the Montana Stockgrowers' Association. It was during this period of time that the big cattlemen were having a lot of trouble with cattle rustling along the Yellowstone, the Tongue, and the Little Missouri, as well as in the eastern part of Montana, and even on over into the Belle Fourche country of South Dakota. It was reported in later years that at least sixty-three accused rustlers were either shot or hung in the rustler elimination campaign over a period of about five years, in the Territory of Montana and the western part of the Dakotas.

There is, of course, the question as to how many of these lynchings of accused rustlers were justified. The best that can be said of the cattleman's law is that it was probably better than no law at all. Miscarriages of justice do occur, even under due process of law, but it is certainly questionable whether injustices occur as frequently under regularly constituted processes of law as they did under cattleman's law. However, it has been said that, regardless of the question of injustices, these activities on the part of the cattlemen did keep the rustler problem from getting completely out of control in the West during that period of time.

20 The best-known cattle detective of the Wyoming Stockgrowers' Association, or at least the one who received the most adverse publicity as a cold-blooded killer, was Tom Horn. He first showed up officially on the Wyoming scene in 1894, when he was employed as an undercover cattle detective by the Swan Land and Cattle Company (or Two Bar outfit) at Chugwater when John Clay was general manager. There have been reports that Horn actually was in the Territory of Wyoming as early as 1892, but his first employment of record in that part of the country was when he went to work for the Two Bar at the headquarters ranch, masquerading as a horse breaker. Horn had been recommended for this job of cattle detective by Jim McParlan, who at that time was superintendent for the Pinkerton Detective Agency in Denver, where Tom was then employed as a private detective specializing in cattle stealing and bank robbery cases.

Tom Horn was born in Scotland County near the small town of Memphis, Missouri, on November 21, 1860. This was, of course, only a year before the outbreak of the Civil War. Consequently, Tom grew up during and immediately following that great conflict, when that part of Missouri was going through a very turbulent and lawless period. The country was dominated by Confederate guerilla bands and other renegades from both sides of the conflict, who lived off the country and took from the people whatever they considered necessary for their survival, killing when necessary to accomplish this purpose.

Life was cheap, with violence and bloodshed being a part of the way of life. Therefore, during the period of time that Tom was growing up with this violence all around him, it was impossible for a young boy to differentiate between what was justifiable killing and what was not justifiable, if there were such a distinction. So of course, from the viewpoint of a small boy who was living in this environment, there was not necessarily a question of right and wrong involved. It would appear to him that survival would just depend upon which side you were on at a particular time. Consequently, it was undoubtedly inevitable that the bloodshed and violence which Tom Horn had seen and experienced while he was a growing and impressionable boy in Missouri had a lot to do with the type of man which he became in his later life.

Young Tom left home at the age of fourteen, following a fight with his father, and headed westward across the Missouri. His first job was with a tough construction outfit that was laying track for the Santa Fe Railroad, where they were pushing their line westward across the state of Kansas. From this construction job, the boy then drifted on over into the state of Texas, where he worked for a year as a cowboy with a large Texas cattle outfit. On this job, many of the cowboys and other ranch hands with whom Tom came in contact spoke Spanish. He found that he had a very definite aptitude for learning languages, and before long he was speaking Spanish quite fluently.

In the summer of 1876, this tall boy, now sixteen years of age and very definitely a loner, showed up in Prescott, Arizona. He was a quick and observant youngster who spent most of his time alone and avoided crowds. Also, he cared very little for affection and had no particular interest in women. However, he did have a good sense of humor and people liked him, but at the same time they soon learned that he was a youngster who made friends slowly. Also, he had a lot of raw courage and would not stand crowding. Very few people ever became close friends with Tom Horn, or even got to the point of knowing him well. However, the fact remains that throughout his entire lifetime, he was always intensely loyal to the few close friends that he did make, as well as to the people for whom he worked.

A few weeks after coming to Arizona, Tom took a job of herding the oxen at the army outpost of Camp Verde; and it was here, in the valley of the Verde, that this boy from Missouri was destined to meet Al Seiber, the person with the greatest influence upon the development and the molding of Tom Horn.

Al Seiber was born in Germany in 1850, then had

been brought to the United States by his parents when he was only six years of age. When the Civil War broke out, Al Seiber, then a young man, enlisted in the Union Army, where he served with distinction, having been twice wounded, the last time at Gettysburg. Shortly after he was discharged from the army at the end of the war, Seiber left for the Virginia City gold fields. From there, he drifted on down to Tombstone, Arizona, where he continued his gold mining activities, with only limited success. In 1871, Al Seiber became a scout for the army in Arizona, under General Stoneman. He soon became recognized as a man with considerable ability in that capacity. In 1873 he was sent to Camp Verde, where he was given the assignment of organizing and heading a group of Apache scouts to be recruited from among the peaceful Apaches on the San Carlos Reservation.

Seiber was a large and very powerfully built man, with tremendous strength and endurance, who never avoided a fight and who, when aroused and angry, could become very ferocious and could kill another man, whether Indian or white, without any scruples whatever. This man had twenty-eight bullet and knife scars on his body as proof of his fighting activities over the years. Seiber ruled his Indian scouts at Camp Verde with an iron hand. As a result, he was both feared and respected by all of the Apaches, whether they be peaceful Indians or renegades. They called him "Iron Man."

Seiber was a good judge of men, and when he became acquainted with Tom Horn while the boy was herding the oxen at Camp Verde, he developed a liking for this unusual youngster and sensed that the boy probably had the qualities that could be developed into the type of man that he needed for a particular job. Seiber was in need of a good undercover man, or boy, to live on the San Carlos

Indian Reservation. He had to have the courage, resourcefulness, intelligence, and ability to ferret out information on the planned outbreaks and raids of the renegade Apaches, and then get this information out to him, without being caught, before the raids actually occurred. He believed that Tom might have these qualifications, and was especially interested when he learned that Tom spoke Spanish.

Seiber spoke the Apache language, but not Spanish, which was the language that was spoken by many of the Indians in the Southwest. In addition, there were also many other Spanish-speaking people in that part of the country with whom it was necessary to communicate, and so Seiber needed a good Spanish interpreter. Consequently, quite soon after meeting the tall, sixteen-year-old boy from Missouri, the chief of scouts arranged for Tom to go with him on a trip to the San Carlos Reservation, without telling him what he had in mind. While they were at San Carlos, there happened to be a council meeting where there were some Spanish-speaking people present. Seiber called Tom in and asked him to act as interpreter. The next day, after the meeting, Al Seiber left for a visit to some of the other army outposts in the area, leaving Tom with a peaceful old Indian chief at the San Carlos Reservation, until his return.

Tom had many of the characteristics of an Indian and he got along famously with the young Indians on the reservation. He liked them and their wild way of life and they liked him. As a result, when Seiber returned to San Carlos, he was quite pleased with the progress that had been made, and when they arrived back at Camp Verde, he had a long talk with Tom, telling him of what he had in mind for him and at the same time outlining to him what his duties would be. Shortly afterward, he put the boy on the army payroll as a scout and interpreter and advised him to continue to cultivate his friendly relations with the Indians on the reservation in every way possible.

As a consequence, after two or three more trips to the reservation, the old chief asked the boy to come and live with him, telling him that there was an Indian girl who wanted to throw a stick at him, or, in other words, wanted him to be her man. Soon afterward, with Seiber's approval, Tom went to live with the Apaches and to become one of the tribe. This sixteen-year-old boy was now on a very dangerous assignment. If the renegade Indians who were on and off the reservation were to suspect that the boy was spying on them, they would kill him without mercy or hesitancy. Regardless of this danger, the hazards and challenge of the assignment appealed to this venturesome youngster, and as a consequence, the experience and methods of operation which he developed here on the reservation, particularly those of gaining the confidence of the people whom he was spying on, would continue to be the methods that he would use in this type of work for the rest of his lifetime.

Tom lived the life of an Apache for almost two years, mixing with the young Indians on the reservation, learning their culture, and speaking their language. They called him "Talking Boy" and much of the fame that Al Seiber gained as an Indian scout was due to the information that young Tom Horn was funneling out to him. The renegade Indians could not understand how Al Seiber could anticipate their every move, even before their raids occurred. To them, Seiber became a mystery man with big medicine and supernatural powers. Seiber encouraged this belief on the part of the Apaches in every way possible, even staging performances designed to accomplish that purpose.

It was in the summer of 1878 that Al Seiber induced Tom to come back to Camp Verde and to become an official interpreter, in both Spanish and Apache, for the army, when they were involved in council meetings or other dealings with the Indians, as well as to become Seiber's right-hand man in handling the Apache scouts.

The Seiber scouts were being used at that time in the campaign against the renegade band of Chiricahua Apaches led by the great and cunning outlaw Indian, Chief Geronimo; who, with his followers, refused to stay on the reservation and carried on an almost constant series of depredations and raids against the white settlements in the Territory of Arizona, as well as against the Pima, Maricopa, and other peaceful tribes of Indians who had their little farms along the Gila, Salt, and Verde Rivers in the low country of Arizona. Whenever the United States Army would get hot on his trail, the wily old outlaw Indian chief would take his band of followers across the border into old Mexico, where the army could not follow him without being in violation of international law. There in Mexico, he would start raiding the Mexican settlements until the Mexican army would begin to close in on him; he would again duck back across the border into the United States where he would then hide out in the Superstitions, Magollons, or some of the other mountain ranges in the Territory of Arizona.

For several years, Tom Horn spent most of his time with the Seiber Apache scouts, chasing renegade Apaches, including Geronimo, as well as some of the white outlaws who were wanted by the federal government for various crimes. In the process, he naturally became involved in several good-sized battles, as well as many skirmishes between the army and the renegade Indians, and also in the hunting down of individuals, or small parties, where only the Apache scouts who were under Seiber's or his own command were involved.

Under these circumstances, it was only natural that the methods of operation, as well as the code by which Al Seiber lived, would become the code of Tom Horn. In the process of his training and experience, he became a man hunter, with all of the cunning and craftiness of the Indian, which he had acquired while living with the Apaches. He could crawl for great distances on his belly like a snake, or sit motionless for hours with his back against a tree or rock, while at the same time seeing and making mental notes of everything that went on around him.

Tom had filled out and developed into a large and powerful man. Although not as large as Al Seiber, he stood six feet two inches tall, with muscles of steel and nerves of iron. He could fight like a tiger with his fists and was deadly with a gun or a knife. Tom Horn was considered, by those who knew him, to be a tough man to fool with. He was referred to around army posts and cow camps as a "white Indian."

It was in the spring of 1882 that General George Crook, who was referred to by the Apaches as "Grey Fox," was reassigned as commanding general of the troops in Arizona. In the process, General Crook was returning to Arizona, where he had previously seen service for several years before leaving for the campaigns against the Sioux and the Cheyenne in the northern high plains country of Wyoming and Montana. Although this smart old Indian fighter had been gone from the southwest for eleven years, the Indians in Arizona still remembered and respected him as a man who kept his word and who did not speak with a forked tongue. In that same year, Al Seiber was appointed as chief of scouts for the entire Territory of Arizona, with Tom Horn as his assistant.

The trouble with Geronimo and his Chiricahua Apaches had reached a very critical stage by the time of General Crook's arrival in Arizona, with the settlers in both the United States and Mexico demanding action, and a "Hot Pursuit Treaty" under consideration by the governments of the two nations. This treaty, if it became effective, would permit the troops of either country to cross the border, when in actual pursuit of thieves and bandits who had violated the laws in the country involved and had crossed the border in order to avoid being captured. Soon after arriving at Fort Bowie, which was to be his headquarters, General Crook left for Guaymas and Hermosillo, Mexico, where the details of the Hot Pursuit Treaty were being finalized. This treaty, when approved by both nations, applied to the international border lying along the northern boundary of the Mexican states of Chihuahua and Sonora where they joined the southern boundary of the United States.

After the signing of this treaty, General Crook organized a punitive expedition, in May of 1883, and crossed the border into Mexico with the objective of capturing Geronimo and his followers and returning them to the reservation in Arizona. However, before the expedition got under way, there had been some minor trouble developing with the Indians at San Carlos, and General Crook had sent Al Seiber back to the reservation to handle that problem. He then appointed Tom Horn as temporary chief of scouts for the expedition. After this detail was handled, the troop column, consisting of several hundred mounted men and a pack train of three hundred fifty animals, carrying enough supplies to last for sixty days, left from San Bernadino Springs.

After traveling southward for several days and crossing the Sierra Madre mountains, the troops caught up with and surrounded Geronimo and his renegades near the town of Bavispe, on the Yaqui River. Some skirmishing occurred until Geronimo, seeing that he was badly outnumbered, sent in a messenger under a white flag asking for a council meeting, which was granted by General Crook. After arguing for several hours, with Tom Horn acting as interpreter, Geronimo, with his band of about two hundred bucks and at least an equal number of squaws and papooses, finally agreed to go back and stay at the San Carlos Reservation, and not give any trouble in the future.

Eighteen months later, Geronimo and his renegades again jumped the reservation. This time, when they left San Carlos they split up into several parties, with a planned rendezvous at Durasmillo Springs in old Mexico. As they swept southward across Arizona, they raided numerous white settlements, running off livestock, burning buildings, and killing almost everyone in their path, including women and children. When they were across the border, they moved rapidly south to their hideouts in the Sierra Madre mountains of old Mexico. However, within a few weeks General Crook had organized another punitive expedition that also operated under the Hot Pursuit Treaty, and again crossed the border on the trail of Geronimo, with Tom Horn and his Apache scouts working in advance of the troop column as they searched out and tracked down the wily old outlaw Indian chief and his large band of renegades.

After several days of hard, forced marches, with the troop column traveling principally at night, they caught up with the old renegade and his followers on the banks of the Aros River, south of the border where some heavy fighting took place. Quite a large number of Geronimo's renegade Apaches were killed, as well as several soldiers and a few of the Apache scouts. While this battle was under way, Geronimo managed to slip away and escape under cover of darkness with the remnant of his band, and to get back to his mountain hideout, where he continued for almost a year to play hide-and-seek with the troops from both sides of the border.

In the spring of 1886 General Crook asked to be relieved, and General Nelson A. Miles, who was another of the experienced Indian fighters who had been engaged in the campaigns against the Sioux and the Cheyenne in the northern high country, was sent in to take over command of the troops in Arizona, with instructions from the War Department to capture Geronimo and his Chiricahua Apaches and then return them to the United States, where a decision would then be made as to their future.

General Miles, a man who always moved rapidly, immediately proceeded to organize another punitive expedition into Mexico, and in the summer of 1886, he again caught up with the old renegade while he was camped near the Bavispi River. When Geronimo found that he was very badly outnumbered, he asked for a council meeting. At this meeting, he refused to talk through anyone as interpreter except Tom Horn. After some delay, he finally agreed to surrender, when told by Horn that, unless he did give up peacefully, he and his entire band, including women and children, would be ordered shot by General Miles. After their surrender, Geronimo and his renegade Chiracahua Apaches were herded back across the border to Fort Bowie, where they were loaded on boxcars like cattle and shipped out on a special Southern Pacific train to exile in the swamps of Florida. This was the end of the long trail for the old Apache outlaw Chief Geronimo.

With the end of the Apache Indian raids in Arizona,

the Apache scouts were soon disbanded, and Tom Horn's service as a scout for the army was terminated. For the next four years, he spent most of his time around Tucson and Tombstone, where he worked as a cowboy for some of the big cattle outfits in Arizona, including the Chiricahua Cattle Company. In addition, he competed in the steer roping and other events at rodeos throughout the Southwest, where he was a rather consistent winner of prize money. He also served for a period of time as a deputy sheriff under Bucky O'Neil in Yavapai County, and in the same capacity with Sheriff Reynolds in Gila County. On both of these jobs, Tom Horn was recognized as a fearless and effective lawman.

An event which occurred in the summer of 1889 when he was attending a public dance near Tucson probably changed the entire pattern of Tom Horn's life. While he was at this dance, he became involved in a gunfight, over a girl, with a young Mexican Army officer. In the argument, and fight which followed, the impetuous and hotheaded Mexican pulled his gun and fired the first shot at Tom, who then very deliberately pulled his gun and fired one shot, which killed the Mexican Army officer instantly. Ordinarily, this shooting would not have created any great disturbance, but the young Mexican Army officer was supposed to have been in the United States as a member of a military mission. When a hearing was held, witnesses testified that Tom Horn had shot in self-defense and he was exonerated. Regardless of this fact, an international incident had occurred, and feelings were running high on both sides of the border. As a result of this sentiment, some of Tom's friends who were public officials suggested to him that he might be wise to help to avoid further international friction by moving to some other part of the country, at least temporarily, until things quieted down. In line with these suggestions, Tom shortly afterwards left for Denver, where he went to work for the Pinkerton Detective Agency, using recommendations and references which were furnished to him by the same Arizona public officials who had suggested the move. It was here that he was employed when Jim McParlan recommended him to the Swan Land and Cattle Company officials as a cattle detective to work in their part of the country.

When Tom Horn showed up as a horse breaker at the Two Bar outfit, or Swan Land and Cattle Company, at Chugwater, he was a tall, muscular, mustached man in his early thirties; hardened to the killing of other men to the point that from his point of view, the killing of a white cattle rustler was no different than the killing of an Apache horse thief. Tom soon afterwards became widely known to the cattlemen in Wyoming, when, after a few months at the Two Bar, his name went on the payroll of the Wyoming Stockgrowers' Association as a cattle detective.

Tom Horn was a natural-born man hunter, with catlike movements, who would stalk a suspected cattle rustler like most men would stalk a deer. He was perhaps best described by a man who knew him well, as a strange, incomprehensible person who hated houses and who spent almost all of his time, day and night, out of doors and alone. Tom did almost all of his riding at night. He moved about cautiously over the country, avoiding ridges where he would be silhouetted against the skyline, slipping up draws and ravines with the stealth of an Indian, then hiding out in deep canyons where he would be out of sight in the daytime.

It was not at all unusual for Tom Horn to ride quietly out of the shadows into the firelight at some roundup camp, where he would spend a few days working as a cowboy, then just disappear some night as quietly as he had come, without anyone knowing that he had gone until he failed to show up for breakfast the next morning. Frank Jones, who knew him well, said that Tom always had an instinctive aversion to anyone getting behind him. When he had filled his plate at the chuck wagon, he would always walk to the outside of the circle of cowboys, who would be seated on the ground, with their plates in their laps. He would then sit down, but if anyone went out beyond him, he would pick up his plate and move out still further so that he would still be on the outside of the circle.

In August of 1895, a young Englishman by the name of William Lewis, who had filed on a one hundred sixty acre homestead about thirty-five miles northwest of Cheyenne near Iron Mountain, was found near his homestead — shot to death with a high-powered rifle. Lewis had previously been accused by a neighboring cattleman of being a cattle rustler and had received a notice to leave the country, which he had ignored. At the coroner's inquest, which was called shortly afterwards, it was found that Lewis had been shot three times, from a distance of about three hundred yards, with a .44 caliber rifle. There were rumors at the time that Tom Horn was the killer, but no definite proof was made available, and no one was ever arrested for the killing of William Lewis.

During that same year, Fred N. Powell, another small rancher, with his homestead on Horse Creek about ten miles south of Lewis, received a notice to leave the country immediately or suffer the consequences. Powell, also a man of courage, tore up the notice and defied the cattlemen. A few days later, during the month of September, Powell was shot through the heart from a distance of only about a hundred yards, as he worked in a meadow near his cabin. Riders who were in the area at the time, but some distance away, said that he was shot by a tall man who was riding a black horse. Fred Powell's six-year-old son, who was with his father at the time of the shooting, identified Tom Horn as the killer; but, due to the age of the boy, his testimony was not considered to be competent, and no one was arrested for the murder of Fred Powell.

By this time, Tom Horn's reputation as a ruthless killer had become widespread; public sentiment built up to the point that he was finally dismissed as a cattle detective by the Wyoming Stockgrowers' Association. From that time on, at least as far as the records were concerned, he was apparently on the payroll of certain individual cattlemen, or of small groups of cattlemen, as a private cattle detective. However, with his intense loyalty to the people for whom he worked, Tom Horn never did divulge the names of any of his employers. He did, however, continue to spend the greater part of his time at the John Coble ranch. Consequently, it was rumored that Coble at Iron Mountain in southeastern Wyoming, and Ira Haley, with his headquarters ranch near Green River in southwestern Wyoming, were two of his principal employers, but there was never any valid proof of this report.

It was during the summer of 1900 that Tom Horn was supposed to have been working around Green River (under the assumed name of Tom Hicks) for some of the big outfits in that part of the country; including that of Ira Haley, whose operations and interests extended over into the Brown Park country of northwestern Colorado. During the month of July of that year, a small rancher by the name of Matt Rush, whose homestead was in Brown Park and who had been accused of being a cattle rustler by some of the big cattlemen in that part of the country, was found shot to death in his own cabin.

Shortly afterwards, in November of that same year,

another small rancher, by the name of Isam Dart, who had been accused of being an associate of Matt Rush, was also shot and killed from ambush — with the shot being fired from a distance of about one hundred fifty yards while Dart was chopping wood at his woodpile near his cabin. Tom Horn was suspected of having been responsible for both of these killings. However, alibis were provided for him covering the period of time in which these murders occurred, and no action was ever taken against him in either one of these cases.

During that same summer, Tom Horn was also involved in a barroom fight with a man by the name of Jim Davis, at the well-known Four Ace saloon in the small cow town of Baggs, Wyoming; only a short distance from the headquarters ranch of Ira Haley. While this fight was under way, Davis pulled a knife and cut a very deep gash in the neck and shoulder of Horn before he could grab Davis by the arm and force him to release the knife. Horn was reaching for his gun when some of the spectators stepped in and stopped the fight. However, Tom carried a large and jagged scar from that fight for the rest of his life.

John C. Coble, the owner of the ranch at Iron Mountain where Tom Horn spent most of his time when he was in that part of the country, was the well-educated son of a wealthy and very influential Pennsylvania family. Coble first came to the high plains country in the early eighties and became associated with a large British syndicate which was then operating in the Powder River country under the name of the Frontier Land and Cattle Company. However, like many of the other big companies that were operating in the cattle business at that time, this outfit was completely wiped out by the hard winter of '86-'87. Shortly after this disaster, Coble arranged for new personal financing, through his family connections in the east, and acquired new ranch holdings in the upper Horse Creek and Iron Mountain country, near Cheyenne. He began to restock that range and soon had a large outfit operating, with his headquarters on the headwaters of Chugwater Creek, near Iron Mountain.

About the same time that Coble (who had become a very domineering and vindictive man) was getting his operations underway, two small ranchers, Kels P. Nickell and James V. Miller, both filed on homesteads which were only a short distance from the big Iron Mountain headquarters ranch of John Coble. The result was that almost immediately, trouble began to develop in the area, with relations between the three neighbors in a constant turmoil and with feelings becoming extremely bitter on all sides. Coble was supposed to have made statements in which he accused both Nickell and Miller of stealing his cattle. A fight developed between Coble and Nickell in which Nickell was supposed to have pulled a knife on Coble. A few days later, Coble had Kels Nickell arrested, charging him with attempted murder. Nickell claimed self-defense and was acquitted by the jury.

In addition to the trouble between Coble and Nickell, there was also bad blood between the two small ranchers, Nickell and Miller. They also had had a knife fight which had resulted in a court battle. Kels Nickell then brought in a band of sheep and started grazing them on the open range, which added additional fuel to the fires of hatred which were already burning in the Iron Mountain country.

While all of these conflicts were occurring, the Iron Mountain School Board had employed Miss Glendolene Kimmel; a very attractive young lady with very definite oriental features, who had been born in the Hawaiian Islands to a German father and a Polynesian mother, as the teacher of the local school, with arrangements having been made for her to board at the James Miller home.

When Tom Horn returned to the Coble ranch in the spring of 1901, he soon became acquainted with the new school teacher and found her to be quite interesting. Consequently, he began to spend quite a lot of his time at the Miller ranch. Glendolene fell hard for this big, dashing, mature cowboy, with his striking features and his stories of adventures in the Southwest, including his involvements in the Indian wars. This colorful cowboy was soon her ideal, and she refused to believe the stories that were going around about Tom Horn being a professional gunman and a ruthless, cold-blooded killer.

At the same time that Tom Horn was carrying on his flirtation with Glendolene Kimmel, he was also starting to cultivate a friendly relationship with Kels Nickell, to gain his complete confidence, apparently with a very definite plan and purpose in mind. In carrying out this plan, Tom would stop in at the Nickell ranch quite frequently and listen to the stories that Nickell would tell of the reasons for his hatred of Coble. Horn would give the impression of being in sympathy with Nickell's sentiments, and would express personal dislike for John Coble. He would also pretend that the only reason that he was staying at the Coble ranch was so that he could watch Coble and try to get something on him.

It was at daybreak on the morning of July 18, 1901, that Willie Nickell, the thirteen-year-old son of Kels Nickell, put on an old hat and coat of his father's as protection against the chilly morning air in that high country and went out to the barn, where he saddled a horse that his father usually rode and left for the Iron Mountain railway station to take care of an errand for his father. About ten minutes later, when young Willie Nickell reached the horse pasture gate, about three quarters of a mile from his home, and had stepped off his horse to open the gate, there was the sudden sharp crack of a rifle shot. The bullet struck the boy in the back, spinning him around, then knocking him to the ground. His body was found by his brother later that same day.

When an investigation of the tracks at the scene of the killing was made the next day, there were indications that the boy had regained his feet after having been struck by the first shot, and had walked a few steps before being hit in the back by a second bullet. This time he did not get up.

A search was made by the sheriff of Laramie County, with the help of riders from some of the adjoining ranches, of the entire area near where the shooting had occurred, in the hopes of finding tracks or other evidence that would give some indication of who the killer of the boy had been. Some tracks were found in a pile of rocks about three hundred yards from where the body had been found, which gave the appearance of having been made by a man who had stood there for some time in his stocking feet. Other indications were also found that the killer had left his horse tied to a tree some distance from the scene of the killing, and that he had then walked to the pile of rocks, where he had taken off his boots and had been hidden among the rocks, waiting for his victim to appear. It was assumed by the sheriff and the neighboring ranchers who had helped with the search, that the killer had mistaken the boy for his father, Kels Nickell, due to the fact that the boy was riding his father's horse, and also wearing his father's heavy coat and hat.

When a coroner's inquest was held shortly after the killing of the boy, Kels Nickell accused James Miller of the murder of his son. However, Miller had no trouble in furnishing proof — testimony by several people, including visitors at his ranch — that he was at home at the time of the shooting and could not possibly have committed the crime. When the name of Tom Horn was mentioned at the hearing as a possible suspect, Kels Nickell came to his defense, saying that he knew that his friend Tom Horn did not kill his boy. In addition, an alibi was also furnished, to the effect that Tom Horn was on a train between Cheyenne and Laramie at the time that the shooting occurred. This left the authorities without anyone as a logical suspect.

Early on the morning of August 4, about two weeks after the killing of Willie Nickell, Kels Nickell, the father, was shot three times from ambush as he walked from his cabin to the corral to feed his sheep. When an investigation was made, it was determined that these three shots were fired from a distance of about six hundred yards, with a high-powered rifle. The first shot knocked Kels Nickell to the ground, with a bullet though his hip, the second shot broke his left arm, and the third shot just grazed his left side.

After the shooting, Nickell's wife and remaining son loaded the wounded man into a wagon and took him to a hospital in Cheyenne, thirty-five miles distant, where he eventually recovered. In the meantime, however, while Kels Nickell was in the hospital recovering from his wounds, a group of unidentified riders rode into his band of sheep while they were grazing near his ranch, and clubbed a large number of them to death. When Nickell was released from the hospital, he again accused James Miller and his two sons of this attempt upon his life and the slaughter of his sheep. After these charges were made, the three Millers were all arrested and taken to Cheyenne, but when no evidence of their guilt was produced, they were all released from custody. Tom Horn, among others, was also questioned in connection with this case, but he furnished the alibi that he was in Denver with a carload of horses when the shooting of Kels Nickell occurred.

It was about this time that Deputy United States Marshal Joe Le Fors, who was working out of the Cheyenne office of the United States Marshal, was brought into the case of Willie Nickell by the sheriff of Laramie County. Le Fors had the reputation for being a very thorough and persistant peace officer who would take any steps that he considered necessary to accomplish his purpose. Within a few weeks, this Deputy U.S. Marshal was spending a considerable amount of his time in the Iron Mountain country, going over the ground and questioning all of the people in the neighborhood, including Glendolene Kimmel, who gave the Deputy Marshal the impression of being very anxious to divert suspicion from Tom Horn. As Le Fors continued his investigation, he spent several days in Laramie, where he found a liveryman who remembered that Tom Horn had brought a hard-ridden horse to his barn on the day that Willie Nickell was killed, and that it had taken the horse over a week to recover from the ride.

As his investigation of the case progressed, Joe Le Fors became convinced that Tom Horn was the killer and that the only question was one of developing the evidence, and proof, that would stand up in court. With this thought in mind, he worked quietly for two or three months and then set a trap for the suspected killer. His first move was to send word by John Coble to Tom Horn that he knew of a cattleman in Montana who wanted to hire a good cattle detective. Within a few days, Horn contacted Le Fors to check on the job. At this time, the Deputy Marshal took the position that he would need to get more information from the Montana cattleman. He made an appointment for Horn to come to his office at a certain time in the near future. Joe Le Fors then brought in a carpenter and had him make certain alterations in the partition between his office and an adjoining room, in such a manner that voices would carry clearly through the partition.

When Tom Horn came in at the appointed time, Deputy Marshal Joe Le Fors greeted him in a very friendly manner and then brought in the letter from the Montana cattleman, along with a full bottle of good whiskey. At the same time that the letter and the job in Montana were being discussed, heavy drinking also got under way, with Joe Le Fors (who was a good, two-fisted bottle drinker himself) leading the conversation as he told wild stories of his own experiences, some of which bordered upon the illegal. As the storytelling gained momentum and became more confidential, Tom Horn, the man who had always been extremely closemouthed and cautious during his entire lifetime, under the influence of the liquor and led on by the confidential and leading questions of Joe Le Fors, opened up and began to tell of his accomplishments as a gunman and also to brag of the men that he had killed.

Le Fors, feeling that now was the time, finally asked the question, "You got six hundred dollars apiece for killing Lewis and Powell, didn't you, Tom? You were paid three hundred dollars for the Nickell job. Why did you cut the price?"

Horn said, "I got twenty-one hundred dollars for killing three men and shooting five times at another."

"Tell me about Willie, Tom."

"I shot the kid at three hundred yards. It was the best shot and the dirtiest trick that I ever done."

"You are the best man to cover up a trail that I ever saw. I found no trail at the Nickell killing and I am a good trailer."

"Sure you didn't, I pulled off my boots."

This conversation between Tom Horn and Joe Le Fors was transcribed in the adjoining room by Charlie Ohnhaus, who was a court reporter. The information which was contained in this transcription of the conversation was the basis for the warrant which was issued on Monday, January 13, 1902, for the arrest of Tom Horn. This warrant was served on the same day that it was issued, in a very cautious and careful manner. Tom Horn was approached as he was walking down the street, by Laramie County Sheriff Ed Smalley, Deputy Sheriff Dick Proctor, and Cheyenne Chief of Police Sandy McKneal. While these three officers were talking with Horn, Joe Le Fors, who had also walked up, reached out with an apparent gesture of friendship, to shake hands with Horn. Then, just at the same instant that Le Fors had a strong grip on Horn's hand, Ed Smalley reached across and pulled Horn's revolver from the holster. He then covered Horn with his own gun and placed him under arrest.

The date of the trial was set for October 7, 1902, with Judge Richard H. Scott presiding, and with Tom Horn well represented by a battery of high-priced attorneys (who were apparently being paid by people other than Tom Horn), consisting of John W. Lacey, T. E. Burke and associates, Clark Watson, and T. Blake Kennedy. The testimony introduced at the trial by the prosecution was based principally upon the transcript of the conversation which had taken place in Joe Le Fors' office between Horn and Le Fors. The attorneys for the defense based their case almost entirely upon the fact that Tom Horn was drunk at the time that this conversation took place. They contended that all of the statements that were made by Horn, under the circumstances, were just drunken bragging which were made while he was attempting to match the stories that were being told by the Deputy United States Marshal. The attorneys for the defense also claimed that all of the other testimony which had been presented by the prosecution was purely circumstantial, and that a man should not be convicted of murder on this type of evidence.

When the jury finally came back into the courtroom, after having been out for several hours, it was with the verdict, "Guilty of murder in the first degree." Sentence was then passed on November 12, 1902, by Judge Scott. "It is ordered that you, Tom Horn, may be taken hence to the jail of Laramie County and there confined until Friday, the 9th of January, 1903, on which day, between the hours of nine o'clock in the forenoon and three o'clock in the afternoon, you will be taken by the Sheriff of Laramie County to a place prepared by him, convenient to the jail and there hanged by the neck until you are dead, and may God have mercy on your soul."

Frank Jones, along with Charlie Irwin, a neighboring rancher, visited Tom Horn in his cell in the Cheyenne jail, while he was awaiting execution. When they returned home after the visit, they said that they found Tom busy and apparently contented, as he worked at his favorite hobby, which he had learned while he was living with the Apaches in Arizona. This was the braiding and plaiting of hackamores, quirts, and bridles from strips of whang leather and rawhide, which he intertwined with various colors of hair that had been pulled from the tails of horses, of different colors, then brought to him in the jail by people on the outside. They also said that Tom appeared to be in good spirits and laughed and joked as though he did not have a care in the world. Perhaps he did not. He just realized that the string had run out.

Appeals, of course, were made to the higher courts by

Horn's attorneys for a new trial, during the period of time before the date set for the execution, but these appeals were not successful. However, temporary stays of execution were granted up to the final date of November 20, 1903. Then shortly before the execution was to occur, a last, desperate appeal for clemency was made to Governor Chatterton by John Coble, Duncan Clark, and Glendolene Kimmel, but the governor declined to intervene.

When the day came that was set for the hanging, a completely calm and composed forty-three-year-old Tom Horn, joking with the few friends who had been admitted to the hanging, stepped up on the gallows without the slightest indication of fear or concern. When Charlie Irwin, one of the few friends who had been admitted, asked him whether he would like for him and his brother, Frank Irwin, to sing a song before the hanging, he said, "Yes, Charlie, I would like that." The two Irwin brothers, in their tenor voices, then sang that old song, "Life is Like a Mountain Railroad," which was quite popular around cow camps at that time. When the last notes of the song had died, the trap was sprung; with the large hangman's knot, with its conventional thirteen wraps, striking the condemned man alongside of the head as he fell, knocking him unconscious. Sixteen minutes later, Dr. George Johnson and Dr. John H. Conway, the two doctors in attendance at the hanging, pronounced Tom Horn dead.

Glendolene Kimmel, the woman who probably had the greatest influence of any woman upon Tom Horn during his lifetime (except his mother), continued to plead his case with anyone who would listen. In addition, she also visited him every few weeks during the entire time that he was in the county jail in Cheyenne awaiting execution. She went to her grave many years later (still unmarried) with a remaining faith and conviction that Tom Horn did not kill Willie Nickell.

Regardless of any other conclusions that might be reached in connection with the life of Tom Horn, or with the motivation which influenced him, the fact remains that beyond any other factor, he was obviously a product of his environment.

21 The appointing of territorial governors for the territories of the West by the presidents of the United States prior to statehood was the source of many bitter conflicts and controversies between the federal government and the people of the West. This was particularly true with the cattlemen, who were a proud and independent lot under any set of circumstances. As a matter of fact, there has always been something about sitting high on a good horse that seems to give the man on horseback a feeling of power and importance. Perhaps there is also something in the feeling of self-confidence, gained in this manner, which is responsible for inspiring the man on horseback to do big things. At least, a large number of the West's outstanding members of the Congress have been men who got their start and gained recognition as men of courage and ability in the cattle business, and then went on to make a place for themselves in the history of their country.

One of the most controversial of the appointments as territorial governor of Wyoming, was that of cattleman George W. Baxter. A graduate of West Point, he had served as a cavalry officer with the army in the territories of Wyoming and the Dakotas from 1877 until the fall of 1881. He resigned from the army and started in the cattle business for himself, in the Territory of Wyoming, with the headquarters of his LU outfit on Grass Creek, in the southern part of the Big Horn basin. Later, at the time that the Union Pacific Railroad Company had offered its land for sale in southeastern Wyoming, this ambitious young cattleman expanded his operations still further by purchasing thirty thousand acres of railroad land in the area east of Cheyenne. All of this land was of course in alternate sections, which resulted in a checkerboard ownership. Baxter, as was customary, had then fenced the outside perimeter of his purchase, which had the effect of enclosing all of the alternate sections of public domain, or government land.

The appointment of George W. Baxter as territorial governor of Wyoming, was made by President Grover Cleveland about two years after his election for his first term as president, with Baxter being sworn in as territorial governor on November 11, 1886.

At the time of his appointment, the conflicts between the cattlemen and the federal government over fences on government land had been building up to the point where

President Cleveland had developed an obsession on the subject and was fully determined that he was going to force the removal of all fences from government land. With this tough attitude on the part of the president, territorial appointee George W. Baxter had been questioned at some length at the time of his appointment as to whether he had any government land under fence. Baxter had declared that he did not, basing his position upon legal opinion to the effect that the fencing of the outside boundary of railroad land, where alternate sections were involved, did not constitute a violation of the federal laws pertaining to the fencing of government land. However, when President Cleveland learned later that George Baxter actually did have government land enclosed within his fences, he apparently felt that, regardless of legal opinion, Baxter had willfully deceived him when he did not divulge all of the facts in connection with his fencing of the alternate sections of railroad land. Consequently, the president had the cattleman removed from office after he had served only forty-five days as territorial governor, with the effective date of the removal being set for December 20, 1886.

Following the removal of George Baxter, Grover Cleveland, on January 24, 1887, appointed Thomas Moonlight (a resident of the state of Kansas) as the governor of the Territory of Wyoming. Moonlight, a Democrat, was a strong Cleveland supporter who had just been defeated in a race for the governorship of the state of Kansas. Consequently, this appointment by Grover Cleveland was construed generally as a very definite political appointment and was deeply resented by the proud and independent people of the Territory of Wyoming. From their point of view, there was an implication involved in this appointment to the effect that there was no one in the Territory of Wyoming who was sufficiently competent or trustworthy to serve as governor of the territory. This sentiment was especially prevalent among the big cattlemen, who were furious anyway over the removal of George Baxter, particularly when this removal was over the controversial fence issue and in the face of what they considered to be competent legal opinion that, in this instance, there was no violation of federal law involved.

With this increasing bitterness, and the general feelings of animosity over the appointment that existed among the people of the territory, Moonlight was soon embroiled in bitter conflicts, not only with the cattlemen, but also with the territorial legislature, which was composed and controlled, to a great degree by the big cattlemen of the territory. Territorial Governor Moonlight was also a man with an almost complete lack of tact and diplomacy in dealing with the people of the territory. The ultimate result was that the administration of Governor Thomas Moonlight was one of almost complete failure.

There were changes, however, in the relationship between the cattlemen and the federal government when, in the presidential election of 1888 Benjamin Harrison, a Republican, who was much more cooperative with the cattlemen of the West, was elected president of the United States. Shortly after President Harrison took office, he appointed Francis E. Warren, also a Republican (who of course was a livestock man), as governor of the Territory of Wyoming. Governor Warren had previously served in that capacity from February 28, 1885 to November 11. 1886, during the administration of President Arthur. Warren was recognized not only as a good administrator, but also a man who understood the problems of this young and developing territory of the West.

Some of the more judicious and level-headed of the

cattlemen, including Judge Joseph Carey and Governor Francis E. Warren, had come to the conclusion that the time had arrived for some of them to start a movement to get the Territory of Wyoming admitted to the Union. It was their belief that, in addition to the other benefits of statehood, the very serious lawless situation which existed in the territory, which was becoming increasingly critical, could be brought under closer control through a greater degree of local responsibility. Consequently, a petition for statehood was drafted in committee and approved by the 1888 session of the territorial legislature. This petition was then forwarded to Judge Joseph M. Carey, who was serving at that time in Washington, D.C., as a delegate to Congress from the Territory of Wyoming. When Judge Carey received this petition, he immediately presented it to Congress and also arranged for the introduction of bills, in both the House and the Senate, to provide for an enabling act. These bills, however, became pigeonholed in committee and did not receive prompt action.

In the meantime, Governor Warren, impatient with the progress that was being made by the Wyoming statehood bills in the Congress, proceeded with the calling of a constitutional convention, to be convened in Cheyenne during the month of September, 1889. Of the fifty-five delegates who were elected to this convention, eighteen were attorneys, and they, of course, actually handled most of the work in connection with the drafting of the constitution. However, the cattlemen were well represented by several influential men who were competent in matters of this nature, including the very eloquent and persuasive George W. Baxter, who exerted considerable influence upon the provisions which were contained in the final draft of the constitution, which was submitted to the people and approved by them in a special election held on

November 5, 1889. Following the ratification of the constitution, a committee was selected from among the members of the constitutional convention to present a memorial to the Congress, "praying for admission of Wyoming as one of the States of the Union."

When Wyoming had first been given recognition as a territory in 1869, the territorial constitution had contained a provision giving women the right to vote within the territory. When the constitutional convention was convened, this was one of the first subjects that came up for discussion. Many of the delegates argued that, if this provision was contained in the constitution, the application for statehood would run into stiff oppositon in the Congress from many of the United States congressmen and senators, who would contend that a precedent was being established which could ultimately create a situation where women would also be demanding the right to vote in their states. Regardless of these arguments, when the Wyoming constitution was finally unanimously adopted by the convention, in a roll call vote, it still contained the provision for women's suffrage.

When the petition for statehood by the Territory of Wyoming, along with the constitution and the necessary enabling legislation, came up for discussion in the Congress, there was, as had been anticipated, strong opposition to the women's suffrage provision. There was additional opposition based upon the proposition that Wyoming, according to the best estimates, had a population of only about 60,000 whereas the generally recognized requirement for statehood was 100,000. There had, however, been previous exceptions made to this requirement; as when the adjoining states of Montana and South Dakota had been admitted to statehood in 1889 with considerably less than the 100,000 minimum population required. Another point that was heavily stressed by delegate Carey in his arguments before the Congress was the need for greater local responsibility in coping with the problems of lawlessness which existed in the territory, in addition to the desire of the people to elect their own governor and other public officials, instead of having them appointed by presidential decision, which was oftentimes motivated by political considerations.

When the debate ended, the Congress then approved the bill for Wyoming statehood, which was signed by President Harrison on July 10, 1890. As of that date, the Territory of Wyoming became a state. This bill, when signed by the president, still contained the provision for women's suffrage. Consequently, Wyoming gained the recognition as being the first state in the Union to grant its women the right to vote. In a speech which she made in Cheyenne following the signing of the bill, Susan B. Anthony, the great national women's suffrage leader, hailed Wyoming as the first true republic that the world had ever seen. Also, in a speech that George W. Baxter made at the Wyoming statehood celebration, held in Cheyenne shortly after the president's signature to the bill had been obtained and Wyoming had officially become a state, he said, "It means the dawning of a brighter day: the beginning of an era of unparalleled prosperity for the State."

Only five days after the signing of the Wyoming statehood bill, territorial Governor Francis E. Warren issued a proclamation calling for an election to be held on September 11, 1890, to elect a governor and other state officials, in compliance with the requirements of the federal laws pertaining to the admission of a territory to statehood. In this election, Francis E. Warren, who at that time was serving as territorial governor, was elected as the first governor of the state of Wyoming. Also, in a meeting of the state legislature, held in November of that year, Joseph M. Carey, who was referred to for many years afterward as the "Father of Wyoming Statehood" due to his dogged determination and perseverance in getting the statehood bill approved by the Congress, was elected by the legislature as the first United States Senator from Wyoming. A few days later, the legislature also elected Governor Francis E. Warren as the other senator from Wyoming. Shortly afterwards, Warren resigned from the office of governor. The secretary of state, Amos W. Barber, automatically became the governor of the new state of Wyoming, to serve until the next general election.

The two senators continued to be the wheelhorses in Wyoming politics and governmental affairs for many years afterwards, with Joseph M. Carey serving in the United States Senate until 1895. In the election of 1910, he again ran for public office, this time as a candidate for the office of governor of the state of Wyoming. Carey was elected to this office by quite a substantial margin. During this same period, and for many years afterward, the venerable Senator Francis E. Warren continued to represent the state of Wyoming in the United States Senate, until he had served for a total of thirty-seven years, one of the longest periods of service of record in that branch of the government. *The New York Times* said of Senator Warren, "few Americans have led such useful lives." In addition to their lifetimes of activities in public affairs, both Francis E. Warren and Joseph M. Carey continued their large ranching activities in southeastern Wyoming, where they also maintained their homes for the rest of their lives.

Another pioneer Wyoming cattleman who made a substantial contribution to the early political life and development of the state of Wyoming, was John B. Kendrick, who became known as the "Cattle King of Sheridan County." This fine cattleman was born in Cherokee County, Texas, on September 6, 1857, where his father and grandfather before him had been among the early cattlemen in the state of Texas. As a consequence, young John Kendrick had grown up and had spent all of his early life in the cattle business in that state. When he was twenty-one years of age, he made his first trip north, with a trail herd from Matagorda Bay on the Gulf of Mexico, to the headwaters of the Running Water in Wyoming. Young Kendrick liked what he found in this northern high plains country and as a result he stayed on, working as a cowboy and saving his money, until he eventually became foreman for a large cattle outfit which was operating in the Powder River country of central Wyoming. In 1884, he made another trail drive with a herd from Williams County, Texas, to the headwaters of the Cheyenne River, in eastern Wyoming. Shortly afterward, this venturesome young man decided to go into the cattle business on his own, and within a few years he had built up a large outfit, running many thousands of head of cattle in Sheridan County in the extreme northern part of Wyoming.

John B. Kendrick first entered into the political life of the state of Wyoming when he served for a period of time in the state legislature, where he soon became recognized as a man with ability in public affairs. Then, in 1914, this cattleman ran for the office of governor and was elected by quite a substantial margin. Two years later, before his term as governor had expired, he entered the race for the United States Senate, and, with the strong backing of the cattlemen of the state, he had no problem in winning that election. During his many years of service in the United States Senate, John B. Kendrick became recognized as a very able statesman, and he continued to serve in that capacity until his death, seventeen years later.

The West was a big country, and produced many other men of exceptional ability from among its pioneer settlers. These men were molded in a life of danger and hardship, and were accustomed to meeting the challenges of life as they occurred. They were from this big country, where there were no particular restrictions to their way of life; nor were there any built-in restrictions to their vision. In this big country, a man could "see" for quite a distance.

22 The coming of statehood to Wyoming did not immediately bring an end to the many conflicts and controversies which existed and had been building up for many years between the big cattlemen and the small ranchers. These conflicts were particularly bitter in the Powder River country, with the center of this conflict being in Johnson County, which included the Hole-in-the-wall country. The small ranchers in Johnson County were an especially independent lot who deeply resented the controls which had been imposed upon them under the maverick law. This situation had continued to become more aggravated until open revolt against these controls was in the process of developing, and armed conflict with the big cattlemen seemed inevitable.

The situation finally reached the point where, in defiance of the big cattlemen and the Wyoming Stockgrowers' Association, the small ranchers of Johnson County had formed a livestock association of their own, which was called the Northern Wyoming Farmers' and Stockgrowers' Association, with its offices at the county seat in Buffalo, Wyoming. This association did not, of course, have official recognition or any authority from the state of Wyoming. The fact of the matter was that many of its members had been blackballed as rustlers by the Wyoming Stockgrowers' Association, and had been denied permission to work with the regularly authorized roundup wagons.

It was true that there were many cattle thieves and rustlers in Johnson County, as there were in all of the other areas of the high plains country. Also, there had always been a long string of grub line riders (in the wintertime) in the Powder River country, with practically all of these carefree riders of the grub line being cowboys who worked for the big outfits in the summertime and then rode the long grub line from ranch to ranch in the wintertime. Under these circumstances, it was generally considered (in that part of the country) to be the responsibility of, or at least a courtesy on the part of, the grub line rider, when he stopped in at a small ranch for a stay of a few days or a few weeks, for him to furnish the meat for the outfit while he was there.

The little ranchers did not ask too many questions about the kind of meat that they were eating or where it came from. This grub line rider meat was just generally referred to as "elk," but then it was also common knowledge among the people in that part of the country that there were two kinds of elk. In addition to the kind that grew antlers, there were also the "slow elk" that usually had long horns and wore the brand of some big cattle outfit. These animals did not have as much of a wild taste as the kind with antlers, and were oftentimes preferred by some of the small ranchers and their families. Naturally, it was always the desire of the courteous grub line rider to try to please his host and provide the type of meat which would be most acceptable.

Regardless of the losses which were occurring due to the activities of the cattle thieves and rustlers and to the limited amount of beef which was being furnished to the small ranchers by the grub line riders, the loss situation was being exaggerated by the big cattlemen out of proportion to the actual size of the problem. In many instances, the shortage of cattle count being blamed upon the rustlers by the big cattlemen resulted from other natural causes, such as winter blizzards, poison weed, black leg, and from many other hazards of the cattle business.

As these exaggerated claims of losses continued to build up among the cattlemen, some of the younger and more impetuous members of the Wyoming Stockgrowers' Association were advocating that an armed force be organized for the purpose of going into Johnson County and "wiping out" all of the small ranchers and others who had been accused by members of the Wyoming Stockgrowers' Association of being rustlers, as well as to deal with the leaders of the revolt against the jurisdiction of the Wyoming Stockgrowers' Association. In their opinion, complete control had been vested in the association, under the maverick law and was not subject to any other interpretation by the small ranchers.

To add fuel to this fire, a notice was received by the Wyoming Stockgrowers' Association early in 1892 from the Northern Wyoming Farmers' and Stockgrowers' Association, in which they stated that they would hold an independent roundup, beginning on May 1 of that year. This was a month before the regularly and officially scheduled roundup that was held under the auspices of the Wyoming Stockgrowers' Association. This declaration on the part of the small ranchers of Johnson County was taken by the members of the Wyoming Stockgrowers' Association as being definite, open defiance of their authority under the maverick law. This action immediately brought the conflict to a head.

Almost immediately after receiving this notice, meetings of the big cattlemen were being held, in which the desirability of taking quick punitive action against the rebellious small ranchers of Johnson County was seriously discussed. Almost all of the conversations in connection with this plan took place around the bar, or in the meeting rooms of the Cheyenne Club, where the liquor flowed freely, firing the imagination and impulsiveness of some of the younger men, many of whom were anxious to impress the really big and influential cattlemen with their courage and their willingness to risk their lives for the cause. As a consequence, they were quite extreme in the statements that they made and the viewpoints which they expressed, with the result that when the effects of the liquor wore off, they felt that they could not back down on the radical positions which they had taken in the open meeting.

As a result of the positions which were taken in these meetings, a wild scheme was soon actually underway to organize a punitive expedition to invade Johnson County and to wipe out the rustlers, as well as to punish their tormentors among the small and independent ranchers in that area who were defying the association. To some degree, this activity was being led by ex-Civil War army officers who were living in the past and were visualizing themselves as leading a big military expedition against their enemies. As a matter of fact, the entire planned operation was a matter of shadowboxing with a somewhat imaginary, large force of organized rustlers.

While this planning was under way, the really big and influential cattlemen more or less sat on the sidelines, where they appeared to give support and encouragement to the plan but at the same time were very careful to keep their own skirts clean. They were staying in a position where, if the big invasion plans worked out satisfactorily, they could claim their share of the credit but, if the big deal backfired and wound up in trouble, they could disclaim any personal responsibility and involvement in what obviously had been an illegal operation.

In the early spring months of 1892, a large number of well-known professional gunmen, with low-slung open hosters, from Texas and Arizona began to show up on the streets of Cheyenne and Denver. Many of these men had, at different times during their lifetimes, been on both sides of the law before they had been recruited as paid gunfighters by representatives of the Wyoming cattlemen to participate in the invasion of Johnson County. In later years, there were reports that Tom Horn was the man who actually handled the recruiting of the hired gunmen from the Southwest for the Wyoming cattlemen while he was still working out of the offices of the Pinkerton Detective Agency in Denver, but this report has never been confirmed.

Among the leaders who were active in organizing and promoting the Johnson County War and who were also active in arranging for the hiring of the professional gunfighters, were Major Frank Wolcott, who had fought as an army officer during the Civil War and was considered to be an impetuous fire-eater; ex-Governor George Baxter, who was vice-president of the Wyoming Stockgrowers' Association and a former army officer; and H. B. Ijams, the secretary of the Wyoming Stockgrowers' Association, who furnished the list of names from the records of the association of the men in Johnson County who had been accused from time to time of being rustlers by the members of the association, as well as the names of the leaders of the revolts against the controls of the association. The Johnson County invasion was never admitted, or proven, to have been an official action of the Wyoming Stockgrowers' Association. However, it was so closely interrelated that it would be impossible to entirely separate its activities in connection with the invasion from the offical acts of that organization. Regardless of the question of the association's participation in the developing of the plans for the invasion, the fact remains that, according to the plan which was adopted by the big cattlemen, all of the people whose names were on the list were to be wiped out, either with bullets or on the end of a rope.

The twentieth annual meeting of the Wyoming Stockgrowers' Association was convened in Cheyenne on Monday morning, April 4, 1892, with a roll call of the attendance being taken, and with George Baxter, vice-president, presiding. The president, John Clay, was on a business trip to Scotland. The attendance, as reported by the secretary of the association, was the largest on record in several years. However, the minutes that were written and all other records of the proceedings at the meeting are extremely brief. Regardless of this fact, it was said afterwards that there was a lot of excitement and an air of anticipation around the meeting, particularly on the afternoon of the second day of the convention, when a special Union Pacific train from Denver pulled into the railroad yards at Cheyenne.

This special train, consisting of three passenger cars with all blinds drawn, was immediately shunted onto a siding, away from public view. Frenzied activity was carried on during the rest of the afternoon and far into the night, with seventy-eight head of fine, grain-fed saddle horses, including a few broken to harness (branded only with an "A" on the left shoulder), being loaded on cattle cars. On this same siding, wagons, harness, saddles, tents, rifles, ammunition, and other supplies of various kinds were being loaded onto other railway cars. All of these cars were then coupled onto the special train waiting in the railroad yards.

In the meantime, the meeting of the stockgrowers' association had adjourned and many of the cattlemen who had been attending that meeting found their way to the special train in the railroad yards. Quietly, during the night, the special train pulled out over the tracks of the Cheyenne and Northern Railroad, bound for Casper, one hundred eighty miles distant. Many of the men who were on board the train were the professional gunfighters who had been imported from the Southwest, with the greater number of them having come into Cheyenne on the special train from Denver. There were also quite a large number of local cattlemen on board, including some of the foremen from the big outfits. One thing, however, was very noticeable: when the chips were down and the hot lead about to fly, many of the big cattlemen who had talked the loudest and who had been the most vociferous in advocating the invasion of Johnson County found at the last minute that they had "urgent business" elsewhere and were not on board the train when it moved out of the railroad yards at Cheyenne.

When the "Special" pulled in before daybreak on a siding at Casper, the railway cars were spotted without delay at the stockyards, where the horses and wagons were quickly unloaded, with all of the supplies and equipment being transferred to the chuck and supply wagons. While this loading was going on, a few small groups of riders from some of the big outfits in the Casper area rode in quietly and joined the invading forces at the railway siding. When this cavalcade, composed of fifty-six riders with four chuck and supply wagons, pulled out on the trail and headed northward into the Powder River country, they were under the command of Major Frank Wolcott, assisted by W. C. Irvine (another large operator in the cattle business from the Cheyenne area) and Frank Canton, an ex-sheriff of Johnson County who at that time was in the employ of the Wyoming Stockgrowers' Association.

The destination of this punitive expedition was the small cow town of Buffalo, the county seat of Johnson County, located approximately one hundred miles to the north. When the column of riders and wagons was six miles out on the trail to Buffalo (with a light snow falling, whipped by a cold north wind), orders were given to the cooks on the chuck wagons to pull into some rough country nearby, where there was some shelter, and set up their tents and cook breakfast.

While this was being done, the leaders of the expedition spent considerable time in getting the outfit shaken down and organized. Consequently, it was late the next evening when the cavalcade of tired men rode in at the Tisdale Ranch on Willow Creek, sixty-five miles north of

Casper. The owner of this ranch (not related to the Tisdale who had been dry gulched the previous year as a suspected cattle rustler) had been working closely with the big cattlemen in their plans for organizing the punitive expedition to wipe out the suspected rustlers in Johnson County.

Early the next morning, Mike Shonsey, the foreman for George Baxter's cow outfit who had been scouting ahead of the main column, rode back into the camp at the Tisdale Ranch and reported to the leaders of the invasion forces that there were thirteen suspected rustlers who were on the list, including Nate Champion, who was one of the leaders of the revolt against the controls of the Wyoming Stockgrowers' Association. They were holed up at the KC Ranch (near where the town of Kaycee, Wyoming, is now located), on the north fork of the Powder River, about eighteen miles north of their camp at the Tisdale Ranch.

A conference was immediately held among the leaders of the invasion forces. Differences of opinion occurred, with some of the leaders wanting to make a raid that night against the men who were holed up at the KC Ranch, while others advocated bypassing the KC and moving on quickly to the town of Buffalo with the objective of capturing Red Angus, the sheriff of Johnson County, and his deputies. They also wanted to get possession of the rifles stored at the courthouse, belonging to the local militia, before they could be distributed to the residents of Johnson County.

In the end, the opinions of the leaders who were advocating the raid on the KC Ranch prevailed. Consequently, during the night, the column of riders moved out from the Tisdale Ranch, with the words "wipe 'em out" being heard on all sides.

In the early morning hours of April 9, 1892, with the

cold wind still blowing, the heavily armed raiders moved in and surrounded the KC ranch buildings, with some of the men taking cover in the barn while others hid in the willow thickets along the creek, and still others burrowed into the deep snow banks where there was some cover behind small ridges near the cabin. There they all waited for daybreak and for some signs of activity around the big log cabin.

It was shortly after daybreak when a man carrying a water bucket walked out of the cabin door and went to the creek for water. There he was quietly captured, bound, and gagged by some of the raiders who were hidden in the brush along the stream. A few minutes later, another man left the cabin and went to the barn, with the intention of feeding the horses. He, too, was captured without disturbance by the raiders who had taken cover in the barn. It was later learned that the two men who were captured by the raiders were trappers by the names of Jones and Walker who had stopped in at the KC Ranch the evening before in order to get out of the snowstorm.

The third man to leave the cabin that morning was Nick Ray, who was on the list of rustler suspects who were scheduled to be wiped out by the invaders. When Ray was only a short distance from the cabin door, he was knocked to the ground by a volley of rifle fire from the raiders who lay hidden only a short distance away. Nate Champion, who was the only other man in the cabin and who was also on the list, hearing the rifle fire, stepped to the door of the cabin, where he appeared momentarily with his gun in his hand. However, due to the heavy rifle fire, he was immediately forced to duck back inside of the cabin. While this was occurring, Nick Ray, although seriously wounded, was trying to drag himself back to the cabin. When the wounded man was a few feet from the door,

Nate Champion ran out, picked him up like a baby, and carried him back inside of the cabin, where he died shortly afterwards from his wounds. Consequently, Nate Champion made his stand alone for the next several hours while he hoped that help would show up.

While the battle was under way, Jack Flagg, another small rancher on the Powder River near the KC (and who was also on the invaders' list of suspected rustlers), happened to ride up on a hill overlooking the KC Ranch. There, he saw what was happening. Though he was on horseback, he was accompanied by his seventeen-year-old stepson who was driving a team of horses hitched to a light wagon. The Flaggs, seeing that there was trouble ahead, immediately turned back, with the team at a run until they were well out of range of rifle fire, where they quickly stripped the harness from one of the horses, which the boy then mounted bareback. The two of them headed across Crazy Woman Creek and on into the little cow town of Buffalo, with several of Wolcott's gunmen in hot pursuit. However, the Flaggs were both well mounted on fresh horses and made their escape without too much trouble, spreading the alarm as they made their way rapidly on into their county seat town of Buffalo.

As the fight at the KC continued, Nate Champion knocked some of the chinking from between the logs on all four sides of the cabin and then fired alternately from all sides, giving the impression to Wolcott's gunmen that there were several men inside the cabin. With this strategy, Champion continued to carry on his courageous defense against fifty to one odds, until four o'clock in the afternoon when the raiders finally loaded a hayrack, which was mounted on a wagon, with dry hay and wood and then, setting the hay on fire, they pushed the wagon before them until they had shoved it alongside the cabin. It was only a few minutes before the cabin, which was built from pine logs, was also on fire. When the heat inside of the cabin became unbearable, Nate Champion finally ran from the doorway shooting as he ran, for a distance of about fity yards before he was cut down with twenty-eight bullet holes through his body.

Obviously, if the raiders had known that there was only one man inside of the cabin, instead of the thirteen that had been reported by Mike Shonsey, they would certainly have forced the issue much sooner. However, this single-handed defense of the cabin by Nate Champion is certainly one of the most outstanding and remarkable feats of sheer courage and fortitude to be found anywhere in the history of the West. Perhaps most remarkable is the fact that, in addition to defending himself against such overwhelming odds for over eight hours, this unusual man also wrote a very vivid account of the fight while it was under way in a small talley book which he had in his pocket. This blood-stained notebook, which was made public, was found on Nate Champion's body after the fight had ended. He tells his own story in his own words.

> Me and Nick was getting breakfast when the attack took place. Two men here with us. Bill Jones and another man [Walker] the old man [Jones] went after water and did not come back. His friend went out to see what was the matter and he did not come back. Nick then started out and I told him to look out, that I thought there was someone at the stable and would not let them come back. Nick is shot, but not dead yet. He is awful sick. I must go and wait on him. It is now about two hours since the first shot. Nick is still alive. They are still shooting and are all around the house. Boys there is bullets coming in like hail. Them fellows is in such shape I can't get at them. They are shooting from the stable and river and back of the house. Nick is dead, he

died about 9 o'clock. I see smoke down at the stable I think they have fired it. I don't think they intend to let me get away this time.

It is now about noon. There is someone at the stable yet. They are throwing a rope out at the door, and drawing it back. I guess it is to draw me out. I wish that duck would get out further so I could get a shot at him. Boys I don't know what they have done with them two fellows that staid here last night. Boys, I feel pretty lonesome just now. I wish there was someone here with me so we could watch all sides at once. They may fool around until I get a good shot before they leave. It is about 3 o'clock now. There was a man in a buckboard and one on horseback just passed. Flagg and his stepson. They fired on them as they went by. I don't know if they killed them or not. I seen lots of men come out on horses on the other side of the river and take after them. I shot at the men in the stable just now, don't know if I got any or not. I must go and look out again. It don't look as if there was now much show of my getting away. I see twelve or fifteen men. One looks like [name scratched off notebook]. I don't know whether it is or not. I hope they did not catch them fellows who ran over the bridge towards Smiths. They are shooting at the house now. If I had a pair of glasses I believe I would know some of those men. They are coming back. I've got to look out. Well, they have just got through shelling the house like hail. I heard them splitting wood. I guess they are going to fire the house tonight. I think I will make a break when nite comes, if alive. Shooting again. I think they will fire the house this time. Its not night yet. The house is all fired. Goodbye, boys, if I never see you again. Nathan D. Champion.

When Jack Flagg and his stepson rode into Buffalo, they immediately went on to the county courthouse where they told Sheriff Red Angus the story of the large force of armed riders that they had seen making the attack upon the men in the cabin at the KC Ranch. Shortly afterward Terence Smith, another small rancher on Powder River near the KC, also rode into town upon a winded horse and reported to the sheriff that, after hearing the shooting at the KC, he had formed his own conclusions as to what was happening and that from his observations from a distance the men who were at the KC had apparently all been killed, with the buildings also having been set on fire and still burning.

Upon getting this information, Sheriff Angus, a man of action, immediately issued a proclamation deputizing the entire male population of Johnson County to assist him in resisting the armed invasion of the county. Within minutes after the issuing of this proclamation, riders were fanning out over all of Johnson County, notifying the small ranchers along the streams that the country was being invaded by the big cattlemen and a large force of heavily armed professional gunslingers. Within a few hours, hundreds of angry and determined small ranchers and other citizens began riding into Buffalo on lathered horses, ready to go to war to defend their lives, their property, and their independence. As they arrived, they were immediately sworn in as deputies by Sheriff Red Angus and also advised by the sheriff and other public officials that they were legally justified, under the circumstances, in defending their property as well as the lives of the citizens of Johnson County against an invasion of this type.

By evening, with several hundred deputies sworn in, Sheriff Angus proceeded to get them organized. With the assistance of some of the leaders from among the small ranchers and businessmen of the town, a plan of defense was soon in the process of being put into effect. Guards were being posted all around the town, and scouts were out riding the country nearby to watch for developments and to give warning of any approach to the town by the invaders. In cooperation with this plan of defense, the hardware stores threw open their doors and told the ranchers and other citizens of Johnson County to help themselves to any rifles or ammunition that they might need. In addition, the operators of the restaurants, assisted by the women in the town, took charge of the preparation of the food, the necessary groceries and other supplies being furnished without charge by the local merchants, and with the lumberyard furnishing all of the lumber necessary for setting up the serving tables to handle the long lines of hungry deputies. This work of getting organized went on thoughout the night, with some of the business buildings and residential houses being barricaded in such a manner as to furnish cover for the defenders. Shortly after daylight the next morning, the scouts who were out on the range reported that the armed force had moved in to within about seven miles of the town.

The invaders, however, also had their scouts out, and when they learned that Sheriff Red Angus had raised a small army of angry citizens who were well-prepared and waiting for them in the town, they quickly held a meeting of their leaders and changed their plans for moving against the town of Buffalo. Instead, they changed directions and headed for the T Open-A Ranch, located about twelve miles south of Buffalo on Crazy Women Creek. This ranch was owned by Dr. William Harris, who was friendly with the big cattlemen and had known of their invasion plans.

Within a few hours after moving in at the T Open-A Ranch, the invaders had fortified and barricaded the ranch buildings in the best manner possible with the material which was available, and had also thrown up a limited amount of defensive earthworks. The leaders had apparently decided that, being greatly outnumbered, their best strategy would be to wait at this ranch in the hopes that the Johnson County people would come to them.

It was on the morning of April 11 that Sheriff Red Angus met the challenge and moved in with about two hundred of his well-armed deputies and laid seige to the invasion forces holed up in the buildings at the T Open-A Ranch. In the meantime, the local people had learned of the murder of their two friends and neighbors, Nate Champion and Nick Ray, and were demanding revenge. It reached the point where Sheriff Angus sent a delegation to Fort McKinney to ask the commanding officer to loan them a cannon, which, of course, the colonel in command declined, with regrets.

The sheriff's next move was to have his deputies nail heavy planks of lumber to the sides and ends of wagons. Then, with men stationed inside of these wagons and other men taking cover behind them, these reinforced vehicles, which were not greatly different from the first tanks used during World War One except they were armored with wooden planks instead of steel, were pushed up alongside the barricaded buildings, where heavy rifle fire was exchanged at close range. These improvised "battle wagons" proved to be very effective for this purpose. Someone than came up with another idea: why not place a dynamite charge with a long fuse in one of the wagons, then push the armored vehicle up alongside of the barricaded buildings and light the fuse?

While a wagon was being sent to Buffalo for the dynamite, the invaders inside the buildings learned of the plan and realized that their situation was becoming precarious. They managed to slip one of their men out under cover of darkness to Fort McKinney, where he sent a telegram to acting governor Amos W. Barber (who was apparently aware of the plans by the big cattlemen for the invasion of Johnson County), advising him of their predicament. When Governor Barber received this telegram in Cheyenne, he immediately declared that a state of war existed in Johnson County. However, instead of calling out a unit of the state militia that was stationed at Buffalo, which he probably did not do because of local sentiment and the involvement of the people of Johnson County in the battle at the T Open-A Ranch, he sent a telegram to President Benjamin Harrison in Washington, D.C. In the telegram he said, "An insurrection exists in Johnson County . . . against the government of the . . . state open hostilities exist and large bodies of armed men are engaged in battle." In his telegram, the governor also suggested to the president that the U.S. Army troops which were stationed at Fort McKinney, only thirteen miles from the ranch where the battle was in progress, could be used to suppress the insurrection, and requested that this be done.

Upon receiving this information, and after a brief delay, with several consultations with his advisors, the president finally authorized the use of the federal troops, and issued orders through the War Department for the commanding officer at Fort McKinney to handle the problem.

In carrying out this order, Colonel J. J. Van Horn, the commanding officer at Fort McKinney, went in to the ranch on April 13, 1892, with three troops of cavalry under a flag of truce, and intervened in the struggle in Johnson County. He obtained the surrender of Major Wolcott and his greatly subdued and deflated bunch of big cattlemen and gunfighters, who were apparently quite relieved to get themselves out of this fix that their arrogance and belligerance had gotten them into.

Colonel Van Horn then declared martial law in Johnson County and escorted the invaders to Fort McKinney under heavy guard to protect them from the still angry people of Johnson County, as well as to hold them to answer for the murder of Nate Champion and Nick Ray. As a result of these measures being put into effect, the situation in Johnson County was soon brought under control, with the forty-three invaders being moved to Fort D. A. Russel, near Cheyenne, about two weeks later, to be held for trial.

The bodies of Nate Champion and Nick Ray were brought into Buffalo for burial by the local people. Nate Champion, who had come up the trail from Texas, had been a very popular and highly respected leader of the small ranchers in the Powder River country. He had been the roundup captain for his district and was a friend of almost everyone who knew him. Frank Jones, who knew Champion well, described him as a fine-looking, soft-spoken man who would stand his ground and who could not be pushed around. He was recognized as a natural-born leader of men. He also said that his friend Nate Champion, like many of the other cattlemen in that country, both large and small, may have branded a slick or two during his lifetime, in violation of the highly unpopular maverick law, but that Nate was definitely not a cattle thief. The two men who were killed at the KC Ranch were buried in a small, quiet cemetery in Buffalo, with a very impressive funeral attended by almost everyone in Johnson County.

The news stories, headlines, and editorial comment in the newspapers at the time that the Johnson County War was under way, and for several weeks afterwards, varied to a great degree, depending upon whether the personal interest and sentiments of the individual newspaper publisher were with the big cattlemen or the small ranchers. The *Cheyenne Sun,* for instance, declared: "in Johnson, Natrona and Converse Counties, the rustlers are all powerful . . . . then let us have no mamby-pamby sentimentalism about the killing of a few stock thieves." Other newspapers in the state had an entirely different viewpoint. The *Lusk Herald* said, "they [the invaders] have proved themselves blood-thirsty murderers and should be given the full extent of the law." The *Laramie Sentinel,* in its editorial comment, said, "Of all of the fool things that the Stock Association ever did, this takes the cake." Other newspaper articles stated that, fortunately, no one had been killed, although several had been wounded in the siege at the T Open-A Ranch and two of the invaders, by the names of Dudley and Lowther, had later died from the wounds that they had received at the time of this battle.

It was common knowledge among the people who lived in the Powder River country at the time of the Johnson County War that a small book had been found in one of the cattlemen's wagons after the fight at the ranch, which contained the names of about seventy small ranchers and other citizens of Johnson County, including Red Angus, the sheriff, and the mayor of Buffalo. They were all slated to have been wiped out at the time of the invasion, either by being shot, strung up, or run out of the country. This book was later destroyed by some of the men whose names were listed, due to the reflection which might have been cast in the future upon their reputations. Therefore, the names which were listed in this book were never published.

When the president of the Wyoming Stockgrowers' Association, John Clay, returned from Scotland, he disclaimed any personal involvement in the affair, taking the position that he had been told by Major Wolcott, several months before he left on his trip to Scotland, about the plan that was being discussed by some of the cattlemen of going into Johnson County with an armed force on a punitive expedition, and that he had discouraged the idea as being impractical. He further stated that he was not aware that the plan had been carried out, or of its results, until his return to the United States. He did, however, publicly express himself, after his return, as being in sympathy with the objectives of the invasion, and he was a heavy contributor in helping to pay the ultimate costs of the Big Johnson County fiasco.

One of the other prominent Wyoming livestock men who were indirectly involved was Senator Joseph M. Carey, with his big CY outfit on the Platte and with his cattle ranging over into Johnson County. Although there is no evidence that Senator Carey was personally involved, he apparently knew of the invasion plans and was in sympathy with the movement. On the other hand, Senator Francis E. Warren was probably not aware of these plans at the time that they were being formulated; but he did exert considerable influence on behalf of the big cattlemen in the months that followed when Major Wolcott and his followers were facing murder charges in the courts of Wyoming.

The forty-three invaders who were being held at Fort D. A. Russell were eventually released by the army to civilian authorities at Cheyenne to face murder charges there in the civil courts. However, in early July, 1892, a change of venue was obtained and the prisoners were all taken to Laramie, in Albany County, for a hearing. After about two weeks of legal maneuvering, the very prominent attorneys for the defense — M. C. Brown, Willis Van Devanter, W. T. Stoll, and Hugo Donselman, all men with considerable political influence in the new state of Wyoming — succeeded in getting a ruling by the court that the trial be held in Cheyenne, which was the area where public sentiment was the strongest for the invaders. This ruling by the court was generally considered to have been a very definite legal victory for the defense.

While these legal maneuvers were under way and time was being gained by the defense, the two principal witnesses for the state, Jones and Walker, the two trappers who had been at the KC Ranch, who had been held prisoners by the invaders while the fight was underway, and who were there as eye witnesses to the killing of Nate Champion and Nick Ray, suddenly disappeared from the state, and could not be found when the court convened. Reports afterwards were to the effect that the two witnesses had been spirited out of the state by the big cattlemen, then paid a substantial amount of money to keep out of sight, and were hidden out in one of the New England states during the period of time that the criminal action was pending in the courts against the invaders of Johnson County.

When the prisoners were moved back to Cheyenne and a hearing was held before District Judge Richard H. Scott, they all pleaded not guilty and a trial date was set by the judge for August 22, 1892. Due to the fact that there was not sufficient room for holding all of the prisoners at the county jail, the judge concurred in having them held temporarily at Keefe Hall, where they came and went as they pleased during the time that they were there. However, when Judge Scott learned later that no provision had been made by Johnson County for paying the bills for board and room of the prisoners, he ordered them all released from custody; the Wyoming men on their own recognizance and the Texans and other out-of-state gunmen upon bond signed by prominent Wyoming citizens, most of whom were big cattlemen. The local men who had been held as prisoners returned to their homes, while the out-of-state gunmen went to Omaha, where they were paid off for the time that they had spent on the punitive expedition into Johnson County and while in custody afterwards. These hired gunfighters who had been brought in from the Southwest promptly left for parts unknown.

When the court was called to order on January 21, 1893, after the trial had been postponed for about six months due to what Judge Scott described as his "need for holding court in Weston and Crook counties," it was with the following men appearing before the court; from Wyoming: Frank M. Canton, Joseph Elliot, William J. Clark, Frank H. Laberteaux, William C. Irvine, John N. Tisdale, Frederick O. DeBillier, Herbert E. Teschemacher, William E. Guthrie, Frederick G. S. Hesse, Michael Shonsey, Charles A. Campbell, Frank Wolcott, Arthur B. Clark, Elais W. Whitcomb, Alexander D. Adamson, Charles S. Ford, Benjamin M. Morrison, La Fayette H. Parker, D. R. Tisdale, A. R. Powers, W. S. Davis, and R. M. Allen; from Colorado: W. B. Wallace; from other states: (all absent) William Armstrong, Alexander Hamilton, William Little, Alexander Lowther, Thomas Smith, Buck Garrett, J. C. Johnson, J. B. Mynett, J. Barlin, S. S. Tucker, B. Wiley, J. M. Buford, K. Richard, B. C. Schultz, W. H. Tabor, G. R. Tucker, D. E. Brooke, W. A. Wilson, M. A. McNally, and Robert Barlin.

Hundreds of veniremen were called as the judge attempted to empanel a jury. However, when these potential jurors were questioned by the attorneys for both the prosecution and the defense, they practically all expressed strong sentiments for one side or the other or admitted close friendship, relationship, or association with some of the cattlemen who were involved. Some of them had been represented at some time in the past by one of the several attorneys who were handling the case for either the defense or the prosecution. After several days of this type of legal procedure and maneuvering, with the attorneys for both sides challenging jurors right and left, the judge still did not have a jury. Costs of the trial were building up, with Johnson County broke and Laramie County, where the trial was being held, refusing to assume the responsibility for paying the costs of continuing with the trial. As a result, several conferences were held by the judge with the authorities from Johnson County and, in view of the financial circumstances in their county, they finally agreed to having the case dismissed.

Following the dismissal of the case, the cattlemen who had been summoned before the court demanded that they be completely exonerated of the charges which had been made against them in court. As a result, the accused who had been present for the trial, as well as those from out of state (who were still all absent), were freed by the presiding judge of the charges that had been preferred against them. So ended the Johnson County War.

The net result of the conflict and of the ill-advised invasion of Johnson County by the big cattlemen was two men murdered, and costs which had accumulated in the process of carrying out the invasion and which had to be paid by the cattlemen, amounting to over one hundred thousand dollars. In addition, a serious blot had been made upon the good name of the new state of Wyoming, where statehood had been granted only two years before. Many of the cattlemen who had become involved in the Johnson County War had previously been members of the constitutional convention which had drafted the state constitution, and who had participated in pleading for its adoption by the Congress of the United States, where they had used as one of their principal arguments the need for the elimination of lawlessness from the territory.

The strong sentiments and the bitterness which had

been built up over the state by this conflict continued to live for many years afterwards, and did irreparable harm to the development of satisfactory relationships between the people who were living in the different sections of the state. There were many versions and differences of opinion as to the motivations of the people who were involved in the conflict, and also as to the justification for the actions which were taken.

The opinions of the writer, as expressed in this book, are based to a great degree upon information which I have gathered over a long period of years from listening to discussions among people who were in the Powder River country at the time of the Johnson County War, or who were actually involved in the conflict. Among these was my father (Frank E. Jones), who punched cows in the Powder River country before the invasion, and knew most of the people who were involved on both sides of the conflict. I also had several other close relatives who were living in Johnson County at the time of the invasion; including an uncle, Jess Ammerman, who was foreman for the OX Bar on the Powder River at that time. An aunt, Mrs. Emma Baldwin, who lived in Buffalo, Wyoming, at the time of the siege at the T Open-A ranch, and had some very vivid memories of the excitement and consternation in the little cow town of Buffalo when Red Angus was raising and swearing in his small army of deputies, while at the same time the people in the town, including the women, were working feverishly to barricade their homes and places of business against the expected attack by Major Wolcott and his small army of professional gunfighters.

In retrospect, it is quite obvious that the entire bizarre concept of the big cattlemen organizing what amounted to a punitive expedition — to go into Johnson County with a small army of heavily armed men who were without legal authority under the law for the purpose of trying to eliminate the rustlers, and also to punish the small ranchers in that part of the country who were revolting against the controls which had been imposed by the Wyoming Stockgrowers' Association under the maverick law — was, to say the least, a very ill-advised approach to the problem. The very impractical methods which went into the carrying out of this plan were so ill-conceived they made the overall conflict between the big cattlemen and the little fellows appear in their true perspective. The end result of this big fiasco was to bring the people in that part of the country to the realization of the need for recognized legal authority and the lawful administration of justice throughout the West.

23 In the decade following the Johnson County War, great changes were beginning to occur throughout the West, with law and order becoming the way of life, and a period of prosperity in the process of development. Networks of railroads were building over the northern high plains, many kinds of small industries were coming into the country, and giant federal reclamation projects were under construction or in the planning stages. Some of the cattlemen were also increasing the size of their privately owned irrigation systems to the point where the availability of hay for winter feed and meadows for winter pasture was rapidly increasing.

There were still occasional local flare-ups in the country; the old hatreds and animosities which had existed for so many years between the big and the small cattlemen would make themselves felt, but these deep-seated controversies of long duration were beginning to die out. A very vital factor in this improvement of relations was the fact that a new generation of younger men, born before the turn of the century (of whom the writer was one), were beginning to make their weight and influence felt.

This new generation of cowboys were the sons of the pioneer cattlemen who had first come into this western country from the eastern states, or who had come up the cattle trails with the early trail herds from the Southwest, or who had even come from Europe. These younger men did not retain the feelings of animosity and resentment to as great a degree as did their fathers. Consequently, the lines which had been drawn between the big cattlemen and the little fellows were fast disappearing, and a fine spirit of friendship and cooperation was in the process of developing. There were now dances and other social functions where the young people got together in an atmosphere where the prejudices of the fathers did not prevail.

Up until this time, all ranch houses had been built with logs, rock, sod, and such other building materials as were readily available in the country. Now, with these changes occurring, some of these old log and sod houses were being torn down and replaced with good-looking ranch houses built with lumber, some of them two and three stories in height. Some of the women were even insisting upon having water piped into the house. In addition, the women were also forming their ladies aid societies and other community organizations; some of the small ranchers were even burying the hatchet and joining the stockgrowers' associations. With some of the large outfits getting smaller and some of the small outfits getting larger, these organizations were becoming much more democratic and were now representing the interests of all the cattlemen, whether large or small.

This, however, was still an open-range type of cattle country, with the roundup wagons pulling out in the spring and returning to the headquarters ranches in the fall. The young cowboys still in their teens were beginning to do a man's work and to pull their end of the load. They went out when the wagons first pulled out in the spring and stayed out all summer. They did everything that the older cowboys, who had spent many years on the range and in the saddle, were accustomed to doing, from roping steers to riding the rough string. These boys did not ask for any special favors and they did not get any. The tough old wagon bosses felt that these youngsters had grown up in the cattle business and had started riding horses almost as soon as they could walk, so they should be able to hold their own.

This younger generation of native-born cowboys were very proud of their heritage. They found their wild and carefree way of life to be very fascinating. There was danger, excitement, and challenge in the way that they lived. This was their life and they lived it fully. Here in this new country, they had everything that appeals to the active imagination and dreams of a youngster. This was truly a land of abundance; especially in the late spring, when the blue stem and the wheat grass were growing green in the native meadows, and the cattle were grazing fat on the buffalo and gramma grass which formed a soft carpet over the rolling hills, with deer in the mountains, antelope on the plains, and speckled trout in the cold, clear mountain streams. Was it any wonder that the Indians had fought so long and so hard to retain this which had been theirs for thousands of years?

It was only natural that tragedies, where cowboys were

crippled or lost their lives, would occasionally occur in the process of working with cattle on the open range. One of these instances occurred when Billy Wilde, the young wagon boss for the Two Bar outfit, was crossing a herd of cattle across the North Platte River on June 29, 1903, at the Rock Ranch crossing, only a few miles below Fort Laramie. This was the time of year when the heavy snow was melting rapidly in the mountains, resulting in a heavy runoff of water, with very strong currents running in the big river.

While the crossing of the herd was under way, two young cowboys with the outfit, Eddie Woods and Fred McCarty, neither of whom could swim, were working the downstream side of the large swimming herd when a tree, with long, out-stretched branches, which had become uprooted by the flooding waters, came floating and tumbling with the strong current, down through the center of the herd.

This dangerous tree was apparently not seen by either of the young cowboys, with their horses swimming low in the water until it was too late for them to get out of its way. Eddie Woods was immediaely knocked from his saddle by the trunk of the tree. This young cowboy grabbed desperately for a limb, missed, and was quickly sucked under and disappeared in the turbulent swirling waters. The other young cowboy, Fred McCarty, in an effort to save his drowning companion quickly turned his horse downstream in the strong current. However, before McCarty realized what was happening and that he could not save the life of Eddie Woods, his own horse had become completely exhausted in fighting the current and was floundering badly in the water, at times going completely under. Consequently, this young cowboy, in order to relieve the horse of his weight, left his saddle, while still hanging onto his rope tied hard and fast to the horn of his saddle.

When the other cowboys near the river became aware of the trouble that Fred McCarty was having, they tried to save the young cowboy by swimming their own horses out into the strong current and throwing ropes to the drowning boy. However, with the strong current running, they failed to reach him. Finally, in grabbing for one of the thrown ropes, the young cowboy missed at the same time that he lost his grip on his own rope. Both horse and rider were immediately caught in a giant whirlpool and sucked under, with neither of them reappearing, except for a brief instant when one of McCarty's arms appeared momentarily above the surface of the water as though he were waving good-bye to his friends who were in the river trying to help him.

It has always happened, in any line of activity which is dangerous and where a very high degree of skill is required, for some of the people who are engaged in that activity to become exceptionally expert in doing the things which are required. Consequently, contests and competitions between these people, which give them an opportunity to prove their respective capabilities and to satisfy their natural desire to excel, will develop. This was true with the cowboys in the cattle country, where the rodeo first became popular as a public attraction at the turn of the century. The first Frontier Days celebration (with the slogan of "Daddy of them all" later adopted) was held at Cheyenne in September of 1898. The first Miles City Roundup was also held at about the same time. The rodeos that were held at that time, which later became contests between professionals, were strictly competition between working cowboys.

In addition to the rodeos, there were also the traveling

Wild West shows of Buffalo Bill Cody, Irwin Brothers, and the Hundred and One Outfit. These shows traveled over the country in specially-built, highly colored, and elaborately decorated railway cars of the same general type as those used by the big circus companies. These Wild West shows made one-night stands in practically all of the larger cities and towns over the United States and Canada. In some instances, they even shipped their show stock, cowboys, and equipment overseas, where they staged their shows in some of the larger cities of Europe.

The rodeos and the colorful Wild West shows were naturally of particular interest to the younger generation of cowboys, who had grown up in the cattle business and who were a rather wild and reckless lot to begin with. The adventure, competition, and challenge, as well as the thrill, danger, and limelight of the rodeos and Wild West shows, were a very definite attraction for these youngsters. As a result, the interests of many of these young cowboys were being diverted from the cattle business by these attractions, to the point that conflicts and bitter feelings soon began to develop between these show outfits and the older local cattlemen who deeply resented the fact that the Wild West shows, with their glamour, were luring some of their sons away from the ranches to follow the rodeo circuit or the traveling Wild West shows. These sentiments on the part of the fathers continued to build up until they became convinced that no good would come from it all and their sons would either wind up getting their necks broken or become worthless traveling-show bums, with their interests becoming centered upon how fast they could tie steers instead of in building irrigation ditches. Most of the fathers had been pretty wild and reckless themselves when they first came into this country, but from their viewpoint things were different *now*, and there was no reason for their sons "who should know better" to act the same way. Surprisingly, most of the sons lived through it all and in the end settled down and became good conservative cattlemen themselves, with boys who gave them a lot of trouble.

There were a few people remaining in the high plains country who brought back memories to the older cattlemen of the days of the great British cattle outfits. This was especially true with the remittance men, who in most instances had been the sons or other relatives of some of the prominent Scots or English with interests in the big British syndicates. Often, this particular young man had become involved in some kind of trouble at home, generally minor, like having an affair with the gardener's daughter. In order to avoid further embarrassment to the family and reflection upon the family's good name, the young man was bundled up, put on an allowance, and shipped out to the States where it was hoped that he would take an interest in the cattle business and become a credit to the family. Some of these remittance men did eventually become successful cattlemen, or later returned to Scotland or England to claim the family fortune or title upon the death of the father. However, most of the remittance men continued to live in the West on their remittances, and could in later years be found hanging around the bars and clubs of the larger cow towns, where they could easily be identified by their British accent.

There was also an occasional character in this big country, like old Military Jack, who ran a bunch of broomtailed mares up in the YBO hills, along the west rim of the Goshen Hole. He lived in an old, tumbledown log cabin that had been built by an old buffalo hunter in a small grove of box elder near a little stream of clear water. Here, this slightly built, elderly man, with high cheek bones, a long, handlebar mustache, and a military bearing, lived the life of a hermit. Military Jack was always considered, by the few local people who ever came in contact with him, as not only being eccentric but as also being somewhat off his rocker. He was always obsessed with the idea that someone was trying to steal his horses, which he considered to be the finest of animals. As a matter of fact, they were an almost completely worthless bunch of inbred broomtails, but in Military Jack's opinion the local people just did not realize how valuable his horses were.

When the roundup wagons were working in his part of the country, this gaunt, solitary, phantomlike figure of a man would oftentimes be seen on guard against his imaginary horse thieves, as he sat his horses, silhouetted against the skyline on some ridge. Wearing an old, faded blue Civil War uniform, his long, yellow hair falling almost to his shoulders and a rifle across the pommel of his saddle, this striking figure of a man would give the impression of being something out of the past, as he watched every move being made by the cowboys working in that area. If some cowboy should take a notion to ride into what Military Jack considered to be his own private domain, a rifle bullet would probably kick up the dust a short distance in front of him. If the cowboy did not take the hint and decide that he was not welcome on Military Jack's range, the next rifle bullet would probably be a lot closer. After this, the phantomlike figure would take off, with his horse running at full speed, to a point where he would again take up the same position on another ridge ahead of the cowboy, and repeat the performance. Sooner or later, the cowboy would get the general idea and decide that he had better look for cattle on some other part of the range; always a wise decision.

One of the instances in which the old animosities

among the cattlemen broke out, occurred in the Powder River country in the summer of 1897, when R. M. Devine, wagon boss for Joseph M. Carey's CY outfit, was pulling his roundup wagon into the Hole-in-the-Wall country and became involved in a shoot-out with Bob Smith, a small rancher in the Hole who was an old enemy of Devine. In this gunfight, Smith, who was quite popular in the Hole, was killed by Devine. As a result, with public sentiment building up in the Hole over the shooting and a major battle imminent, the CY outfit, under orders from Joseph Carey, pulled their wagon back out of the Hole until things quieted down. After a hearing was held about a week later, at which Devine was exonerated in the killing of Bob Smith on grounds of self-defense, the wagon boss again pulled his wagons into the Hole-in-the-Wall country with a larger roundup crew of about forty men, including several officers of the law, and continued with the roundup. Working that part of the country very thoroughly and finding it to be quite free of rustler activity, with the exception of finding a few calves whose brands were subject to question, they did find where one gang of outlaws had been holed up in an old deserted cabin, where they had been in the process of altering and burning over the brands on twenty-eight head of big four-year-old Ogallala steers. However, when these outlaws had learned that the CY wagon was working in that part of the country, they had abandoned the twenty-eight steers and lit a shuck out of the country. The big Longhorns were all picked up in the roundup and reclaimed by the Ogallala outfit.

This was the period of time when the market prices for cattle had been going up steadily for several years. The quality of the herds had been improving and the cattlemen were making good money. Consequently, when these pioneer cattlemen of the West looked out upon their ranges of good grass, their large grazing herds, and their sons growing into good cattlemen, they were quite proud of what they had accomplished since coming to what had been a wild and lawless country. They had fought Indians, outlaws, and blizzards. They had endured depressions, droughts, and hardships of many kinds. Some of them now owned stock in the local banks, while others were deacons in the church. They now felt secure in this new country with great opportunities ahead of them.

This period of peace and prosperity in the cattle country had continued for several years with the cattlemen assuming that it would continue indefinitely. However, change is inevitable, and regardless of these feelings of pride and security, the storm clouds were beginning to gather and the cattlemen of the West were about at the end of an era. For some time, changes in the motivations of people had been occurring over the country, with the urge of people to move ever westward gaining momentum. As a result of these changes, the pioneer cattlemen and their sons would soon be facing a far greater challenge than ever before to their way of life in this big new country.

24

The passing of the Mondell Act; which was introduced in Congress in 1909 by Frank W. Mondell of Wyoming, which provided for homesteads of three hundred twenty acres of land instead of the previously allowed one hundred sixty acres; triggered a tremendous influx of homesteaders to the northern high plains country. An additional incentive to the homesteading of public lands was added in 1912 when the residence requirements on homesteads was reduced from five years to three.

They came by the thousands, many of them overland, with teams and covered wagons. They came principally from the midcontinental states along the Mississippi and the Missouri rivers. Previous to this time, the few homesteaders who were coming into the high plains country were principally interested in grass and water for cattle. These new people now coming in were looking for farmland where they could plow up the grass and raise crops, as the homesteaders in western Nebraska had attempted (with some degree of success) to do twenty years before. As these immigrant wagons rolled slowly westward — some of them traveling as far as a thousand miles over the rough, dusty, and wind-swept wagon trails of that time, with all of their personal belongings loaded in the wagon and with any surplus livestock trailing along behind — it was with confidence in their own abilities and faith in the future.

Others came into the country with their families, furniture, and household goods loaded in one end of a railroad immigrant car (a boxcar partitioned down the middle) and their teams of horses, wagons, harness, milk cow, breaking plow, and any other equipment they might own loaded in the other end. Many of the homesteaders who came west in this type of railway car were fresh over from Europe. They had been attracted to the United States by the advertisements which were being run in European newspapers by the American railroad companies who were using this method of advertising for attracting new settlers to the government land along their railroad tracks in order to increase the traffic on newly built lines. In these advertisements, the railroad companies told glowing stories of this wonderful new farming paradise where the land was free and where the immigrants could build homes and a new way of life for their families, while becoming prosperous American farmers.

It was like an avalanche. There was no stopping them. They were wild-eyed and eager, and filed upon anything where they could get a plow in the ground. They came from everywhere: Germany, Holland, Russia, the Scandinavian countries, and the rest of Europe. The immigrants who spoke the same language naturally got together, filing in the same general area. All of these new people, regardless of where they came from, deeply resented any advice from the local people who would tend to question their ability to make a living farming this high, dry, plains country. This was the land of their dreams; they had seen the advertisements and they believed what they had read.

The railroad companies, in their advertisements, also featured the new dry farming methods that were being developed and promoted by government experiment stations established in several areas of the West. These stations dealt with the conservation of the limited available moisture in these areas. Claims were being made by these experimental stations that, by following these recommended scientific dry farming methods, crops could be grown with success upon land that had previously been considered too dry for farming. It soon became apparent to the homesteaders, however, that these scientific methods of dry farming did not, in actual practice, prove to be all that was claimed for them in the railroad company advertisements or government bulletins. It was found that it was impossible to conserve moisture that did not fall; that, although the soil would grow a good crop of native grass, the topsoil was not of sufficient depth in most areas, or with the necessary qualities in the soil, to grow satisfactory crops of agricultural products.

Regardless of these facts, the dry farmers continued to turn over the soil, plant the seed, and then watch their crops slowly burn up from lack of moisture while their dreams were also slowly fading away into disillusionment. The dry farmers generally did manage to raise enough grain to feed a flock of chickens and a few pigs, as well as to raise feed for their work horses and two or three milk cows. In addition, they generally managed to keep small gardens growing by watering them from the well or, in some instances, by hauling water in barrels from some nearby water hole or stream. They shot jackrabbits for meat, and traded butter and eggs or home-cured bacon and ham to the little country store for flour, sugar, coffee, calico, and a few of the other necessities of life. To some degree, the life which these people lived was a repetition of what had occurred in western Nebraska many years before.

As another means of getting a few of the necessities of life, or at least of getting a few dollars in cash, some of the homesteaders turned to picking bones. There was a market, at that time, for dry bones to be shipped by rail to eastern markets, where they were ground into fertilizer and used to spread upon the land to enrich the soil for agricultural purposes. There were quite large quantities of these dry bones, of the buffalo who had been slaughtered by the hunters for their hides, as well as of cattle and other animals. These bones were to be found (bleached white from their long exposure to the sun and wind) lying scattered over the prairie, or piled up and accumulated in large quantities in some of the draws, arroyos, and dry washes, where the animals had drifted over cut banks and cliffs and had died there in large numbers.

The bone buyers paid seven dollars a ton for these bones at points where they were weighed and loaded onto railroad cars. These cars were spotted on sidings at some of the small towns that were springing up along the lines of the new railroads that were building in the cattle country. These dry bones were quite light and it took a lot of them to make a ton. Consequently, it usually took the average homesteader and his family about two weeks to gather a ton of bones, haul them to a railroad station anywhere from ten to a hundred miles distant, and then to get back home again; all for seven dollars.

As a result of the homesteaders turning over the sod with their breaking plows and attempting to raise crops with their dry farming methods, the cattlemen were soon finding themselves faced with an increasingly serious problem. The filings of the newcomers naturally resulted in a decrease in the availability of grass for cattle. The cattlemen were soon being forced to reduce the size of their herds because of this shortage of grass; while the big outfits, with requirements for hundreds of thousands of acres of rangeland for their operations, were being rapidly forced out of the cattle business.

Some of the more unscrupulous and vindictive of the cattlemen attempted to fight back against this encroachment upon what they considered to be their range. They used every means that was available to them — including wire cutters, stampedes, fire, threats, and even bullets — all to no avail. The land-hungry homesteaders just continued to come in ever-increasing numbers. Whenever the cattlemen succeeded in running one dry farmer out, there would be three or four new ones waiting at the land office to file on the same land.

As these filings continued to increase, the cattlemen were soon finding themselves being forced to pull their reduced herds back to the range which they themselves had under fence; which was, of course, principally government land that was illegally under fence. However, even here the cattlemen were not secure, for it was not many months before some of the more bold and land-hungry of the homesteaders began to file on this government land which was within the cattlemen's pastures; sometimes with these filings running right up into the cattleman's dooryard!

This was naturally a very bitter pill for the old pioneer cattleman to swallow. Although he realized that he did not hold title to this land, it had been inside his fences for many years, and a man can become very much attached to the land. The Indian understood this deep feeling of attachment to the land for it was a part of his religion. He knew that he belonged to the land, and that the land would eventually reclaim him.

It soon became obvious to those of mature judgment, that in this contest between the cattlemen and the dry farmers there was a very basic issue in question: the best usage of the land. Would this high, dry country, with its short seasons and long bitter winters, be hospitable to agriculture over a long period of time; or was its best usage being destroyed for many years to come through the turning over of the sod and the elimination of the native grass from the prairie in an attempt to raise crops in what had always been buffalo and cattle country?

With the passing of time, it became very apparent that, regardless of the desire and the need of the homesteaders for homes for their families, and a way of life for themselves, in the end, this basic question of the best usage of the land would prevail. In the meantime, all that the cattlemen could do was to try to hang on until this attempt to change the usage of the land had been given an opportunity to run its natural course. Time and the elements would eventually determine whether this land was better suited for agriculture or for cattle.

The last blow for the cattlemen fell when the controversial issue of fences on government land came to a head in January of 1907. It was at that time that President Theodore Roosevelt, due in part to political pressures from the homesteaders, issued a directive ordering that all fences be removed from government land by April 1 of that year. The cattlemen could not understand how this man Roosevelt, who had been a rancher on the Little Missouri for so many years, could have been subjected to the kind of political pressures which would have caused him to turn against his old friends and associates and deal them what they considered to be their knockout blow.

Within a few days after the issuance of this presidential directive, special agents, operating as Deputy United States Marshals, were riding the range, issuing written notices to the cattlemen with fences on government land to pull these fences down by April 1 or be subject to arrest after that date for violation of the federal land laws pertaining to the illegal fencing of government land.

The removal of these fences was a personal blow to the old-time pioneer cattlemen. However, regardless of their sentiments in the matter, most of the cattlemen soon sent out fence crews and began to pull them down. As a result, great piles of fence posts and rolls of barbed wire could soon be seen scattered over the prairie, while at the same time the cattlemen were freely expressing their opinions, in language that could not be printed, of any president of the United States who would subject his old friends to this kind of treatment. Even the old drift fence, which ran for over a hundred miles along the state line between Wyoming and Nebraska, from the North Platte River to the Colorado line, came down where it had been built on government land. However, some of this historic old fence, where it had been built on state or deeded land, was still standing and being used many years later.

Although it soon became apparent that the efforts of the homesteaders (in most cases) to farm this high dry plains country was doomed to failure, the greater number of them continued to stick it out for the required full three years before they could make final proof and get a federal patent as proof of their ownership. In most instances, when this was accomplished, these new landowners would start shopping around among the cattlemen for the best price that they could get for their land, then sell and load their personal belongings on their wagons and head for parts of the country where they might buy a little piece of land where the seasons were longer and the moisture more plentiful.

There were some exceptions to this practice of selling. Some of the more enterprising and tough-minded younger men who liked this country and were in a position to raise a little money bought out some of their discouraged neighbors and began to put together enough land to get started in the cattle business for themselves. There were also a few areas in the high plains country where the soil was sufficiently productive to grow good crops. A few of the original homesteaders remained in these areas and continued to make a living from the soil. However, most of the high plains country was sold to the cattlemen and started slowly going back to grass.

It was soon quite obvious that the days of free grass on the open range were about at an end. From now on, the rangeland would practically all be deeded. Someone would own, fence, and control it. There would be no further need for the roundup wagons, or for the large number of cowboys that were needed for that type of operation. This was the end of an era which would long live in the history of the West.

The blemishes and scars where the buffalo grass had been turned wrong side up would take many years to become grassed over, and would long remain as a reminder that this was cattle country. Eventually, however, even these scars would heal, and the cattle would continue to eat the good grass in pastures which would be fenced and cross-fenced by the cattlemen. Regardless of these facts, the glamour, danger, and adventure which had existed during the days of the open range would be gone forever from the cow country. The young men would go away to agricultural colleges and would come back with a lot of new ideas about how to raise cattle under these changed conditions (methods which they had learned from the book). Some of these changes would have merit, while others would not. However, in general, the old pioneer cattlemen who had started this business and who had learned the hard way would still insist that their methods were the best, and they would generally have their way. Change comes slowly to the cow country.

Perhaps the greatest loss that occurred during this period of transition, was in the shattered hopes and dreams of the thousands of defeated homesteaders who had come here with high hopes, believing without question that they could build homes for their families, as well as farm and grow crops, in this rugged, tough high plains country; where before there had only been a land of grass for the buffalo and later for the cattle. Now, regardless of this attempt to change its usage, it seems apparent that this counry will continue to be cattle country for many years to come.

The hundreds of little homestead shacks, with their windows knocked out and with gaping doors hanging half off their hinges, as well as the tumble-down barns, sheds, and corrals, were all mute evidence of the failure of these people to violate and change what the old-time cattlemen claimed was the plan of the Almighty, when He created this land for the white man's cattle and the Indian's buffalo. In riding past some of these old deserted homestead shacks in later years, when the first signs of spring were in the air, one would probably see a single crocus blossom or other spring flower beginning to pop out of the ground as a lingering reminder of the faith of some woman in the fertility of the soil. These restless people had continued to surge westward, searching for a new life and fighting for survival in a rugged country where the price was high and the rewards could be substantial and gratifying, or could result in the complete destruction of the individual and his dreams.

This has long been the way of life for the pioneer with a venturesome spirit, as he reached out in a big country where there were frontiers to conquer, in search of a new life.

25

Three years after the passing of the Mondell Act in 1907, the once great Swan Land and Cattle Company (or Two Bar outfit), which at one time had been running in excess of a hundred thousand head of Longhorns over most of Laramie, Goshen, Platte, Carbon, and Albany counties in southeastern Wyoming, was in the process, like most of the other big outfits, of going out of the cattle business due to the depletion of the open range. This outfit did, however, continue to run a limited number of sheep on their deeded range for several years afterwards.

At the peak of its operations, the Two Bar outfit had operated five roundup wagons on the range, and had over a hundred cowboys on their payroll who were busy throughout about six months of the year, branding calves and gathering beef cattle for shipment to market. However, during the last summer of their cattle operations, when the writer repped with that last Two Bar wagon, they were down to one roundup wagon and a good crew of old-time cowboys who were gathering the last of the remnants of the once great Two Bar herds and loading them out for shipment by rail to one of the Missouri River cattle markets.

The wagon was camped on Fox Creek when I threw my string of cow ponies into the cavvy and joined the outfit. They had already been out for several weeks on this last roundup and were all cleaned up and ready to pull the wagon in for the last time, except for working the Goshen Hole country. Dinky Moore was the wagon boss of that last wagon, and some of the regular old-time Two Bar punchers who were working with the outfit at that time were: Jim Mallory, Morris Thomas, Billy Wilde, Claude Sage, Bob Braziel, Hank Greyser, Dempsey Thomas and Billy Chaffee, with Carl Spencer repping for Johnnie Boyles' OP outfit, and Nick Marr repping for the Open-A X outfit of Yoder and Marsh.

After working out the Fox Creek country, Bear Creek, and the Chugwater flats, the wagon pulled out for an overnight camp at the Big Willows. From there, we worked on down Horse Creek to the big bend at Jay Pens, where we swung the drive westward across the center of the Hole, with overnight camps at Greasewood, Bull Camp, and Bogville. After the last drive had been made and the last herd had been worked, the wagon boss pointed the herd toward the crossing of the Platte River. Here, we swam them across the big river at the old Texas-Montana Cattle Trail crossing, a few miles down river from Fort Laramie. Shortly afterwards, we loaded out that last Two Bar beef herd on stock cars of the Burlington Railroad which were waiting on a siding near the river.

After the steers had all been loaded, the horse cavvy was brought into the stockyards by the horse wrangler, where the wagon boss gave each of the Two Bar cowboys the pick of one top horse from his own string of cow ponies as a gift from the company. After this the balance of the cavvy, consisting of about two hundred head of top cow ponies, were all loaded out on stock cars for shipment to South America, where these horses had been sold to a large cattle company that had begun operations on the pampas in Argentina. A few of the Two Bar cowboys who had signed two-year contracts with the South American company to punch cows for them in that country also shipped out on the same train as the horses.

The next morning, we broke camp on the Platte, with the cook pulling his pot racks from the fire and loading his Dutch ovens into the chuck wagon for the last time. The wagon boss was heading the remnant of the once proud Two-Bar outfit upstream toward Fort Laramie, where the cowboys would be paid off and the outfit would break up. The roundup wagon was pulled into an old wagon yard, where it would remain along with the other old abandoned army transport wagons, buffalo hide wagons, stagecoaches and other types of horse-drawn vehicles; all relics of bygone days. Here they would all remain for many years, reminders of the days of the buffalo, the turbulent period of the Indian wars, the emigrant wagon trains, and the days of the open-range cattle operations; that way of life that had passed forever from the American scene.

So ended the colorful open-range era in the history of the West, which became a part of the great American heritage.

BRANDS

Brand	Name	Brand	Name	Brand	Name
¥	Y CROSS	T+T	T CROSS T	D	THE D
	BLOCK QUARTER CIRCLE	LC	THE L C		SHIPWHEEL
◇	KEYSTONE	A∕U	A U SEVEN	OP	THE O P
o—o	BRIDLE BIT	OX	THE OX		SPADE
FF	F F BAR	FS	BAR F S	LO	THE L O
	HASH KNIFE	CY	THE C Y		QUARTER CIRCLE L
	MILL IRON	Ⓒ	QUARTER CIRCLE C	CO	THE C O
DS	D H S	CK	THE C K		CIRCLE DIAMOND
VVV	THREE V	O	CIRCLE BAR	76	SEVENTY SIX
₩	PITCHFORK	101	HUNDRED AND ONE	LU	L U BAR
W	W BAR	J	LAZY J	777	SEVEN SEVENTY SEVEN
N	N BAR	79	SEVENTY NINE	◇	BAR DIAMOND
	MALTESE CROSS	FUF	F U F	SL	THE S L
	ELK HORN	ML	THE M L		SEVENTY SIX
	TURKEY TRACK	Ǝ2	REVERSED E TWO	TE	THE T E
	MATADOR		FLYING E BAR		R O L REVERSED
44	FORTY FOUR CONNECTED	LU	THE L U		BUG
◇A	DIAMOND A	Y	Y SIX	M	M BAR
	TWO BAR	KC	KAYCEE	XIT	THE X I T
⦁⦁⦁	THREE CIRCLE	TA	T OPEN A	T7	T SEVEN
OX	OX BAR	71	71 QUARTER CIRCLE	4W	FOUR W
+S	CROSS S		INVERTED THREE T	JD	J D BAR
ΛX	OPEN AX	PO	THE P O	X	HAT X
	FOUR BAR O	WR	W H R	KJ	THE K J